To Coleman:

Best of luck to you

Regards ~

J. Seale

EYES
ON
TOMORROW

The Evolution of
PROCTER & GAMBLE

EYES ON TOMORROW

The Evolution of
PROCTER & GAMBLE

BY OSCAR SCHISGALL

Published by J. G. Ferguson Publishing
Company, Chicago, a subsidiary of Doubleday
and Company, New York. Distributed to the
trade by Doubleday.
1981

Library of Congress Catalog Card Number: 81-66073
ISBN:0-89434-011-5

I-10

*"In a moment this moment will be but a memory.
We cannot change it. Let us therefore fix
our eyes on tomorrow."*
Anon.

IN APPRECIATION

For more than a hundred and forty years Procter & Gamble has been an integral part of the nation's history. As an example of what free enterprise can achieve, its story is true Americana.

Much of the material in this account came from the company's archives. But the *spirit* of Procter & Gamble, its fundamental and unchanging character, emerged principally from my talks with people who had given years of their lives to P&G.

To name them all would require page after page of listings. Many are identified in this chronicle. I must, however, express special gratitude for the help, the recollections, and the time so generously given by Chairman Emeritus Howard J. Morgens, Chairman Edward G. Harness, Vice Chairman Owen B. Butler, and President John G. Smale—to use the titles they held while this book was being written.

And for the editorial assistance I received from him, and for the long months he gave to guiding my research, I am deeply indebted to S.A. (Gus) Shaddix.

To all these and countless others who assisted me, I gratefully dedicate this book.

Oscar Schisgall

CONTENTS

AN OVERVIEW

In the spring of 1837 two earnest men in their mid-thirties worked day after day in the yard behind their small shop in Cincinnati. Lean, black-bearded William Procter and the shorter, clean-shaven James Gamble stirred boiling animal fats in a large iron kettle slung over a wood fire. The fats were essential ingredients of the soap and candles they manufactured, products that William Procter himself would later deliver to local customers in a wheelbarrow.

At the time there were eighteen other soap and candle manufacturers in Cincinnati, yet the business established by Messrs. Procter and Gamble is the only one that has survived. Moreover, it has survived to become one of America's industrial leaders despite one hundred and forty years of wars, depressions, riots, panics, periods of desperate shortages, and other hazards that have beset the nation. It ranks today among the largest corporations in the United States.

So one asks: How did it happen? Did the founders have a formula different from all others?

Although they were doing business together earlier that year, William Procter and James Gamble signed their partnership agreement on October 31, 1837. They did so with a total capitalization of $7,192.24. That amount, contributed in equal shares, had not been easy to raise. It had in fact required months of scrounging and sacrifice. In the end, the financing had been accomplished by pooling savings, borrowing from friends, even selling William Procter's most cherished possessions—two wagons, a carriage, and two horses. He must have yearned for the wagons and horses as he hunched over a loaded wheelbarrow on Cincinnati's streets.

The first employee hired by the partners, when at last they could afford it, was a man-for-all-jobs named Barney Krieger. (Krieger stayed with them forty-seven years, setting a precedent for longevity that many others have followed.) A hundred and forty-four years later, Procter & Gamble employed more than 60,000 people—39,800 in the United States and 20,900 in its international operations. By 1980, the iron soapmaking kettle in the Cincinnati backyard had expanded to forty plants throughout the United States and major operations in twenty-four foreign nations.

As for the initial investment of $7,192, it has risen to corporate assets of $6.5 billion. Modest 1837 sales of a few pennies here, a few dollars there, all carefully recorded in William Procter's ledger, have climbed to annual revenues exceeding $10 billion. And what was once a simple trade in candles and soap encompasses more than fifty household products in the United States, hundreds more overseas.

One may expect sales in billions of dollars in connection with high-priced aircraft, automobiles, computer installations. One hardly thinks in such terms when it comes to soaps, toothpastes, detergents, paper towels, and similar household items that sell for a few cents or a dollar or two. Simple arithmetic suggests that Procter & Gamble's contemporary sales represent well over 10 billion individual transactions a year at retail counters. And it has been estimated that the company's products can be found in 97% of all American households—apart from those that pour into homes in more than a hundred other nations.

In addition the company sells scores of items in bulk to industry and institutions. These run from foods to chemicals, from car wash cleaners to cellulose. They produce sales of about $1.5 billion a year.

When Howard J. Morgens was P&G's chief executive officer he once remarked, "You might call us the General Motors of the light industry field." In turn, a gallant officer of General Motors countered, "You might call us the Procter & Gamble of heavy industry."

Impressive as all such facts may be, perhaps the most surprising aspect of Procter & Gamble's modern operations lies in its thirty-four separate sales forces, twelve of them in the United States. Sales representatives of different domestic divisions often call on the same customers in the grocery trade. To an outsider such a system may appear unwieldy, even inefficient. Yet it reflects the manner in which Procter & Gamble is now structured, and it works smoothly. In fact, today it would be hard to imagine the company operating in any other way.

One practice that has caused editorial comment in many publications is Procter & Gamble's policy of stimulating competition within the company. Its brands compete with one another as vigorously as they compete with the products of other manufacturers. Thus P&G's Ivory soap competes with P&G's Camay, Zest, and Safeguard, and vice versa. P&G's detergent, Tide, competes with its Cheer, Dash, Bold, Oxydol, and Era. P&G's Crest and Gleem dentifrices compete with each other, as do Charmin and White Cloud toilet tissues, Prell and Head & Shoulders shampoos. Moreover, year after year the company introduces new brands which challenge its existing products. And each brand is required to be profitable on its own merits. A weak brand cannot "borrow" from the company in order to stay alive. This attitude has long been fundamental within Procter & Gamble.

Internal competition of a different sort is likewise a major concern of the corporation. This is competition among its people. Procter & Gamble has long been known as a company which does not hire its executives; instead, it hires able people and gives them intensive personalized training so that each may move up the executive ladder as fast as his or her abilities permit.

In the years since its incorporation in 1890 Procter & Gamble has had only six chief executives. Every one of them has come up through the ranks. Since all were trained in the same milieu, they shared the company's objectives, aspirations, and above all its principles: "to foster growth in an orderly manner, to reflect the standards set by the founders, to plan and prepare for the future."

Preparing for the future has recently involved capital spending of as much as $750 million a year, much of it to build new plants for products to be sold in the years ahead. It has meant budgeting over $200 million a year for the research and development of these products.

Obviously such expenditures imply confidence in the future—the kind of confidence that can be traced back to the founders. Even before they formally became partners they signed personal notes for the purchase of a plot of land on which they hoped some day to build a factory. More to the point, they did this at a time when the nation itself was in economic distress.

In 1837 no one knew what the money of the United States was worth, or if it was worth anything at all. Individual banks had been printing their own bank notes, and many of these "greenbacks" had no tangible support in reserves of gold or silver. Their value had become so questionable that in July, 1836, the Treasurer of the United States had stunned the nation by announcing that the federal government would accept no more greenbacks in payment for public lands. Until the federal government issued its own money the Treasury would insist on "payment in specie"—that is, in gold or silver. The specie circular precipitated financial panic. Was paper money worthless?

Frightened depositors rushed to their banks, clamoring for their money in gold or silver. But there was not that much specie in the land. On May 10, 1837, several New York banks, unable to meet depositors' demands, shut their doors in the face of screaming mobs. The panic of 1837 was underway. More than 600 banks fell that year. Terror spread across the country. Were all lifetime savings to be lost? Was the nation bankrupt?

This was the economic hysteria in which William Procter and James Gamble calmly launched their business. In analyzing what carried them through this and other financial crises, some business publications quoted a simple, practical, and understandable statement made by a company officer: "P&G's products have always been relatively inexpensive, quickly consumed, and an integral part of the life-style of people. They are essentials."

Admittedly this is a persuasive prescription for success. No one denies it explains much of Procter & Gamble's growth. Still, there are a number of retired P&G executives who look at the company with a nostalgic perspective of their own. They quietly assure you that the real explanation for the company's status in the industrial world is more difficult to describe. They speak of things that have little to do with the price of products. They talk about "enduring policies based on the high sense of ethics that dates back to the founders." They speak of business integrity, of fair treatment of employees. "Right from the start," said the late Richard R. Deupree when he was chief executive officer, "William Procter and James Gamble realized that the interests of the organization and its employees were inseparable. That has never been forgotten."

Granting that the instincts of the founders were noble, that their principles were lofty and their behavior beyond reproach, one does not have to be a cynic to ask: Can any corporation exist through scores of years under unvarying high-minded principles? Surely, one would think, there must have been periods of crisis when principles had to be sacrificed because of circumstances beyond anyone's control. Could P&G have survived all difficulties, its own and the nation's, without sometimes yielding to expediency?

And there is this to consider: In an organization as old as Procter & Gamble, could generation after generation of employees have been induced to share the same philosophy? Was this possible in a corporation whose divisions were to become scattered across the United States and into many foreign countries? If so, one wonders how such homogeneity was achieved. And what exactly was the so-termed "spiritual inheritance" that came down through generations from the two founders of Procter & Gamble?

These are questions worth exploring if one is to understand the workings of the American system of free enterprise. Few have profited from that system as consistently or as spectacularly as has Procter & Gamble. This book will seek to discover, in the company's history and in its present operations, how one of the country's largest corporations achieved its stature.

1

THE FOUNDING FATHERS

.

Each of the founding partners of Procter & Gamble owed his presence in Cincinnati to the need of medical attention.

James Gamble came to America first. His father, George, an itinerant Methodist minister in Northern Ireland, had sought to escape the dreadful depression which throttled that country in 1819. He had heard of prosperity that Irish friends were finding in a place called Shawneetown somewhere in Illinois. So the Reverend George Gamble took his wife and family across the Atlantic to seek a better life in Shawneetown.

By the time they reached Pittsburgh they had all but exhausted their funds. The only accommodation they could afford, sailing down the Ohio River, was space on a flatboat. Young James, age 16, became violently ill on the boat. At the Cincinnati stop his worried parents hurried him ashore to find a doctor.

What they saw must have amazed them. The city was one of the busiest in the United States. Shipbuilding was a major industry, the river wharves constantly teeming with activity. "Not less than forty to fifty 'floating palaces' were launched from Cincinnati's shipyards every year," wrote historian Edward Hungerford. Yet even shipbuilding was not the city's most vital industry, nor was the brewing of beer. The distinction of being the leading business was pre-empted by packing houses that specialized in the slaughter of hogs. People were facetiously calling Cincinnati "Porkopolis."

While James was convalescing, his parents, still astonished by the city's liveliness and prosperity, lost interest in going on to Shawneetown. By the time James had regained his health they had decided to stay. They rented property from the wealthiest man in town, Nicholas Longworth. Finding no local demand for another preacher, the clergyman began his new life by opening a greenhouse on West Seventh Street. No doubt he continued his preaching at home, imbuing his son with his own religious fervor.

James, a stocky, muscular lad, worked at the greenhouse for a brief time before being lured by one of the city's more lucrative industries, the making of soap. Determined to learn the trade thoroughly, he apprenticed himself to William Bell, one of Cincinnati's veteran soap manufacturers. He spent eight years with Bell before he and a friend, Hiram Knowlton, opened a soap and candle shop of their own.

The first few years of the venture could scarcely be termed a spectacular success. Nevertheless they were sufficiently lucrative to enable Gamble, at the age of thirty, to marry Elizabeth Ann Norris, the daughter of Alexander Norris, a respected local candlemaker.

Elizabeth Ann was not the only Norris girl to be married that year. Her sister, Olivia, became the bride of a man from England named William Procter.

* * * * *

Procter had come to America from England because of a devastating financial shock. In London, on a Monday, he had opened a woolen goods shop. The next morning he unlocked the door to discover that burglars had stolen every item in the store. He owed the British equivalent of $8,000 for the vanished merchandise. Stunned and demoralized, he saw no immediate way of paying the debt.

In this situation of utter defeat he and his first wife, Martha, considered letters they had been receiving from a faraway place in America. Some identified it as "The Falls of Ohio," others as Louisville, in Kentucky. All who had emigrated to the distant town extolled its opportunities. If a man was not afraid of hard work, the letters said, fortunes could be made.

William Procter determined to rebuild his life in the New World. Promising his creditors to send payment on his $8,000 debt, he took his wife overseas.

Strangely, like the Gamble family before them, he and Martha could afford nothing better than passage down the Ohio River on a flatboat. And on that boat Martha was stricken with cholera. At the Cincinnati stop William frantically rushed her ashore to seek help, but there was little doctors could do. Within a few terrible days Martha died.

William Procter (left), James Gamble and the Signature Page of the original partnership agreement.

After her burial Procter was too broken in spirit to travel farther. In his dejection he found some sort of temporary employment in a bank, but on the low wages offered he saw no way of ever repaying his $8,000 debt; and that debt, despite his grief, he was determined to honor. He needed a better source of income.

In his youth he had been apprenticed for seven years to the owner of a general store where he had learned to make dip candles. When he discovered that many Cincinnati merchants were earning fair incomes in the candle trade, he went into the candle business for himself.

His interest was stimulated by the fact that many candles were being shipped into Cincinnati even though the basic raw material for candles was plentiful locally. So Procter began to make, sell, and personally deliver candles from a shop that he rented on Main Street in downtown Cincinnati. The previous tenant had left a large doghouse. Unable to afford a dog, Procter fastened both ends of a 30-foot chain inside the house and looped the remainder on the ground. For added effect he strewed some bones about. Would-be burglars had every reason to think that a large and unfriendly dog resided in the doghouse.

Even while paying off the London debt, Procter did well enough to buy a wagon and a team of horses. But it was a lonely life. And when he came to know Olivia Norris, whom he met at church services, he asked her to become his wife. They were wed within months of James Gamble's marriage to Elizabeth Ann.

So now they were brothers-in-law, William Procter, the candlemaker, and James Gamble, the soapmaker. Both were buying the animal fats essential to their separate products. That made them buying competitors, a situation that seemed illogical and impractical to their father-in-law, Alexander Norris. He urged them to complement each other's efforts by becoming partners.

It took several years but the brothers-in-law finally agreed to join forces. In early 1837 James Gamble ended his partnership with Hiram Knowlton. Gamble's share of the stock on hand was moved into Procter's premises near the northeast corner of the intersection of Sixth and Main Streets. Although no contractual agreement had been signed, records indicate the two men considered themselves partners as early as March 9, 1837. On that date, their names were first linked by an ampersand. Their letterhead read: "Procter & Gamble's Manufactory."

On June 22, 1837, there was recorded in the title records of Hamilton County, Ohio, a deed which conveyed to James Gamble and William Procter a tract of land adjoining the Miami-Erie Canal, close to the edge of the city. The selling price was $1,000, and Messrs. Procter and Gamble paid $346 in cash and signed notes totaling $654 to be paid off within two years.

Thus, more than three months before signing a partnership agreement on October 31, 1837, the two committed themselves to place dollars behind their staunch faith that their business would grow and need a good site for a soap and candle factory. In this simple act of faith and foresight one finds the genesis of a persisting characteristic of Procter & Gamble: careful planning for long-term growth, no matter what specific business problem— even crisis—the company might be dealing with at the moment.

Recognition of the importance of research was also manifest to some degree in those pre-partnership days. James Gamble contacted a consulting chemist in Philadelphia to request the latest information on soap and candlemaking.

* * * * *

The sign on their little shop proclaimed "Procter & Gamble & Co." The "& Co." was not an affectation. For about a year, probably because they needed funds, they took in a third partner, Fenn E. Tarrant. Mr. Tarrant, however, for reasons unknown, soon withdrew. Perhaps he could not tolerate the air of religious righteousness with which William and James conducted their affairs, an air that had no counterpart among less pious merchants.

Both partners were devout Protestants. Their religious convictions were unshakable. To their dealings with others they brought a kind of Biblical rectitude. Even in the photographs they left in later life one can detect stern dignity and probity. To make an untrue claim for their products would have been to utter a falsehood, and this they refused to do. ("You shall not lie or speak falsely to one another," said the Bible.) They might lower their prices to meet competition, but as for lowering quality, they would as soon have condoned larceny.

A newspaperman reported, "Suppliers of fats and oils could take a signed order from Messrs. Procter & Gamble and pass it along in lieu of cash." In observations like these one can see why, more than a century later, P&G executives would be speaking of "the high sense of ethics" bequeathed by the founders. They

5

Original site of P&G plant and office, second door north, at Sixth and Main Streets, Cincinnati.

might also speak of a high sense of thrift. For a practice the partners soon adopted was to sell the by-products of their trade. Hog fats, when boiled, left a residue of thick oil that could not be used for candles or soap. Yet it had other uses. So the firm's first advertisement, appearing in the *Cincinnati Gazette* of June 29, 1838, used two inches of space to announce:

> *Oils for lamps and machinery. A fine article of clarified Pig's Foot Oil, equal to sperm, at a low price and in quantities to suit buyers. Neat's Foot oil ditto. Also No. 1 & 2 soap. Palm and shaving ditto. For sale by Procter & Gamble Co., east side Main Street 2nd door off 6th Street.*

In these formative years of Procter & Gamble, funds were so limited and output so scanty that the firm could seek little business outside Cincinnati itself. All their interests were local. In the outside world the Republic of Texas might be recognized as an independent nation. The first covered wagon might reach California via the Oregon Trail. An American expedition might lay claim to the continent of Antarctica, and an Ohioan, William Henry Harrison, might be elected president of the United States.

But for Messrs. Procter and Gamble, the most important news of the day generally centered on the arrival of this or that riverboat.

If the vessel had pushed its way upstream from New Orleans, it was likely to unload barrels of rosin, a vital ingredient of the soaps manufactured by all local companies. One or both of the partners had to be at the wharf to claim their share of the rosin cargo amid the din of their shouting competitors. In all probability, these were the only times when they lost the quiet decorum of their everyday lives. "When they had to yell for their rights," one commentator wrote, "they yelled as loud as anyone else."

* * * * *

From the outset James Gamble supervised production. William Procter was in charge of the office and sales. In these early years candles were their principal source of income. The candles were painstakingly made by looping a wick on the end of a stick, dipping it into the melted tallow, then hanging it up while the wax on the wick cooled. The process was repeated again and again until each candle was of the proper thickness.

As for soapmaking, it was equally primitive. In the morning hours Gamble collected meat scraps and wood ashes to make the lye he needed. Paying for the meat scraps with small cakes of soap, he went from house to house, to hotels and riverboats, collecting his raw materials.

With the increase of sales, more and more materials were necessary. The collection of meat scraps and wood ashes had to be extended throughout nearby Hamilton and Butler Counties and even into Indiana. Their first employee, Barney Krieger (who did every kind of chore during his forty-seven years) was of inestimable help in these daily rounds.

Of course, all eighteen Cincinnati soap and candle manufacturers were doing the same thing. It was not unusual for several of them to knock at the back door of the same house in a single morning. Procter and Gamble had to learn to compete for needed supplies. In this they developed buying skills they were never to lose. They sought every possible opportunity to store raw materials for the future. It was wiser to tie up funds than to risk a future without products to sell.

In the matter of selling, the ethical standards of the partners were often at odds with the practices of some others. What angered them most was the advertising of fraudulent claims. One

7

advertisement in particular roused their fury. It was for a soap sold by a Cincinnati druggist. Among the many claims he made were:

> It will remove tetter, salt rheum, pimples, tan, freckles, and all cutaneous disorders.
>
> It is a very superior article for washing and cleansing sores and wounds and preparing the flesh to heal.
>
> By washing children therewith, it prevents sore ears and ruptures of the skin. It will strengthen the muscles and prove a preventative to many diseases ... It will thicken the hair and prevent baldness ... It will cure the scurvy in the gums and prevent the teeth from rotting and aching, preserve the enamel, and cure offensive breath.

The druggist who inserted this advertisement professed to be the agent of an unnamed manufacturer. His store, at the corner of Fifth and Race Streets, was only four blocks from the Procter & Gamble office. One can visualize the outraged partners marching into the store to confront the man, perhaps even to threaten him with biblical damnation, and demand that he stop circulating such patently false claims.

All things considered, the methods pursued by William Procter and James Gamble must have been sound, for during that first decade their business steadily continued to grow. By 1848, according to a William Procter notebook, their firm was earning an annual profit of $26,000.

* * * * *

One morning in 1851, observing the loading of P&G candles on a riverboat, William Procter saw a wharfhand painting crude black crosses on each wooden box. Puzzled, he asked, "Why are you marking the crates that way?"

"Lots of folks working on the boats and wharves can't read," the man answered. "They don't know which is crates of candles, which is soap, so we mark the candles so's they can tell the difference."

Because candles were the firm's predominant source of revenue, Procter had no objection to the special marking. Shortly later, some artistically inclined wharfhand changed the black cross to a star and put a circle around the star. Another decided there should be a cluster of stars within the circle; and part of the circle became a quarter-moon drawn as a rough sort of human profile.

With the partners' approval a stencil was cut for the crude "moon and stars" emblem, and the design was painted on the ends of all the firm's candle shipping boxes. A little later they decided that the man in the moon was somewhat superfluous and eliminated that element of the emblem.

Thereupon came an urgent message from New Orleans that a jobber had rejected an entire shipment of P&G candles. Because the boxes didn't have the full design, the jobber thought the candles were imitations.

He wrote, "We want P&G's Star brand candles and no other ... the only kind we can sell."

Not only was the man in the moon promptly called back into service, but William Procter himself suggested a refinement. The cluster of stars should number thirteen, he decided, matching those on the first flag of the United States. With further artistic modifications—especially to delineate more sharply the profile of the man in the moon—the "Moon and Stars" was eventually registered as a trademark in the U.S. Patent Office when federal legislation made it possible for businesses to have legal protection against trademark infringement.

Meanwhile, Procter & Gamble's business outgrew the production facility at Sixth and Main Streets. Now the partners profited from the foresight of their 1837 purchase of land adjacent to the Miami-Erie Canal about a mile to the northwest. Not only did the canal offer a prime shipping route to markets north of Cincinnati (it was to stretch all the way to Toledo), but the land was close to the meat packing houses which were increasingly becoming the firm's key source of fats.

An early Procter & Gamble advertisement, 1838.

The partners decided to construct a factory on their property on the eastern side of Western Row, a street later named Central Avenue. The first Central Avenue unit in the mid-1850s was a modest building one story high, 32 feet wide, and 65 feet long. Among its production facilities were two soap kettles, each of which could turn out about 1,000 pounds of soap a week.

With the factory now separated from the city office, Procter continued to tend to sales and finances and seldom visited the plant. Conversely, Gamble ran the factory and seldom felt a need to go to the office. The result was that the partners rarely saw each other except on Saturday nights. Then they regularly met at Procter's house to consider the firm's financial situation, discuss current business problems, and make future plans.

Not long after the Central Avenue plant was built, the business office was also relocated in a leased five-story building and warehouse at 24 West Second Street. At about the same time P&G's letterhead also indicated growth in its product line:

PROCTER & GAMBLE
Manufacturers and Wholesale Dealers in
STAR, ADAMANTINE, & TALLOW CANDLES
Rosin, Palm, Oleine, Toilet & Shaving Soaps;
Pearl Starch, Lard Oil, Etc.

The "Wholesale Dealers" portion of the letterhead had special significance. Procter & Gamble actually sold more products than it manufactured during those early years. For example, P&G made tallow candles but sold Star and Adamantine candles that were made by others. (Star candles, a generic name, were made from the stearic acid of lard. Adamantines were made from the stearic acid of tallow. Adamantines had a higher melting point than Star candles, and because they were firmer their generic name was derived from the dictionary's "adamant.")

Finally, tired of selling other firms' wares, William Procter and James Gamble decided they ought to concentrate on making Star and Adamantine candles themselves. But a review of their financial situation made it obvious they couldn't afford to add production equipment for both types.

They chose to concentrate on Star candles since the basic raw material for these, hog fats, was readily available at the nearby pork packing houses. Moreover, they saw an advantage in a by-product of the Star candle process: oleic acid. It was this residue— called "red oil" by the trade—that especially attracted the partners' interest. They were convinced that P&G could use red oil as a raw material for making better laundry soaps than any others on the market.

All in all, the decision to produce Star candles had a powerful influence on the long-term growth of Procter & Gamble. Red oil became a key ingredient in two new P&G soaps. These were so enthusiastically welcomed by consumers that soapmaking received steadily increasing emphasis in the firm.

Red oil was first used to make a hard, white German-type soap with visible red mottles. Other firms also made German-type soaps, but P&G's Mottled German, sold in one-, two-, and three-pound bars, was distinctive. Thrifty homemakers discovered that the soap's mottled appearance meant it did not contain an excessive amount of water. (Mottled German soap became such a consumer favorite that it led in 1875 to P&G's first legal action involving infringement of its trademark. P&G sued a Chicago imitator who called his product "German Mottled," and P&G won the case.)

The other red oil soap the company introduced in the 1850's was Oleine. One of its ingredients, palm oil, gave it a pleasant violet scent. It was a hard, rough-textured soap for general household uses.

Trying to make the most of by-products, the partners were selling increasingly large amounts of lard oil—a liquid by-product of the pressing of hog fat. Lard oil fueled the household lamps that some people preferred to candles; it was equally useful as a lubricant.

But the expected profits of another potential by-product constantly eluded the partners, and this failure was frustrating.

* * * * *

Frugal-minded James Gamble had long been bothered by his inability to find an economical way to recover and refine the crude glycerin present in the residue of Star candlemaking. Each time he walked into a pharmacy and saw retail price tags of up to $1.50 for one pound of refined glycerin, imported from England, Gamble must have groaned at the thought of all the crude glycerin going to waste in the Central Avenue plant.

For a time he thought he had an answer to the problem. High pressure saponification tanks were devised for extracting crude glycerin from the waste water. However, one of the high-pressure tanks exploded destroying much of the equipment, and the process was abandoned. It was too dangerous to employees.

Joining James Gamble in his frustrated mullings over glycerin waste was William Procter's oldest son, William Alexander Procter. He left college in 1851 at the age of 17 with his father's approval to work under Uncle James in the factory. For training purposes his uncle assigned him to jobs in all parts of the plant before eventually putting him in charge of lard oil production. William Alexander did so well in the eyes of his father and uncle that they took him into the partnership in 1857, giving him a 10% interest in the business.

The solution to the glycerin extraction problem, however, came from outside. It was brought to Cincinnati in 1858 by a Philadelphia chemist, Richard A. Tilghman, who had invented and patented the process. Tilghman invited all Cincinnati's soap and candle manufacturers to witness a demonstration of his method. They watched as intently as if Tilghman had been showing them a magic formula for creating gold out of waste—which, in a sense, he was.

Not all were convinced (including James Gamble) that the method would be as effective as Tilghman claimed. Still, even though skeptical, Procter and Gamble felt they could not afford to give up any opportunity to develop another valuable by-product. The partners licensed the process from Tilghman, then began an immediate search for ways to improve both the process itself and the equipment required.

In time Procter & Gamble learned to distill and refine glycerin and to sell it profitably at about half the price of the imported product. Because the imported glycerin had been so expensive, its use had been limited generally for medicinal purposes, and principally for its emollient properties in treating burns and chapped skin. With P&G's lower prices, glycerin—or glycerol, as a chemist would call it—started to become an ingredient in a broad range of products. (In the next century it would become an important ingredient in antifreeze, medicines, explosives, lipsticks, printing inks, cellophane, quick-drying paints, and for countless other uses.)

At the outset, however, the partners had no way of envisioning the millions of dollars the firm would some day earn in glycerin sales. Nor, for that matter, could they have guessed that their licensing of Tilghman's process would involve P&G in expensive lawsuits.

No one thought of such things because Procter & Gamble was doing very well as it moved into its third decade. In just over twenty years the partners had built a business described in an 1859 Cincinnati book as "engaged more extensively in manufacturing operations than any other establishment in our city," and as having "sales largely exceeding $1 million yearly."

Another member of the second generation, George H. Procter, contributed considerably to this growth. He had come home from Kenyon College to travel as a P&G sales representative. His successful contacts with brokers and wholesalers in large eastern cities greatly stimulated sales there, especially sales of Mottled German and Oleine soaps.

Though the partners were doing well, they were certainly not sequestered from events outside their business. The nation they had adopted was divided against itself. In the 1850s the increasing prospects of a war between the states of the North and the South frightened Messrs. Procter and Gamble as they frightened every thinking person. Still in the habit of conferring every Saturday night at the Procter home, now, in these weekly sessions, they were concerned with the ever-growing likelihood of civil war. As patriots and humanitarians, they were distressed. As businessmen—with responsibilities to their families, their employees, and their customers—they had to make contingency plans. Some hard questions had to be addressed.

What, for instance, would happen to supplies of rosin, a key soapmaking material obtained exclusively from Southern sources? New Orleans was the principal rosin trading center and the Mississippi and Ohio Rivers were the delivery routes. If New Orleans were blocked, how could a critical shortage of rosin be avoided?

William Procter and James Gamble knew that other essential raw materials—soda ash, sulfuric acid, candlewick, lard—would also be subject to wartime shortages. However, the availability of these did not depend entirely on Southern sources.

The partners' common trait—advance planning—prompted them to send William Alexander Procter on a rosin buying trip to New Orleans in 1860. As the junior partner's companion on what was to become a momentous venture, they assigned his cousin,

13

James Norris Gamble. Two years younger than William Alexander, James N. Gamble had delayed his entry into the firm while he studied analytic and applied chemistry under Professor Campbell Morfit at the University of Maryland.

As had his older cousin, James N. Gamble started working in the factory. Although still a novice in the soapmaking business, he fully understood the importance of having ample supplies of rosin in the event of war. This trip to New Orleans, he realized, was not only exciting but urgent beyond words.

2

WAR BY CANDLELIGHT

When William Alexander Procter, 26, and James Norris Gamble, 24, boarded the riverboat, the ominous war talk among fellow passengers heightened their feelings of urgency. In New Orleans they rushed to the firm's principal rosin supplier. There they found a vast reserve available for $1 a barrel. William and James exchanged only a quick glance before they reached a decision.

"We'll take a whole boatload," they told the dealers. "We want it shipped immediately." Thus, on their own initiative the young men made the biggest single purchase of rosin any company in Cincinnati had ever made.

The shipment duly arrived. A gang of wharfhands unloaded it. The barrels were carted in wagon after wagon to a vacant lot next

15

(Top) The Cincinnati Riverfront of the 1880s was a key shipping point for P&G products going to cities along the Ohio and Mississippi Rivers. (Below) An early P&G packing line, circa 1881, shows James Gamble's determination to employ labor-saving machinery.

to the Central Avenue plant. Seeing in the passing procession evidence of wanton extravagance, one of the firm's competitors observed, "There goes P&G's funeral."

Whether born of brashness or wisdom, this first major decision of the second generation of Procters and Gambles catapulted the firm into a new era of growth.

When the Civil War broke out three months later, the Union forces needed all sorts of supplies, including vast quantities of soap. To meet the demand, all other soap manufacturers were desperately trying to buy rosin. Where it was obtainable, the price soared to $8 a barrel. Before long it skyrocketed to $15. And Procter & Gamble had more rosin, bought at $1 a barrel, than any competitor.

News of this quickly brought a team of Union Army procurement officers to Cincinnati. They inspected Procter & Gamble's equipment and supplies and asked endless questions. What they reported to their superiors brought immediate orders from Washington: P&G was to supply soap to all Union Army encampments in the West. The Army's needs would require the daily shipping of 1,000 cases.

A month earlier this would have seemed an impossible task. Now, impossible or not, it had to be done.

Procter & Gamble threw itself into the kind of production never before attempted. It had to hire 300 additional workers and put many employees on night shifts. It had to buy more soapmaking kettles. It had to acquire nearby buildings for extra space. Contacting every available source of supply, the firm purchased thousands of wooden crates for shipping. No factory in Cincinnati was busier.

When Confederate troops were reported to be only a few miles south, martial law was declared in Cincinnati. Local factories were shut down, but not Procter & Gamble. A supplier to the Union had to continue producing.

Yet war or no war, the plant closed on every Sabbath. The law of the Lord superseded all else. One commentor remarked, "It was as if Procter & Gamble had a demanding third partner named God."

Though nobody was yet aware of it, something was happening in Union Army camps that could not have been anticipated. When the wooden boxes carrying the firm's name and trademark were emptied of soap and candles, they served in tents as chairs and tables and repositories for personal belongings. Every Union soldier was constantly exposed to the Procter & Gamble name and trademark. This serendipitous form of advertising helped the firm become one of the best known in the Northern states.

Of course, the government had its quality control inspectors. When an order of soap was ready for shipment, an inspector came to the factory, selected and opened random boxes, carefully weighed and scrutinized the contents. Records indicate that not one box ever failed to contain the weight and quality of soap marked on it at a time when some manufacturers were taking advantage of wartime conditions by turning out inferior products. Records also show that Procter & Gamble made no more than its normal profits on its wartime production, and this despite the competitive advantage it held as a result of the prewar purchase of rosin.

The war was at its height when, in the midst of feverish production, fire blazed up in the P&G plant. An accident? Sabotage? Nobody knew. Shouting employees joined the fire brigade to battle the flames. By good fortune the fire was limited to one factory wing.

But the troubles were not ended. Late one night a gang of hoodlums hurled stones at the Procter home. Windows broke and rocks flew into the house. By the time William reached the front door, the rowdies were racing away. He stood glaring after them, furiously shaking his fist, not understanding why they had done this. A reporter soon had an explanation. "Both William Procter and James Gamble," he wrote, "had been denouncing manufacturers who were cheating the government and the troops. In particular, William Procter had exposed the Ohio company which was supplying the soldiers with supposedly woolen blankets which actually were made of shoddy, really only converted rags. It is believed that the stoning of Procter's home was in reciprocity for the 'shoddy' practice he had exposed."

As the war went on, Procter & Gamble's problems became more serious because their rosin inventory was dwindling to dangerously low levels. The partners daily counted their remaining barrels and held worried conferences. They knew of no way to get additional rosin. The question was—could anything be used as a substitute?

For an answer they looked to young James Norris Gamble. He had been maintaining regular correspondence with chemists in several universities. Now he hastily mailed a number of inquiries. Could there be a substitute for rosin? From one of his correspondents he learned that a soap company in Philadelphia had indeed found a replacement—silicate of soda. James at once obtained the material and steeped himself in experiments. He produced varying batches of soap, subjecting each to comparisons with cakes containing rosin. In the end he had to admit failure. Silicate of soda simply did not yield the results he had hoped to find. To maintain its quality standards, P&G would still have to rely on rosin—even while its inventory steadily, and alarmingly, dwindled.

One can be sure that some employees urged the use of the substitute ingredient. No doubt they argued, "What if we do turn out a poorer grade of soap? It's an emergency measure. Better to have a poor soap than none at all."

The idea of deliberately producing an inferior product, even in such an emergency, was as repugnant to William Procter and James Gamble as the sale of "shoddy" blankets. They flatly refused to do it. Every box of soap and candles they had been shipping carried a guarantee of weight *and* quality, and they would not violate that assurance. So the erosion of the rosin continued. The partners' anxiety worsened with every disappearing barrel. By April, 1865, they were almost at the end of their resources when Appomatox brought a cessation of hostilities.

* * * * *

Soap and candle production had reached undreamed of figures during the war. The Central Avenue plant had been expanded not only by new construction but by the purchase of adjacent buildings. With the Civil War at an end, however, the firm's great production capacity became a reason for anxiety. There would be no more government orders. How could the enormous wartime output be adapted to peacetime civilian conditions? Would there have to be a drastic curtailment of production? Would parts of the plant have to be closed, workers laid off?

Interoffice records indicate that though the Procters and the Gambles were worried, there was no need for such apprehension. Wartime shortages that had been accumulating in the civilian sector brought an overwhelming, unexpected rush of orders. The

Central Avenue plant had once more to be expanded, not closed. Employment increased rather than declined.

At the same time there arose the problem of how to handle customers in the devastated South. Though they constituted a major market, Southerners had exhausted their finances and energies in the war. Most Southern brokers and wholesalers could not buy from Procter & Gamble unless the firm would extend long-term credit. Was the risk worth taking?

At the insistence of William Procter, P&G decided to do so. "But only," he stipulated, "if each individual decision is based on an evaluation of character rather than assets. Cash balances may vary from year to year, but a reputation for integrity is constant." It proved to be an attitude that won P&G many loyal Southern customers in the years that followed.

As raw materials again flowed freely into Cincinnati, the company expanded into new markets and with new products. This growth and expansion was especially significant in the case of one product that was an outgrowth of wartime experience, kitchen lard. For some time P&G had used lard stearin for making Star candles; but the price had risen so high that the company had been forced to make tallow candles only. As for lard stearin, James Norris Gamble and his associates found a way of refining it into a fine lard for household frying and baking. After the war, sales of this kitchen lard—especially in the South—became an important source of revenues for more than two decades. (Moreover, this first food product later turned the firm's interests toward other edible products.)

*   *   *   *   *

No doubt inspired by booming postwar business, the younger members of P&G intensified their efforts to seek ways of increasing the factory's production while reducing operating costs. Every appropriate new type of equipment that was invented received careful study. Whatever proved feasible was installed in the Central Avenue plant.

One day the office was visited by a young man who worked for the Western Union Company in Cincinnati. He introduced himself as Thomas Alva Edison. He had noted, he told James Norris Gamble, that P&G was exchanging messages between its office and its plant by couriers in horse-drawn carts. Edison proposed an electrically operated system over which the two locations could communicate directly and instantaneously. Probably because he was impressed by the ingenuity of the idea, James Norris Gamble approved and the system was created. It did not function very well, but Edison did not remain in Cincinnati long enough to evaluate his work. No one at Procter & Gamble heard of him again until word came to Cincinnati in 1879 that this same Edison had mortally wounded the candle business with his invention of an incandescent electric light bulb.

With Procter & Gamble now approaching its thirtieth year, the founders, each by this time in his middle sixties, began to leave more and more of the firm's management to their sons. William Procter, in fact, virtually retired. He gave much of his time to church and civic activities. James Gamble, for his part, continued to come to the plant, working there with his son, James Norris.

On its thirtieth birthday, October 31, 1867, the firm of Procter & Gamble showed capital assets of $800,000. And though things were going well for the company, it was not to be an uninterrupted prosperity. The nation was again headed toward trouble. "The country was being bruised," one historian wrote, "by human greed. A few avaricious men were all but ruining the United States."

During the first term of President Ulysses S. Grant in 1869 a number of these speculators were deliberately trying to corner the gold market. What this might do to the nation's economy did not trouble them. But could they be stopped? President Grant, on the advice of several leading bankers, ordered the immediate sale of $4 million of government gold. (In those days four million could flood the market and precipitate the sinking of gold prices as billions might today.) The attempted corner on gold was thwarted. But the abrupt decline in gold prices brought fear and uncertainty to the entire market. What was the real value of gold? How low would it drop? The uncertainty led to a Wall Street panic on the historic Black Friday of September 24, 1869.

Financial shock waves spread across the nation. People hoarded what money they had rather than pay bills. Procter & Gamble's receipts dropped drastically; so did everyone's. Simultaneously the value of P&G's inventory sank and the start of the new decade saw the first serious financial setback the company had ever known. Profits of $34,000 in the first four months of 1879 dwindled to about $3,000 in the next two months; and after that, for the remainder of the year, P&G operated at a loss. With no earnings, the company had to slash expenses everywhere, cutting

21

average wages of some plant employees from $11 to $10 a week, laying off others.

Moreover, the firm had to cease shipments to those wholesalers and brokers who were deeply in arrears; other customers were served on rigidly restricted terms. The elderly founders, recalled to office conferences, became heavily involved in decisions as to which customers would be served and which would be denied credit. As had long been their practice, the partners' decisions were based as much on the character of the would-be buyers as on their capital assets.

Yet, even while struggling with the difficult problems of 1870, the founders and their sons were looking at the possibilities of future business. The increasingly widespread use of oil lamps for illumination made it clear that candle sales would be declining. On the other hand, it was equally clear that a growing population would be using more and more soap. Such usage was spurred by the spread of public waterworks systems, by the increasing installation of plumbing in homes, and by increasingly enlightened public awareness of the hygienic value of frequent bathing and laundering. Procter and Gamble's future, the partners concluded, was going to depend heavily on the firm's ability to compete against the hundreds of other soap manufacturers.

By this time another of William Procter's sons was ready to contribute his talents to the business. This was Harley Thomas Procter who joined P&G as a sales representative in 1869 at the age of 21. Harley was dynamic, eager, seething with fresh ideas. The fact that Procter & Gamble had grown so much between 1837 and 1869 did not impress him. Impatient with what he regarded as antiquated methods of merchandising, he soon became the rebel of the second generation. And as an inventive rebel he was destined to add new dimensions to all P&G's operations, especially to advertising and sales.

*   *   *   *   *

When the United States celebrated its centennial in 1876, the nation was slowly emerging from another wave of financial woes that had begun with the Panic of 1873. In the ensuing depression, over 5,000 U.S. businesses collapsed.

For Procter & Gamble this first half of the 1870s had brought difficult times. Nonetheless, its total business volume continued

22

to increase. Soapmaking now constituted about 25% of the company's sales, while refined kitchen lard, lard oil, and candles accounted for the bulk of the business.

In 1876, Ohio's Governor Rutherford B. Hayes, a Cincinnatian, was elected president of the United States in a highly disputed election decided by one vote in the Electoral College. This was the year when General Custer and Chief Sitting Bull had their historic confrontation at the Battle of the Little Big Horn; Colorado was admitted as the thirty-eighth state in the Union; Mark Twain's *Adventures of Tom Sawyer* was a best-seller, although banned from numerous libraries around the country as unsuitable for children; and Alexander Graham Bell patented a device called the telephone. The times were exciting.

But in Cincinnati, beyond rooting for the election of Rutherford B. Hayes, local interest was focused largely on the formation of the National Baseball League. A charter member of the league was the Cincinnati Red Stockings, the nation's first professional baseball team. (The new league had seven other members, ranging geographically from St. Louis to Boston; and Cincinnatians were left disconsolate by the fact that the team from Chicago was the first pennant winner.)

Of considerable local interest, too, was the construction across the Ohio River by the Cincinnati Southern Railway of the world's longest cantilever bridge. This was the second distinctive bridge for the community. In 1867, John Augustus Roebling, designer and builder, had connected Cincinnati with Covington, Kentucky, via one of the world's most amazing structures, a great suspension bridge. Its fame was to be echoed a few years later (1883) with the opening of another Roebling-designed suspension span, the Brooklyn Bridge.

Cincinnati had in truth become one of the most enterprising communities in America, vivacious with its beer gardens, German bands, and riverboat traffic. The riverboats brought not only merchandise to the wharves but also "an unending stream of gamblers, theatrical performances, and 'ladies of easy virtue.' " Horace Greeley wrote in his book, *The Great Industries of the United States*:

> *The population of Cincinnati has increased to over 200,000 persons. The city has built nearly a thousand steamboats, and shipped yearly nearly eighty million dollars' worth of produce, importing nearly one hundred million dollars' worth*

23

of materials from abroad. Besides this, the industrial enter-
prise of the city has built up a manufacturing interest which
produced an aggregate of over fifty million dollars' worth of
various articles . . . .

As for Procter & Gamble, though its main office and warehouse were still located on East Second Street near the riverfront, its greatly expanded Central Avenue plant had become a local show-place. *Illustrated Cincinnati* described the facilities in detail: "Its sixteen buildings occupy an area of about 67,000 square feet and contain all the modern appliances for the prosecution of the business on the most extensive scale. The firm is widely known throughout the United States, and their trade extends all over the states and territories."

Ignored by the writer of the article, however, was a makeshift research laboratory which James Norris Gamble had set up in a corner of his machine shop. Working with him in that laboratory, while also superintending the plant's lye house, was P&G's first full-time chemist, an Englishman named Gibson. In that crude research facility, one of the first industrial laboratories in the U.S., Gibson was assigned to assist James N. Gamble and his younger brother, David, in a research project which had been frustrating the company for years: to find a formula for a hard, white soap that would be equal in quality to the fine castile soaps then on the market. (Castile soaps, based on olive oil, an expensive imported ingredient, were too costly for the average American consumer.)

The search for a white soap equal in quality to castile yet lower in price was helped when another soap manufacturer offered to sell P&G a formula he had developed. James N. Gamble recorded in his diary: "We bought the formula for a very moderate sum and proceeded to make soap according to the prescription, but after a little experience we changed it considerably."

As experiments proceeded, James N. Gamble must sometimes have been tempted to recommend to his partners that they simply put on the market the best white soap they could then make. If such thoughts did occur to him, he obviously set them aside and intensified his search for a product which would meet *all* the standards he had set.

Meanwhile, after several years of travel and selling, Harley Thomas Procter attained the position of sales manager, a job which then included responsibilities for advertising and promotion. Of course, advertising was in its infancy at Procter & Gamble as it was everywhere. The firm was producing numerous soaps under names like Town Talk, Mottled German, Princess, Queen, Duchess, and Oleine, but the advertising of these brands was extremely limited. P&G's total yearly advertising budget was only about $1,500—less than half the amount spent on printing wrappers and office stationery.

A few of the nation's 300 soap manufacturers were more enterprising. For instance, the Schultz Company of Zanesville announced that a $1 gold piece would be hidden in every thousandth bar of their Gold soap. This became a highly successful merchandising idea, though the appeal was that of a lottery rather than of a quality soap.

At last, in 1878, after all the years of experimenting with various formulations involving mixtures of tallow with vegetable oils—coconut oil, palm oil, and cottonseed oil—James N. Gamble triumphantly reported that he and his research associates had developed a white soap formula which was satisfactory in every regard.

After seeing the result of the first boiling, all the delighted partners agreed to put the product on the market. It was to be called P&G White Soap.

One thing was wrong: To Harley Procter the name was uninspiring and insipid. "Scores of companies are marketing 'white soaps,'" he argued in family meetings. "Grocery stores are so full of them that neither merchants nor customers have any reason to care which they buy." Harley wanted to find the best possible way to get people to try P&G's White Soap. If they tried it once, he reasoned, they probably would buy it again.

So what, his elders asked, did he suggest? Harley asserted that White Soap needed a distinctive name, one people would recall when they went shopping. A distinctive name, well advertised, would induce customers to buy P&G's White Soap in preference to all others.

The attitude of his associates, while not enthusiastic, seemed to be, "Well, suggest a name, and then we can decide." If his elders were less than ecstatic, perhaps it was because their own low-key merchandising methods, coupled with the good name of the firm, had proved successful enough over the years.

Harley began his search for a distinctive brand name with the nervous intensity that characterized everything he did. His father and uncle seemed content to leave the quest to him—no doubt smiling a bit as they watched him delve into the pages of the thesaurus Dr. Peter Mark Roget had published in 1852, into other lexicons, into lists of soaps being manufactured in foreign countries. Time after time they saw Harley shake his head in rejection of ideas. And the weeks passed.

Like his parents, he seldom missed a Sunday church service. On one Sabbath early in 1879, at the Mount Auburn Episcopal Church, he listened as the minister read from the Psalms. As Harley followed the text in his prayer book, he read, "All thy garments smell of myrrh and aloes and cassia, out of the ivory palaces whereby they have made thee glad."

There Harley abruptly stopped following the minister's reading. His eyes and thoughts focused on the phrase, "out of the ivory palaces." *Ivory*! Ivory was white and hard and long lasting. The word evoked an image of purity and luxury. Harley left church that Sunday morning excited and exuberant. *Ivory soap*! His quest for a name was ended, although he would have to wait until Monday to propose the name to the partners. They would not talk business on the Sabbath.

On Monday, when his elders half-heartedly agreed to adopt the name, Harley faced a challenge to prove the merit of his advertising idea and of the brand name he had chosen.

3

THE BIRTH OF MODERN ADVERTISING

Ivory Soap first wore this wrapper in 1879.

Harley Procter had a consuming personal ambition. He was determined, as he promised his wife, to retire in his early forties with ample funds to insure a good life. Perhaps that was one of the reasons he was so tireless, even frenetic a worker in his early years: a young man always in a hurry.

If his aim to retire at so young an age seemed rash or unreasonable, an accident in early 1879 helped him toward the goal: The ingredients of P&G's new white soap were mixed by mechanical devices called crutchers. The crutcher's arms revolved in the white mixture until an attendant decided by sight, smell, and even taste that it was thick enough to be poured into soap frames. There it would cool and harden into blocks of soap before being cut and packed.

One morning the man who tended the steam-driven crutcher went off to lunch and forgot to stop the machine. He was gone for the better part of an hour. When he returned, he stood appalled. The frothy, puffed-up mixture overflowing the vat made it obvious that the substance had been stirred far too long.

27

Berating himself for his negligence, the workman went off to summon his supervisor. When they inspected the sight together, they made a very practical decision: The ingredients had in no way been changed. They had frothed up more than they should, but what could be the harm in that?

"Let's empty the whole mixture into the frames," the supervisor said. "I don't think any harm will come of it."

It was done. After a few days the aerated mixture, having hardened into bars, was cut into cakes, wrapped, and shipped out, and the incident was forgotten.

A month or so later, however, when reorders began to arrive, there were customers who asked for "that soap that floats." Floats? No one in the Cincinnati office knew what this meant. They knew of no "floating soap." Could the people at the factory clarify what the customers wanted?

Only after a searching investigation did the factory workers recall the accident which had once occurred. Could this have produced a floating soap? To test the possibility the accident was repeated. The result was indeed a buoyant, floating cake.

Word reached Harley Procter that Procter & Gamble could henceforth make a white floating soap without compromising the characteristics which James N. Gamble had worked so hard to incorporate into the formula. Yet the great value of the floating quality as a selling point did not make an immediate impression on Harley Procter. For some time he continued to occupy himself with communicating to American consumers what he felt were the principal attributes of Ivory: its purity and multiple uses—a soap so pure that it could safely be used to bathe babies in the nursery, of such quality that it could effectively serve "the varied uses about the house that daily arise." The first official use of Ivory as a trademark occurred on July 18, 1879.

In the office Harley faced a practical problem: how to convince the other members of the firm that P&G needed to be spending much more money on advertising? He wanted to advertise directly to consumers. This was a new concept to the partners, as it was to the owners of most other businesses of the time. The idea of investing considerable sums of P&G money in advertising represented a major change for a firm which had historically tried to plow back every available cent into the capital assets of the business. Before he could advertise directly to consumers Harley Procter had to undertake a major in-house selling campaign.

"Ivory is the finest soap we have ever made," he said at a meeting of the partners late in 1881. "But how are customers going to know about its virtues unless we tell them?" As eyebrows were raised around him, Harley patiently explained how he planned "to post the public by letting them know of the superior quality of the genuine article" through repetitive advertising in the public media.

Harley's request for funds did not take place under the most propitious circumstances. The firm had recently been the loser in long and costly litigation involving the Tilghman process for extracting glycerin from the residue of soapmaking. Although Procter & Gamble had used the Tilghman method briefly before switching to a drastically modified process, the firm had continued to pay royalties until 1871. Then it had stopped. Tilghman sued P&G and several other alleged infringers of his patents. Eventually, after years of court action, Procter & Gamble was ordered not only to pay back royalties and accumulated interest but was also required to reimburse Tilghman for personal damages. That resulted in the company's having to pay the man nearly $260,000.

In 1881 the entire amount had not yet been paid; yet here was Harley Procter arguing for advertising funds which would place even more strain on the firm's treasury. Harley pleaded, exhorted, and finally made his sale. Reluctantly the partners approved an 1882 advertising budget of $11,000 so that Harley could begin "to post the public" about Ivory soap.

Long before this Harley had drawn and patented a unique design for the product: The laundry-size bar of White Soap was notched in the middle of its long sides so that the homemaker could easily make two toilet soap bars out of the one big bar. (This "notching" of a large bar of Ivory soap remained a P&G practice a century later.)

Harley also had designed what he felt was a "very elegant" Ivory wrapper—a black and white checkerboard pattern dominated by the Ivory name. The wrapper featured the moon and stars trademark.

As P&G's first national sales manager, he was now hectically engaged—as were his assistant, Hastings L. French, and a three-man sales force—in introducing Ivory soap to wholesalers, brokers, and commission houses around the country. The introductory advertisement in the grocery trade press contained a

1851: A rough cross-mark.

Later, the cross becomes a star.

Then, a cluster of stars honoring 13 original colonies.

Next, the "Man-in-the-Moon" profile emerges.

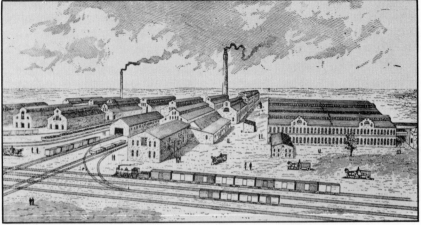

1882: First regis-
tered in the U.S.
Patent Office.

1902: Embellished
with gingerbread
frills.

1920: Back to sim-
plicity.

1932: Final design
by sculptor Ernest
Haswell.

THE "IVORY" is a Laundry Soap, with all
the fine qualities of a choice Toilet Soap, and
is 99 44-100 **per cent. pure.**

Ladies will find this Soap especially adapted
for washing laces, infants', clothing, silk hose,
cleaning gloves and all articles of fine texture
and delicate color, and for the varied uses
about the house that daily arise, requiring the
use of soap that is above the ordinary in
quality.

For the Bath, Toilet, or Nursery it is preferred
to most of the Soaps sold for toilet use, being
purer and much more pleasant and effective
and possessing all the desirable properties of
the finest unadultered White Castile Soap. The
Ivory Soap will " **float.**"

The cakes are so shaped that they may be
used entire for general purposes or divided
with a stout thread (as illustrated) into two
perfectly formed cakes, of convenient size for
toilet use.

The price, compared to the quality and the
size of the cakes, makes it the cheapest Soap
for everybody for every want. TRY IT.

SOLD EVERYWHERE.

THE MANHATTAN.

✦ COMPARISON ✦
— OF —
PROCTER & GAMBLE'S
"IVORY" SOAP
— WITH —
Best "Castile" and "English Standard White" Soaps.

CONSTITUENTS.	IVORY SOAP.	CASTILE. Vegetable Oil Soap.	STANDARD WHITE SOAP.
Water,	14.249	14.50	32.80
Fat Acids,	75.699	76.50	61.00
Soda (combined),	10.052	9.00	6.20
	100.000 (1)	100.00 (2)	100.00 (3)
The fat acids stand to the combined alkali as .	7.535 to 1	8.5 to 1	9.74 to 1
Real Soap in 100 parts,	85.751%	85.50%	67.20%

"This analysis and comparison shows the PROCTER & GAMBLE
'IVORY SOAP' to be of remarkable purity, and in every respect of
superior excellence. As a Laundry Soap it has no superior, and it
is equalled only by the most select vegetable oil Castile Soap.

"All which is respectfully submitted.

B. SILLIMAN,

MEDICAL DEPARTMENT OF YALE COLLEGE,
NEW HAVEN, CONN.

December 23, 1882.

Professor of Chemistry."

Across the Top: The evolution of
Procter & Gamble's Trademark began
as a crude cross, used by wharf hands
to identify P&G's Star Candles.
Opposite Page: (Above) P&G's first
research laboratory, 1887: (Below)
Artist's rendering of Ivorydale in 1890.
This page: (Left) the first advertise-
ment for Ivory Soap, 1882; (Above)
One of Harley Procter's first tes-
timonial advertisements for Ivory
Soap.

31

woodcut of two feminine hands holding a stout string about the notch of the large bar as if about to divide the bar into two cakes. "The IVORY . . . is the only Laundry Soap that successfully answers for Toilet Use," the advertisement said.

Harley and his sales force continued to push, in addition to Ivory, the sales of candles, lard oil, and P&G's other soap products. On one occasion, Harley traveled to San Francisco and returned with an order from a single customer for seventeen railcar loads of P&G soaps and candles. He also brought back from that and other trips further convincing evidence that the increasing use of other means of illumination would be eroding candle sales.

Now, with the advent of 1882, Harley had his $11,000 advertising budget for Ivory. His mind churned over how the funds could be used most effectively, and he decided that he needed independent appraisals of the purity of Ivory soap. James N. Gamble had assured him on that point. But would the buying public need more convincing evidence than just the good name of Procter & Gamble, despite the firm's reputation for "pure goods and full weight"?

Harley knew that the castile type was commonly accepted by the public as a model of purity. However, there was no established definition for "pure soap." He decided to seek a standard from an independent scientific consultant in New York City; and further, to employ that consultant to provide analyses of the contents of the three leading brands of castile soap sold in America.

The chemical consultant performed the requested analyses. He sent his reports to Harley together with his scientific views on what constituted an absolutely pure soap. Such a soap, he advised, consisted of nothing but fatty acids and alkali. Anything else that turned up in an analysis, he said, should be described as "foreign and unnecessary substances."

With the definition of purity now in hand, Harley and James N. Gamble sent samples of Ivory soap to the same chemist for analysis. They offered to pay reasonable fees—in advance if preferred—to analyze Ivory for its purity and efficacy.

When the first consultant sent in his report, Harley carefully perused the figures on Ivory's "foreign and unnecessary substances" and compared them with the earlier analyses of the three top-selling castile soaps. With sudden delight, he saw—using the consultant's own definition of purity—that Ivory was actually purer than the castile soaps. He jotted down the "impurities" shown in the Ivory analysis: uncombined alkali, 0.11%; carbonates, 0.28%; and mineral matter, 0.17%. Total "foreign and unnecessary substances" in Ivory: 0.56%.

Whether Harley's next move was due to instinctive advertising genius or to a leaning toward honest advertising or perhaps a combination of both remains unknown. Whatever the reason, he concluded that Ivory's purity should be advertised exactly as the analysis showed. After deducting the 0.56% of impurities, Ivory could be described accurately as "99 and 44/100% pure." Thus was born one of the most famous advertising slogans in history—a slogan that was still to be thriving a century later.

In late 1882, with technical support for the claims he wished to make to consumers, Harley wrote the copy for the first Ivory advertisement which would address the public directly. To illustrate it, he brought into service the woodcut used earlier in the grocery trade press—feminine hands, stout string, and a notched bar of Ivory—even though that illustration did not directly relate to the principal selling points of his copy.

The first Ivory advertisement appeared on December 21, 1881, in a nationally circulated religious weekly called *The Independent*. Harley's copy read:

> *The Ivory is a Laundry Soap with all the fine qualities of a choice Toilet Soap, and it is 99 and 44/100% pure.*
>
> *Ladies will find this Soap especially adapted for washing laces, infants' clothing, silk hose, cleaning gloves and all articles of fine texture and delicate color and for the varied uses about the house that daily arise, requiring the use of soap that is above the ordinary in quality.*
>
> *For the Bath, Toilet, or Nursery it is preferred to most of the Soaps sold for toilet use, being purer and much more pleasant and effective, and possessing all the desirable properties of the finest unadulterated White Castile Soap. The Ivory Soap will "float."*
>
> *The cakes are so shaped that they may be used entire for general purposes, or divided with a stout thread (as illustrated) into two perfectly formed cakes, of convenient size for toilet use.*

33

The price, compared to the quality and the size of the cakes, makes it the cheapest soap for everybody and every want. Try it.

Sold Everywhere

The first Ivory ad in *The Independent*, including the illustration, occupied only six column inches. It made only a passing, one-sentence reference to the floating qualities of Ivory soap.

Very soon thereafter, however, Ivory ads were occupying full pages in several national magazines, each including testimonials received from the chemistry professors to whom Harley had sent samples of Ivory. Oddly enough, although the advertising copy continued to emphasize the purity and safety of Ivory, the "99 and 44/100% pure" claim did not appear in all the early copy. Also, the fact that "The Ivory Soap will 'float' " only occasionally received special mention. In truth, the famous Ivory advertising slogan, "It Floats," evolved so slowly that it was not used as a principal feature of an Ivory advertisement until ten years later, in 1891.

Nevertheless, these first ads in the years from 1882 to 1885 were enormously effective. As a matter of record, Ivory soap was becoming such a consumer favorite that several other soap manufacturers were advertising that they had products "just as good as the 'Ivory.' " P&G had a strong response to statements like these. In prominent footnotes to Ivory advertisements, it said:

A WORD OF WARNING

There are many white soaps, each represented to be "just as good as the 'Ivory' "; they ARE NOT, and like all counterfeits, lack the peculiar and remarkable qualities of the genuine. Ask for "Ivory" soap and insist upon getting it.

Thus Harley Thomas Procter was not only the father of what is still P&G's oldest and perhaps best known product, Ivory soap, but also the originator of the creative advertising and promotional methods which contributed immensely to the growth of Procter & Gamble long after his own active participation in the business. Years later Harry W. Brown, who joined P&G at the time Harley was searching for a distinctive name for P&G's White soap, was to write: "Harley Procter was the greatest salesman and advertiser I have ever known . . . He was energetic, brilliant, versatile, and ahead of his times."

34

Ahead of his times indeed in the imagination and innovations he brought to the science of advertising. His notebooks, which he kept as efficiently as an accountant keeps his ledgers, indicated that he realized, long before the phrase became a cliché, that one picture is worth a thousand words. He jotted down suggested copy, and every item was accompanied by a suggestion for a drawing that would illustrate it.

This was an era when poets were regarded with more reverence than they are today. Longfellow, Whittier, Whitman, Poe were national heroes. And so, in the idiom of the day, Harley's Ivory advertisements often featured verse. Readers were invited to submit their own poems (together with an Ivory wrapper). For those he published Harley paid anywhere from $2.50 to $10. So many amateur poets responded that he sponsored a contest in which the best poem would receive $300. The poems came in by the thousands, and sales of Ivory boomed.

Other items in his notebooks delved into something else that had never before been tried: the purchase of paintings by distinguished artists which could be used for full-page magazine displays. Of course, they would have to be related to soap, and they could be expensive. But they represented a milestone in American advertising art.

According to his notes, he commissioned works for as much as $1,000 from such outstanding artists as Maxfield Parrish, W. Granville Smith, Alice Barber Stephens. Harley sent two men abroad to study European reproduction techniques; and when he could guarantee good copies of his pictures, his advertisements offered reprints "suitable for framing" in return for Ivory wrappers.

Once, when Harley felt the need for fresh ideas, he called on the public to help. He offered $1,000 for "new, unusual, and improved methods of using Ivory soap." So many replies came that the company eventually published a booklet, "Unusual Uses of Ivory Soap"—everything from massaging sore muscles to polishing jewelry. The man's mind teemed with ideas, and most of them not only worked but became part of American advertising technique.

* * * * *

As Procter & Gamble neared the middle of its fifth decade, the founding partners, both now in their eighties, left most operations to their sons. Still, William Procter occasionally visited the offices and one day he calculated some costs that troubled him because they seemed unnecessary.

A vast railroad system was crisscrossing the United States. Yet Procter & Gamble's plants and warehouses were at locations bound to steamboat and barge operations. Nevertheless the firm was shipping by rail. It was spending about $60,000 a year, William Procter estimated, just to transport products to the nearest railroad siding. Did this make sense?

Another thing disturbed him, too. The Central Avenue plant's production capacity was already strained by a constantly growing demand for P&G products. What should the company do? Expand Central Avenue and have a rail spur built to it? Was this the wise course to take? Or should it build a completely new factory near a railroad and gradually phase out the Central Avenue operation?

The Procters—old William, the founder, and his sons, William Alexander and Harley Thomas—argued that P&G's long-term prospects justified building an entirely new plant. Harley Procter, as sales and advertising manager, strongly advocated this idea. He had become convinced during his frequent traveling that P&G would be increasingly disadvantaged because its major competitors already had rail sidings.

The Gamble family, however, had serious reservations about the wisdom of spending the huge sum of money—perhaps more than $1 million—that would be required for the move the Procters had in mind. Old James Gamble was especially adamant. For the first time in the firm's history the founding families were on opposite sides of a critical issue. The debate was still going on when the weather turned bitterly cold in early January, 1884.

As was the weekday custom of each, William A. Procter was lunching at the Queen City Club in downtown Cincinnati and James N. Gamble at his Westwood home when news reached them that the Central Avenue plant was on fire. Breaking out first in the lard oil factory, the blaze had spread swiftly to the candle works and then—whipped by icy, gale-like winds—into the oil storage area.

William A. Procter rushed out of the Queen City Club and signaled a nearby horse-drawn cab. He could see black smoke sweeping over the city and hear the bells of fire engines. Resisting the impulse to have the driver take him to the plant,

Procter looked beyond the blaze, saw its impact on P&G. What he foresaw aroused deep anxiety.

Red oil, once a lowly by-product of candlemaking, had become one of the most important ingredients of P&G soaps. If the oil tanks were destroyed, production would be crippled. And once it became known to market speculators that Procter & Gamble's supplies of red oil had been decimated, the price would zoom. With decisiveness during a moment of crisis, William Alexander ordered the driver to speed to the Western Union office. There he sent telegrams to the company's buyers in key cities: "Buy all available red oil."

The next day, January 8, 1884, the *Cincinnati Enquirer* reported with the journalistic eloquence of the times:

> *In spite of Chief Bunker's excellent plan to keep the flames from spreading, they finally reached the candle factory, a two-story brick building on the west side. Thick smoke was rolling out of the windows of this structure.*
>
> *It was then plain that the fire was going to be a big one. Immediately adjoining the candle factory were the large four-story soap and candle warehouses filled with stores. Great iron doors were between the two on each floor. In a short time the warehouse was also going, and then the fire was indeed hot and fierce. Under the two were cellars stored with oil, and this, with the combustible material above, made a blaze that for hours shot upward and outward and seemed to laugh at the many streams of water that were being thrown upon it with apparent useless result. By 3:30 [P.M.] the lard oil factory and the soap factory's small buildings etc., could not be saved.*
>
> *The firemen labored under terrible disadvantages, and many were the remarks of sympathy made for them by the spectators. The water froze almost as quickly as it fell upon them, and most of them were covered with a thick coating of ice. Every now and then one was compelled to withdraw from his work for a while to thaw out. Some held the hose until their hands were stiff and covered with ice.*

The issue of "to build or not to build" that had divided the families was now gone, of course. Because a new plant had to be built, the values of building near a railroad and on a site that

37

would provide plenty of room for future expansion were clear to both the Procters and the Gambles.

Some parts of the Central Avenue plant had not been wholly destroyed. They could be put back into production rather quickly. A $209,000 insurance settlement on the fire damage could be used to arrange for stopgap production until the new plant could be built. In a fortuitous move about a year earlier, P&G had purchased, from the heirs of its late owners, a small soap and candle factory about a block away from the Central Avenue plant. That production space was now of great value.

Also, William A. Procter's "buy red oil" telegrams brought unexpected results. The purchases resulting from his orders gave P&G a near corner on the red oil market. The firm later sold the oil it didn't need at a sizable profit, and those profits, too, in effect, went to help build a new factory.

As the partners debated the best location for the plant, William A. and Harley Procter recommended purchase of a 55-acre site near the Bee Line Railroad in Mill Creek Valley, about seven miles north of downtown Cincinnati. (At the urging of railroad representatives, Harley personally examined the site. Not wanting the property owners to learn that Procter & Gamble might be interested in buying and thus tempt them to raise the price, Harley pretended to be hunting quail as he strolled over the brush-filled property with a shotgun under his arm.)

On his recommendation the partners voted to acquire the 55 acres. A critical question remained unanswered, however. Where could the firm borrow the estimated $1 million they needed to build the new plant? All such considerations had suddenly to be postponed. They were thrust aside by family bereavement. Founder William Procter, in his eighty-third year, died in his sleep on April 4, 1884, at his home at Eighth and Race Streets.

* * * * *

The reading of William Procter's will, to which the entire family listened in silence, furnished an interesting record of the company's growth. The elder Procter's share in plants and equipment was valued at $82,575. His part of the firm's cash and ledger accounts came to $208,203. Money owed him on the various loans he had made, mainly to his children, totaled $64,735.25. Adding personal bank deposits, he left to his widow, Olivia, and his sons and daughters an estate worth $367,901.13. (This will carried a clause stipulating that all debts owed him by his children were to be deducted from their inheritance. This stipulation reflected in his personal affairs the same insistence on integrity he had always tried to imbue in P&G's business conduct.)

A decent interval after the funeral the P&G partners returned to the problem of raising $1 million for the construction of the new plant. The only hope seemed to lie with the large New York banks. Harley, viewed by the others as the most persuasive member of the firm, was unanimously chosen to go to New York.

What he said to the officers of the Mercantile Bank when requesting the $1 million loan was not recorded. Whatever Harley's arguments were, they were strong enough to bring the president of the Mercantile Bank to Cincinnati to make his own judgment. What the president heard and saw during that visit led him to approve the loan in late 1884.

Ivorydale, as the new factory site was to be named, went into construction as soon as weather made work feasible. The aging survivor of the original partnership, James Gamble, was given the honor of breaking ground on March 23, 1885, and the strength with which he dug in his shovel brought applause from those who had gathered to attend the ceremony—a group that included many of Cincinnati's dignitaries. And suddenly a crisis had to be met.

Plans for Ivorydale included the building of a railroad spur from the Bee Line tracks to the factory itself. This had been part of the agreement made with the railroad at the time the land was purchased. The spur, though only a mile and a half in length, was incorporated as an entity to be called the Ivorydale and Mill Creek Valley Railroad, a long name for a short line.

Its tracks would have to cross a toll road known as Carthage Pike. The Spring Grove Avenue Company, owners of the road, now demanded payment for the right. As for settling on an equitable price, there was no precedent for such a decision. The matter was amicably taken to court where a jury set a fee of $2,500. Procter & Gamble immediately paid it and ordered the laying of tracks to begin.

The owners of Carthage Pike, for their part, asserted that $2,500 was an outrageously low sum for a permanent right-of-way across their road. They insisted on a much higher price, informing P&G that, jury or no jury, the railroad spur would not be allowed to cross the road for so low a fee.

Understandably this angered everybody at Procter & Gamble. "You go right on laying those tracks!" James Norris Gamble told the construction people. With the hope that the conflict would quickly be settled, tracks were laid from the railroad to one side of the toll road; from the factory to the other. Rails were not yet laid on the roadway itself. Weeks passed in deadlock; weeks of tense, angry, futile discussions. Everybody at P&G lost patience. Finally a new and secret order was issued to lay the last section of track across the pike on a Saturday night when no witnesses were present.

Somehow the Spring Grove Avenue Company heard of this. Its attorney rushed to a judge of common pleas court and obtained an order restraining further construction. The order came too late. That night, before any restrictive papers could be served, the tracks crossed Carthage Pike.

The railroad company had sold P&G a small red locomotive for hauling cars along its spur. This was now brought to the roadside, ready to be shuttled back and forth.

All this activity roused the road owners to fury. They organized a gang of sixty men armed with rifles, picks, and shovels. The little army advanced, ready to fight any force that tried to interfere with their tearing up of the rails on the road.

Procter & Gamble's own laborers also gathered in a fighting mood. Picking up whatever weapons they could find, mostly bats, picks, and crowbars, they started a grim march toward the road. A bloody battle seemed inevitable.

The only thing which stopped it was the presence of guns among the cohorts of the Spring Grove Avenue Company. Shots fired over the heads of Procter & Gamble's forces threatened death if there was a further advance. Nobody wanted to die for that thirty-foot right-of-way. The confrontation subsided, and the tracks were ripped off the pike.

Shortly thereafter, conceding it had lost the dispute and that the best way to insure peaceful operations was to settle on a new price with the road owners, P&G paid an added sum and the Ivorydale and Mill Creek Valley Railroad became an operating reality.

Ivorydale was such an immense project—with more than twenty separate structures connected underground by a network of steam mains and water pipes about ten miles in length—that it received wide public notice during and after construction.

Designed with a consideration for architectural beauty uncommon to factories of that era, the buildings were constructed of gray limestone trimmed with brick. (Excepting the soap kettle house, most were one story in height. The kettle house had to be two stories high to accommodate the huge new soap boiling kettles, each of which held 150,000 pounds of soap.)

Although some businessmen of the day considered the expenses an unwarranted extravagance, well-kept lawns, flower beds, and trees separated the factory from the street and provided on Spring Grove Avenue a general impression of "a nice place to work."

The production capacity for soap at the old Central Avenue plant had been about 200,000 bars per day. The new soap capacity at Ivorydale was more than double that amount. And that capacity was badly needed. Not only were the innovative advertising and promotional techniques of Harley Procter creating a steadily increasing market for Ivory soap, but a new laundry soap formulated by James Norris Gamble was also doing well. This product —Lenox, a yellow laundry bar containing tallow and rosin—was becoming especially popular in hard-water areas.

Meanwhile Harley Procter continued his efforts "to post the public" about Ivory soap in magazines and newspapers. Simultaneously he publicized Lenox with a variety of in-store promotions. As a result of the heavy activity behind Lenox, it was not long before this 12-ounce, oval-shaped bar superseded P&G's Mottled German and Oleine in sales.

So in the late 1880s, with two outstanding soap brands, Ivory and Lenox, each backed by steady advertising and promotion, Procter & Gamble was on the path toward the growth it would continue to enjoy in the decades ahead. The course was clear: The company's future must be based on continuing efforts to develop and market low-cost, highly effective branded products to meet ever-changing consumer needs.

Also, by introducing Lenox despite the near certainty that it would take business away from its Mottled German and Oleine soaps, P&G was committing itself to a willingness to market new products which might take business away from existing P&G brands. If that had to be the way to stay abreast of consumer wishes, so be it.

In the summer of 1887 a young chemist named Harley James Morrison, fresh out of Yale, was employed in a position akin to what is now called a chemical engineer. Within three years, supported by James N. Gamble, Morrison built a laboratory staff of college-trained technicians at a time when almost no such jobs were offered in American industry. By 1890 he won approval of a plan to create something previously unheard of—an analytical laboratory at the Ivorydale plant.

The establishment of that laboratory was to have a major impact on P&G's future. It set the firm on a course of scientific research aimed at translating laboratory discoveries into new and improved products.

4

THE NEW FORCE
IN
LABOR RELATIONS

William Cooper Procter

With the many business problems requiring attention, William Alexander Procter at some time in 1883 decided—as had his father 32 years before—that it was time to bring a new generation into the family-owned firm. His only son, William Cooper Procter, was completing his studies at Princeton University (then still named the College of New Jersey).

Perhaps William Alexander felt a young man could learn more in the business than in academic corridors. Whatever his rationale, he persuaded 21-year-old Cooper, as the family called him, to leave Princeton in his senior year and join the company's workers.

Cooper, whose tall, lithe figure attested to his prowess as an

Early Dividend Day crowd at Cincinnati's Coney Island.

athlete at Princeton, joined P&G at the very lowest level of factory labor. He did every menial job from shoveling rosin and soap to pouring fatty mixtures into crutchers. He brought his lunch in paper bags as the other workers did and sat on the floor and ate with them, learning their feelings about their work.

His early contributions to the firm were to be summarized some years later by economist J. George Frederick.

> *The new day calls for men who do what has never been done before: who break down the traditions and the barriers surrounding business, and who persist in finding a way to do what they see should be done, even if their closest advisers cannot see a pathway. These men set new marks for industry, blaze new trails of progress, and change our whole outlook and attitude toward business. Such a man, I believe, is William Cooper Procter.*

Cooper Procter began "blazing new trails" when he sought out his father one day to lodge a complaint on behalf of his fellow plant employees.

"Our people are working too hard and too long, and I tell you this from personal experience," he said. For six days a week the plant employees labored, with time off for lunch, from 6:30 A.M. until 6 P.M. To Cooper Procter that schedule seemed inhuman. He urged his father and uncle to let the workers have Saturday afternoon off without loss of pay.

In 1884 such a thing was unheard of in American industry. If William Alexander and James Norris were shocked, it was because the idea smacked of out-and-out radicalism. The practices the family had pursued for close to fifty years were being challenged by a youngster just out of college. One can visualize William Alexander striding back and forth, hands clasped behind his back, shaking his head, muttering about the impossible notions of this new generation. At that moment he may very well have been disappointed in his son.

Cooper Procter continued to argue for at least a test of his belief that plant employees would work harder than ever to justify the half day off. This gesture by P&G of interest in employees as individuals might very well lessen costs by increasing production. That silenced the older men. No businessman could afford to ignore a step that promised benefits for both the business and its employees.

Harley Procter, himself an indefatigable innovator, endorsed the half day Saturday proposal. After a good deal of discussion, the partners hesitantly agreed on a trial, and they included the office workers as well. Should it fail, the plan could always be rescinded.

The half-holiday practice was put into effect in 1885, setting another pioneering example for American industry. P&G's plant employees were initially enthusiastic. But to Cooper Procter's dismay, it soon became obvious that the workers thought the afternoon off was an inadequate gesture.

This occurred, coincidently or not, as the newly formed Federation of Organized Trades and Labor Unions (the forerunner of the AFL-CIO) was beginning to assert its strength. Labor wanted a great deal more than the shortening of the work week, and the union leaders expected to give the American workingman the courage to make many more demands.

Also, a very militant group called the Knights of Labor was actually staging street demonstrations in Cincinnati. Shouting as they marched, they denounced virtually every industry in town. Before long a committee of the Knights crowded into the Procter & Gamble offices on Second Street, claiming to represent the firm's plant employees. The venerable William Alexander, looking hard from face to face, could see none of his own people among these delegates. He snapped: "Do any of you work for us?" Nobody answered. Testily, William Alexander said, "We recognize the right of no man to interfere between us and our employees. If *they* have any grievances, we'll be glad to receive a committee from *them.*"

Having delivered this ultimatum, he turned away and walked out of the office. The Knights of Labor left, discomfited, muttering threats to organize a boycott of P&G products by the working class.

The boycott threat never materialized, but the Knights of Labor continued to incite P&G employees. Their credo seemed to be: "If you keep on telling people they are being exploited, if you do it passionately and tirelessly, some will begin to believe you." Apparently many did believe, for P&G soon suffered a number of strikes.

At this point William Cooper Procter had no better solution for labor problems than anyone else. Whenever the employees started a walkout—and there were fourteen in the next two years—he felt there ought to be some way of kindling among the workers a stronger feeling of respect for and loyalty to P&G. How could they be convinced that their overall interests were truly inseparable from those of Procter & Gamble?

The idea which finally suggested itself to Cooper (possibly out of his reading at Princeton) was one that the guilds of Europe had practiced centuries earlier. "We should let the employees share in the firm's earnings," he said. "That will give them an incentive to increase earnings."

The thought was utterly new to Cooper Procter's elders. At the outset it was summarily rejected. Nevertheless, rumors about it were circulated in business circles. Reporters came to the office, seeking interviews. Later a writer for *Industrial Relations Magazine* wrote:

> *When William Cooper Procter suggested that it would benefit employer and employee alike to permit the employee to share in the company's profits, the family thought he had lost his senses. Such a thing was unheard of. Were the men not paid for doing what they were hired to do? Why not give them the business and let them run things to suit themselves? These and similar questions were fired at William Cooper Procter. It was even suggested that his resignation would be acceptable.*

The magazine reporter did not stop with interviewing family members. He went to see the heads of several other companies, all with large rosters of employees, and he added to his story:

Outsiders all agreed it was a foolhardy thing to do. They felt anyone who would suggest such a thing was an out-and-out radical. Such a plan was a shortcut to bankruptcy. Even the Knights of Labor, purporting to hold the interests of the workers at heart, viewed it with alarm. What chance could they have to call a strike in a plant where the workers shared with the management in the profits?

Cooper Procter had not presented the proposal before much study. He recognized that profit sharing was thought of generally as only a sop to erase discontent over wages. Though he rejected profit sharing as a substitute for a fair wage, he still embraced it as a potential means for improving efficiency.

As he studied its pros and cons, Cooper kept a key premise in mind: "Any worthwhile change in the conduct of a business," he

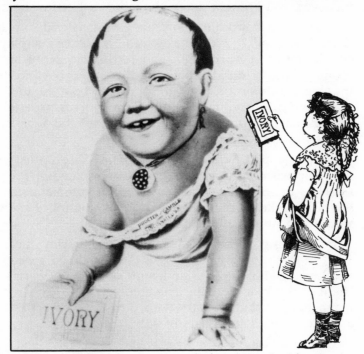

The first Ivory Baby, a cardboard counter-top display piece. At right, drawing from 1885 Harper's Magazine ad.

wrote in his business diary, "must first and last have the element of lessening the cost." And he concluded that the success of any profit sharing plan depended on that simple fact, regardless of how desirable it might be on other grounds.

He felt that profit sharing could not be a viable business proposition unless it increased workers' efficiency at least to the extent of the dividend paid to them. If it increased efficiency to an extent even greater than that, he felt an employer was as much obligated to install profit sharing as to install an improved piece of production equipment.

In presenting the idea to his elders, Cooper pointed out that the root of labor unrest was believed by employers to lie in the fact that "the employee takes no interest in his work and has no consideration for his employer's property or welfare." Profit sharing in P&G, he argued, could supply "the motive which is now admitted to be sadly lacking" *if* it developed the same feeling of self-interest in one's work that a man had in working for himself—and if it reduced the waste of material, cut the labor turnover, and brought down the labor cost of finished products.

His logic was appealing, and the partners decided to give profit sharing a trial. It was announced to factory employees in a circular letter in April, 1887, and further explained at meetings: Profits would be divided between the employees and the firm in the same proportion that total wages bore to total costs of manufacturing and marketing. Each worker would receive a semiannual cash dividend according to the ratio of his or her own wages to total wages.

When the plan was announced, many disgruntled employees viewed it with cynicism. Some expressed contempt. Profit sharing smacked of trickery, a ploy to stave off complaints and strikes. Besides, workers generally felt that the amount of shared profits would probably turn out to be a pittance.

This feeling persisted in a smouldering way until October, 1887. In that month James Norris Gamble called a meeting of 318 employees who, because of length of service, were entitled to share in the year's profits. The eligible participants ranged from managers and skilled soapmakers down to workers earning $4.25 a week for packaging bars of soap.

They all assembled for what was termed "Dividend Day." The company had hired a German band to lend cheerfulness to the occasion. This did not prevent a number of employees from approaching the event with derision. Was music supposed to buoy their spirits when they discovered how little profit sharing would amount to, how thoroughly they had been hoaxed?

When all the employees had assembled, James Norris Gamble, dignified in his cutaway coat, mounted a platform and waved the band to silence. After a short speech in which he emphasized the mutuality of the interests of P&G and its employees, he invited the workers to come forward and pick up their checks. The line formed. Envelopes were torn open, and instantly the meeting hummed with astonishment. Many an employee found himself enriched by 13½% of his annual wages, or seven weeks' pay. Several people got as much as $280. The total distribution of profit sharing dividends amounted to $9,026.66.

James N. Gamble used that dividend day—as he and others often would in the future—to urge employees to "be practical" about the money received. Save and invest, he advised, by putting the money in a building and loan association or using it toward the purchase of a home.

William Cooper Procter spoke briefly at the celebration:

> The first job we have is to turn out quality merchandise that consumers will buy and keep on buying. If we produce it efficiently and economically, we will earn a profit, in which you will share. But the profits can't be distributed unless they are earned. And if the company is to take care of its equipment, expand normally, and remain in a sound fiscal position, part of the earnings must be plowed back into the business. That will safeguard your future as well as the company's.

Although there were only three small-scale work stoppages during the first six months of the plan, there was no appreciable evidence of greater effort on the part of most employees. It was increasingly evident that the plan had a flaw. Employees were coming to look upon their dividends not as rewards for greater efficiency but merely as extra pay they could expect to receive every six months. During the next decade, however, the search for a solution to this problem had to yield to more immediate concerns.

*   *   *   *   *

The year of the fiftieth anniversary of Procter & Gamble, 1887, was eventful in many respects—in the country, in Cincinnati, and within the firm itself.

Among other national happenings that year, the government began free mail deliveries in all communities in the country with a population of at least 10,000, and the United States leased from Hawaii for use as a naval base some sheltered port property called Pearl Harbor.

In Cincinnati, the city's first cable car was two years old but still a delightful novelty. Riders could "speed" at eight miles per hour from Fifth and Walnut Streets downtown out Gilbert Avenue all the way to Peeble's Corner. On a Sunday afternoon in 1887 one of the cable cars ran wild on the inbound route bumping cars ahead until there occurred what one historian reported as "a pileup at Fifth and Sycamore Streets of cable cars, horsecars, people, horses, and bewildered gripmen. More than 10,000 gathered to see the cars, horses, and people untangle. Happily, no one was killed."

As for Procter & Gamble, it had no internal troubles. Its business was steadily growing. The popularity of Ivory and Lenox soaps was contributing substantial revenues. Net profits in 1887 reached $430,000.

In fact, P&G's products were selling so well that the office space, too, had to be expanded to accommodate additional personnel. The main office was relocated in rented quarters in Cincinnati's United Bank Building. There some twenty-five people tended their ledgers and their billing duties under slowly revolving overhead fans; they had the use of four telephones and eight typewriters—a wealth of conveniences that made P&G's quarters among the most modern in the city.

Apart from such physical changes there were others that resulted from the death of co-founder William Procter. A revised partnership agreement was enacted in the spring of 1887. William A. and Harley Procter and James N. Gamble each got a 25% interest. Old James Gamble the founder retained a 17% interest and gave David B. Gamble 8%. This agreement left the Procters and Gambles with equal holdings.

During this process of dividing the families' interests, Harley championed the admission of young Cooper Procter as a partner. In October, 1887, shortly before the semiannual Dividend Day celebration, Cooper Procter was given a 5% interest. Half of the 5% came from the Procters and the other half from the Gambles. As a result, the Procters now owned a majority—52.5% of the firm.

50

Less than four years before, it should be remembered, a deep schism had developed between the two families over the issue of building a new plant at Ivorydale. Now, in two surprising gestures—loaning personal funds to the firm to settle the William Procter estate and giving the Procters control of the company—the Gambles appeared to be tossing aside all fiscal restraints.

This was not so. The Gambles were simply putting their money where their hearts were: the best long-term interests of Procter & Gamble. Cooper Procter ought to be brought in as a partner, the Gambles obviously concluded, because he was the best candidate among the third generation to assume the P&G leadership when the second generation stepped aside.

Although he was the most junior of the partners—but by 1889 essentially in charge of Ivorydale operations—it was Cooper Procter who conceived and nurtured the idea that the partnership should be converted to a public corporation. Looking ahead, he foresaw growth opportunities for P&G that would necessitate additional plants, new equipment, the development and introduction of new products—in short, a need for capital expenditures that would extend far beyond the financial means of the partnership.

His partners agreed in 1889 to explore the idea of incorporation. The firm began making contacts with appropriate financial institutions, with stock underwriting firms, with auditors, and with expert corporate law counsel.

As the voluminous paperwork required for filing certificates of incorporation proceeded early in 1890, those involved attempted to keep some secrecy around their activities. But rumors began to spread in Cincinnati that something big was about to happen at Procter & Gamble. Historian Edward Hungerford commented about those days of community-wide speculation:

> *Cincinnati, where the affairs of Procter & Gamble had become one of its chief business barometers, was having a rather uncomfortable time of it. Rumors were flying around downtown—in the banks, the clubs, and the newspaper offices—that strange things were to happen out at Procter & Gamble. ("In clubs, restaurants, and offices," said the* Cincinnati Times-Star, *"nobody talked of anything else.") It was said that the whole business was about to fall into the hands of one of those great English soapmaking concerns, with*

worldwide ramifications and millions of pounds of sterling banked up behind it. Cincinnati chilled at the thought. That might easily mean almost anything bad for the town, up to the actual closing of Ivorydale and the moving out of its huge mechanical equipment. Not a very likely possibility, but anything is possible to the minds of a panic-stricken town.

The speculative fires were fueled further when word leaked that a new corporation, the Procter & Gamble Company, was to be set up and headquartered in Jersey City, New Jersey. Some Cincinnatians picked up rumors that three men from the New York area—George F. Crane, Horace J. Morse, and William C. Gulliver—would be the sole stockholders.

In fact, as the incorporation plan was implemented, it turned out that the certificates of incorporation did show those three men as sole stockholders. But their role as incorporators was limited to carrying out necessary legal steps to establish an orderly means of transferring the assets of the P&G partnership to a new public corporation.

There was never any thought of P&G leaving its hometown of Cincinnati. The new company would be incorporated in New Jersey only because that state had more liberal incorporation statutes than Ohio. Under its statutes, the company would have to maintain an office in New Jersey which, technically, would be its "principal office."

But the partners clung adamantly to some stipulations: *They would keep control of the business for the indefinite future,* and the Procter & Gamble Company would continue with Cincinnati as its headquarters and "principal place of business."

The first official gathering of the Procter & Gamble Company was the meeting of stockholders held in Jersey City on July 17, 1890. Recorded in the minutes of that meeting was the "certificate of incorporation."* It specified that the company's "principal office" would be in New Jersey, as the state's law required, but the certificate further stated that "the principal office or place of business of said company is to be situated in the city of Cincinnati, Hamilton County, Ohio."

---

* As a minor problem that P&G still has, Procter was misspelled as Proctor in the initial incorporation certificate. The frequency of this spelling error prompted some P&G people later to carry business cards which had a parenthetical footnote: "It's *ER*, dammit!"

5

"INC."

Early share of P&G stock, 1905.

The financial arrangements for the transition revealed months of thorough preparation. The incorporation certificate specified that the "total amount of the capital stock of the company shall be $4,500,000 divided into 45,000 shares of the par value of $100 each." Those 45,000 shares were to be divided into 22,500 shares of common stock and 22,500 shares of preferred 8% stock.

Studying subsequent events, no one could believe that the Procter and Gamble families had any intention of abandoning their business. The eleven-member board of directors (elected at the first stockholder meeting) included five of the six former partners, William Alexander Procter, James Norris Gamble, Harley T. Procter, David B. Gamble, and William Cooper Procter. (In view of his age, founder James Gamble, now 87, chose not to serve, and that was understandable.) Other members were Briggs S. Cunningham, president of the Citizens National Bank of Cincinnati, Henry B. Morehead of Morehead, Irwin & Co., and William M. Kidder of Kidder, Peabody & Co.

Within six days a corporate prospectus was issued. It offered for public subscription an unspecified number of the 45,000 capital shares plus an unspecified portion of $2 million in first mortgage 6% bonds. And this stipulation was significant: "The subscription list will be open on Monday, July 21, and will close on or before Tuesday, July 22, at 3 P.M." The short time allowed, two business days at most, made it obvious that the public offering was primarily a legal technicality, not an effort to elicit substantial public purchase of securities.

At the initial meeting of directors these corporate officers were elected: William Alexander Procter, president; James Norris Gamble, vice-president; Harley T. Procter, second vice-president; William Cooper Procter, general manager; David B. Gamble, secretary and treasurer. Reading this list, Cincinnatians could be assured that the company remained in its historic hands.

Finally, the meeting authorized an agreement by which the six partners of the original Procter & Gamble were to receive a total of $6,500,000 in stocks and bonds for the assets of their 53-year-old firm. William Cooper Procter and David B. Gamble would manage the new company "for a period of five years in consideration of a salary of $30,000 . . . to be divided between them in such proportions as they may determine."

Among themselves, meanwhile, the former partners entered into a new type of partnership which would, in effect, control their total holdings for the next five years. One of its stipulations was that none of them could sell his shares to anyone except "one or more of the other partners." And in the event of the death of any one of them, "this partnership shall not thereby be dissolved; but shall be continued in the same manner . . ." until the end of the five-year period of agreement (January 1, 1896).

This provision, somber as it seemed, was all too soon proven wise. Within one month, on April 29, 1891, 87-year-old James Gamble died at his home at 26 Clark Street in Cincinnati.

His death was a loss not only to his family but to his city. The respect, indeed the affection, he had won was evident in every obituary and editorial eulogy that appeared in newspapers across the country. The church he had attended for so many decades was crowded with standees inside and outside during the funeral services. His pastor spoke with the emotion of one who had lost a personal friend: "For more than seventy-one years Brother Gamble . . . built for himself a reputation and character that are enviable. In business he was industrious and upright. A city paper says that 'not one dollar of his estate carries the odor of fraud or dishonorable dealing.' He was frugal and economical from religious principles. He believed it to be the duty of everyone to try to save some part of his daily earnings . . . His fitting memorials to his beloved deceased wife—the Elizabeth Gamble Deaconess Home and the Christ Hospital—show the great love of his heart for the poor, the afflicted, the suffering, the dying."

Pallbearers were six veteran employees of the old firm of Procter & Gamble. They were now employees of the Procter & Gamble Company, Inc., but clearly personal was their loyalty to a man who symbolized the business life they had all shared decade after decade.

* * * * *

This was not the only loss sustained by the company within a year of its incorporation. The other, though not caused by death, brought its own sting of dismay, even disbelief.

Harley T. Procter, despite his recent election as vice-president decided to keep the promise he had made to his wife—to retire in his early forties. He could certainly afford to do so now. His share of the stocks and bonds received by the former partners was more than $1.5 million. This would easily enable him to move to New England as his wife yearned to do where he planned to breed horses. And it would allow him to travel, another of his ambitions.

Yet he was only 43, an unheard of age for retirement. Though his own family and the Gambles protested, Harley remained resolute. He wanted no further responsibility for the daily operations of the business; the only concession he made was that he would retain his seat on the board of directors and he would attend as many of its meetings as he found possible.

Nothing could deter him. Soon thereafter he moved his family to a new home in Massachusetts. No one in the company could understand how so active, so innovative a businessman could abruptly divorce himself from interests which had absorbed him for twenty-one years. There was no precedent for what he was doing. But then, Harley had been a rebel from the start. He had always followed his own instincts, and he was simply being faithful to himself.

For several years (until 1900) he kept his promise to attend board meetings. Then (until 1906) he confined his business in Cincinnati to annual stockholder meetings. After that, even these were given up, and Harley Thomas Procter lived in complete retirement until his death at the age of 73, on May 15, 1920.

* * * * *

Another of the country's periodic business depressions—this one destined to last several years—began to undermine American industry at the time of the incorporation. Yet, in spite of it, Procter & Gamble was able to announce ("with pleasure," as the president put it) that the corporation's profits were higher than those of the previous year.

"We can see nothing that is in any way discouraging for the future," President William A. Procter declared—reasserting the company's unchanging optimism in the face of national tribulations. "While you must not expect always to have as profitable years as the one just passed, we feel assured that the business outlook for the next year will be decidedly encouraging."

He was right. In fact, three years later, in 1894, he reported: "The company has no floating debt whatever, all bills being paid in cash. The result . . . is strong evidence of . . . how slightly the demand for [our] products has been affected by the general business depression."

Stockholders must have been delighted with such news. Annual reports were stimulating with their details of growth and sound management policies. But suddenly, on August 20, 1895, stockholders got the startling notification that for the indefinite future they would no longer be receiving such detailed reports. What was wrong? Did the company have something to conceal? If so, what was it?

A letter of explanation clarified matters: "Owing to the indiscreet use in the past by some of the stockholders of the published statements of the yearly profits of the company, it is the opinion of the directors that the best interests of the company will be served by not giving out such published statements. The earnings of the past year were in excess of the 12% dividend declared on the common stock. If you will apply in person at the office of the company, you will be given more information if you desire."

Exactly how Procter & Gamble had been embarrassed was not told. In fact, it was never told. Nothing in the company's records reveals the indiscretions of which it complained.

The most serious reaction came from the New York Stock Exchange. It had listed P&G's stock since 1891. Its protest against "the books of the company being closed" was read at the April 21, 1896, meeting of the directors. The letter was disturbing. Yet, after earnest deliberation, the board decided to maintain its secrecy. Correspondence with the exchange continued year after year, but P&G's directors were obdurate. The outcome was inevitable. In 1903 the New York Stock Exchange withdrew Procter & Gamble's listing. Thereafter, the company's stock was traded on other exchanges.

No doubt there were stockholders who regarded this as a defeat for Procter & Gamble, perhaps as a penalty for needless stubbornness. The board of directors, however, persisted in following a course they considered right. And though the policy of secrecy was rescinded ten years later, in 1913, the New York exchange did not restore the listing until 1929.

*　*　*　*　*

It would be folly to assume that every year in a company's history could outdo the previous year in earnings. All kinds of deterrents were bound to arise, especially those caused by sagging national economic conditions, by fluctuations in the prices of raw materials, by extraordinary sales efforts on the part of competitors. Procter & Gamble had no magic formula for overcoming all such obstacles. For two years at the start of the century its profits declined. Measured in decades, however, they continued steadily upward.

The sale of P&G products increased of course with the increase of America's population. At the same time the advertising campaigns instituted by Harley Procter gained momentum. There were beautiful, full-page Ivory illustrations in the leading magazines. Reproductions obtained with Ivory wrappers—especially reproductions of Maxfield Parrish's paintings—hung over the mantel in thousands of American homes. Though Harley had retired, his spirit and his energy remained to inspire his successors. And their efforts were impressive. While the company's profits exceeded $1 million in 1897, by 1904 the figure reached $1,522,000. At that rate it was bound to double in a decade.

During those few years dividends increased from $8 a share in 1890 to $20 a share by 1900. Moreover, in 1901 the directors declared a special cash dividend of $50 per common share, provided the sum was used as part payment for new shares at $100 each. That meant a shareholder could buy another $100 share for $50. Because of such clear evidence of the company's growth P&G stock was selling in 1905 at $390 a share.

It was calculated that anyone who had bought ten shares of common stock in 1890 and who had subsequently availed himself of all opportunities for purchase would, by 1905, have invested a total of $2,100. That year his investment would be worth $10,140. And cash dividends received in the interim would have totaled $2,800. Not bad.

* * * * *

By this time William Alexander Procter as president and his son William Cooper Procter as general manager were virtually running the company. One business publication referred to them as "the architects of growth." Inevitably growth demanded additional management personnel, and managers who were not members of the founding families were increasingly being given prominent roles. All were of course promoted from P&G's own ranks. But more and more able people would be needed in the future, and Cooper instituted a search for them both inside and outside the company. The best places to find such people were the colleges. He sent representatives to college campuses to seek them out, launching a practice that was to be intensified with the years.

But what about those employees who were not potential managers? What about the loyal, run-of-the-mill workers who were giving their lifelong service to the company, though never destined to become executives?

Cooper Procter knew many of them personally. At one time he had labored side by side with them. He had hoped that the profit sharing program he had originated would help provide for the years of their retirement. But in this he was disappointed. Most of them still regarded their profit sharing dividends not as incentives to save but as extra pay; some reacted to the opportunity with complete indifference.

Even before the company's incorporation he had tried various ways of coping with the situation. Once he had contrived a system which would categorize employees in four classes: Those who worked harder, helping to cut operating costs and to increase profits, would receive double the regular dividend. A second class, those whose enthusiasm for responsibility was fair but not overly impressive, would receive the regular dividend. Half a dividend would go to those who showed little interest in their jobs. And those wholly disinterested in their work would get no dividend at all.

The trouble was that foremen and supervisors were unduly burdened with the chore of making subjective decisions about their people. Even reducing the choice to two classes—those who would get dividends and those who would not—brought only grudging results.

Besides, these were days when workingmen were thinking of things that had little connection with the production of soap. They were concerned with the rise of big corporations which were transforming the social and economic structure of the United States.

"The conflicts between capital and labor," wrote historian Henry Bamford Parkes, "were the most conspicuous and acute of the problems presented by the growth of industry."

Violent disruptions of the economy were occurring throughout the United States. In the mining camps of the Rocky Mountains a

Harley Thomas Procter

man named William D. (Big Bill) Hayward organized the Western Federation of Miners. His rallying cry was that the capitalist system had to be overthrown if labor was to achieve justice. (Within a few years Hayward's following was to become the IWW, the Industrial Workers of the World.)

Though Cincinnati itself remained relatively quiet amid scattered social upheavals, Cooper Procter was deeply disturbed by what he saw. He could understand the unhappiness of the laboring class. Many of Procter & Gamble's own employees, reaching retirement age, had meager savings to give them comfort. For them profit sharing had begun too late to enable them to amass enough funds to help them through their declining years. Many were turning to their children for support. It was too late to do much to help them—though Cooper and his father often gave personal funds to people in desperate straits. What, then, could be done to change things in the future?

He tried initiating a stock purchase plan. An employee—any employee—could buy a share of stock on the installment plan: $10 down and the rest payable in installments over a two-year period. Cooper felt the idea had three advantages. First, it offered workers an easy way to save money. Second, the market value of the shares would probably increase as the company grew. Finally, in encouraging employees to become stockholders, P&G would be encouraging them to work harder to raise the company's profits and therefore their own dividends.

Again he was disappointed. Few employees took advantage of the plan. Of those who did, many sold their stock shortly after receiving it. They were fearful of the possible fall in stock prices in a period of depression; fearful of losing hard-earned savings.

Confronted by this unexpected setback, Cooper sought a way of protecting employees against loss of their investment. On December 8, 1896, Procter & Gamble—in an historic move—announced it would guarantee employees who earned not more than $3.50 per day against loss on any investment, up to $1,000, they might make in the stock of the company. "We believe," the announcement said, "the plan forms a practical means of bringing the employer and employee nearer together, by inducing the employees to become part owners in the business. The plan furnishes you with an absolutely safe investment . . . and through your efforts you may increase both the dividends and the value of the stock you buy." The plan had to be dropped in 1931 because of the Great Depression.

Cooper Procter realized, as he wrote in a letter, that the plan still needed improvements to emphasize the "inseparability of interests" of the firm and its workers; but for the time, for several years in fact, he could do nothing about it. There were other problems.

*　*　*　*　*

Procter & Gamble now had to cope with a plethora of competing products—so many of them indeed in the soap field that they were causing a shortage of raw materials, especially of fats and oils. To meet and surpass competition demanded intensified research and development. This in turn would necessitate new manufacturing capacity to keep up with the needs of new products. And there would have to be studies for the possible location of new plants to fulfill future opportunities.

The primary responsibility for all such matters fell to Cooper Procter as general manager. Perhaps it was too much for one man. He often labored fourteen hours a day. Some members of his family saw a kind of religious fervor in the way he worked. He once wrote to his niece, Mrs. Mary E. Johnston: "I never had any patience with any form of religion the main object of which was to save your soul. A religion with plenty of work will save your soul . . ." By keeping you out of mischief, no doubt.

One of his associates later said, "The way that man labored you wondered where he got his stamina. Even in the worst of winter storms he'd walk into the Ivorydale office promptly at 7:40 A.M. every day, coatless even if there was a blizzard. He'd plunge right into work. His speech was rapid, as if the words could never keep pace with his thoughts. And he always looked surprised if people didn't grasp his ideas as quickly as he poured them out."

With so much on his mind and so much to be done, it was not until 1903 that Cooper decided he had found the missing element in the profit sharing plan—an element that would help employees save for retirement without undue financial strain. The new idea, announced on June 16, 1903, bound profit sharing to the purchase of P&G common stock. In Cooper's words, it would "place a premium on thrift by *requiring* our people to save a certain fraction of their wages if they are to receive any extra money from the firm."

To participate in the plan, an employee had to buy P&G stock at current value in an amount equivalent to his annual wage. Payment could be spread over several years with a minimum annual installment of 4% of earnings.

That was only the beginning. Next came the lure, the reward: "To every dollar you save," P&G told its employees,

> "we will add four dollars until as much money as you make in a year has been accumulated. This money is then yours. Our only stipulation is that it must be invested in the common stock of the company. We expect our stock to increase greatly in value. That increase too will be yours. However, we will protect you against depreciation. If you should ever decide to leave the company, and your stock should then be below the market value at which you obtained it, we promise to return to you in such case that full market price."

This coupling of the original stock purchase plan with a profit sharing benefit finally resolved the problem that had puzzled and troubled Cooper Procter for sixteen years. As might have been expected, it brought reactions from many sections of American industry, some in praise, others with doubts and criticism if not downright irritation. Were other firms being challenged to expend four dollars for every dollar an employee saved? It was unheard of—utter radicalism posing as idealism, a few charged.

But after investigating the results at Procter & Gamble a few years later, author Ida M. Tarbell wrote in her book, *New Ideas in Business*:

> I failed to find anyone who had taken advantage of the opportunity [to buy stock and join profit sharing] who was not impressed, some of them to the point of enthusiasm, others to one of bewilderment. I remember a Russian immigrant who years ago was employed as a day laborer and is now earning $100 a month and who had taken all of the stock the plan allowed. He had bought a house and put four children through public school. "It's the greatest thing I ever heard of," he told me, "only I can't get enough."

Nothing could have pleased Cooper Procter more than reading such reports.

6
FROM SOAP TO FOOD

Barrels of Crisco for institutional use are packed at Ivorydale, circa 1915.

Though candle production was speedily declining, in 1909 Procter & Gamble made the world's largest single sale of candles. It went to the Isthmian Canal Commission—10,000 pounds of Star candles for use during the construction of the Panama Canal. Such bonanzas notwithstanding, soap and glycerin were the company's products with the greatest growth rates. Their constantly rising sales necessitated new facilities at Ivorydale: bigger storage tanks, additional soap-framing houses, lye vats, soap kettles. The new kettles were enormous. Some called them monstrous. Each yielded 165,000 pounds of soap at a single boiling.

Yet even these were not capable of keeping pace with nationwide sales. As early as 1900 it had been obvious that Ivorydale itself was not large enough. Whether to build a branch in the East or in the West, nearer other markets, was debated for three years. William A. and Cooper Procter weighed all the facts. They sent scouts to several cities. The final decision was to go west. In 1903 the company bought a site in Kansas City, a growing meat packing center. There it built its first branch.

Within three years Procter & Gamble needed still another plant, this one in the East. Staten Island, New York, was selected, and at an elaborate groundbreaking ceremony the new factory was named Port Ivory.

Such expansion did not occur too soon. Though Ivory and Lenox soaps were P&G's leaders, they were being seriously challenged. Ivory was threatened by a host of new white products, especially Fairy soap made by the N.K. Fairbank Company. Pears', manufactured in England, and many other brands were also nibbling at Ivory's share of the market. P&G responded not only with improvement in its product but by steadily increasing the amount of Ivory advertising.

Still, as Harley Procter had admonished, "Advertising alone cannot make a product successful." Neither could an occasional minor change. The research staff repeatedly found ways of improving Ivory's quality. This greatly helped P&G maintain its strong leadership.

In the laundry field the company had to meet a wholly new type of challenge. For decades home washing had been a back-breaking chore. Clothes were boiled on kitchen stoves or, in rural areas, in backyard iron kettles. This had to be followed by hard scrubbing on corrugated washboards in tubs of steaming water.

64

Few American homes had any mechanical means of making wash day labors easier.

Then, abruptly, there appeared a product that eased the drudgery. It was introduced by another company, and it seriously affected the laundry sales of both Ivory and Lenox. This was Fels-Naphtha, a yellow soap with naphtha as its key ingredient. Its advantages made it a household sensation.

And there was another threat to P&G's laundry business—soap powders. The most popular of these ground-up soaps was Pearline, made by James Pyle & Son, New York. In addition, there was Fairbank's Gold Dust washing powder, the most widely advertised of the new powdered cleansers (featuring "The Gold Dust Twins"). Others, too, were pouring into the market.

The research staff had to embark on a crash program to develop, first, a new laundry soap which would perform better than Fels-Naphtha, and second, a formula and manufacturing process for a P&G soap powder. Neither was an easy undertaking.

To respond to the Fels-Naphtha situation, the company introduced P&G White Naphtha in 1902. It was widely advertised, and by 1920, eighteen years later, it had become the largest selling brand of soap in the world.

The search for a powder was similarly successful. After installing the necessary equipment, P&G began producing Puritan. Even while its initial inventory was being manufactured, competitors learned of P&G's intention to enter the powder field. They promptly instituted a price-cutting war. Startled, not anticipating the move, Procter & Gamble decided to stay out of the fray. Puritan could wait until the competitive frenzy ended.

* * * * *

Not that waiting implied idleness; far from it. In 1903 the Schultz Soap Company of Zanesville, Ohio, whose production consisted principally of a yellow bar soap, Star, and a soap powder, was offered for sale. Seeing an opportunity to enter the powder field with an established brand, Procter & Gamble bought the Schultz firm for $425,000. It changed the powder formula to include naphtha and renamed it Star Naphtha washing powder (which, according to advertisements, could be used for "all manner of rough cleansing, pots, pans, wood floors, etc.").

In the case of Schultz's Star soap, its main selling point had long been that consumers could save the wrappers and receive premiums. For a time P&G continued these premium terms, and Star soap actually surpassed Lenox in sales. But the spurt was temporary. Yellow soaps were losing their appeal, and in spite of premium offers Star began to fade.

Something else was also being eased out of P&G's product list—refined kitchen lard. The prices of lard and tallow had increased to such an extent that it was impossible to market a consumer product at a reasonable cost. The meat packing houses themselves, controlling lard supplies and prices, took control of the lard market.

The same meat packers became major competitors for the country's limited supply of cottonseed oil used in lard compounds. Now Procter & Gamble was really threatened. It needed cottonseed oil for its soap products. It could not do without it. Here was a competitive situation it could not ignore. The time had come to strike back.

The two largest manufacturers of lard compounds were Armour & Company and the N.K. Fairbank Company. Their principal customers were bakeries, restaurants, and other bulk users. It was estimated that these two firms were buying nearly half the cottonseed oil crushed in the United States.

How could Procter & Gamble insure the adequacy of its own supplies? The challenge was the more vital because in meeting after meeting, P&G executives had been considering the use of cottonseed oil for edible products as well as soap. Why ignore so obviously synergistic a market?

True, the company had certain sources of guaranteed supply. Far back in the 1890s it had contracted for the total output of some southern crushing plants; some others it had bought outright. But this supply was no longer sufficient. Moving quickly, P&G organized a subsidiary, the Buckeye Cotton Oil Company. Its first act was to lease and operate a mill in Greenwood, Mississippi. This was the beginning; rapid expansion followed. By 1905 Buckeye owned and operated eight cottonseed crushing mills. Three of them it had bought; five it had built. For a time supply was assured.

Meanwhile, in 1905, mysterious things were happening at Ivorydale. Plant workers, stepping out for a bit of sunshine during their lunch hour, watched enormous presses being moved into the laboratory building. These were followed by a huge refrigerating device. When onlookers asked questions, nobody explained anything. To make matters even more puzzling, frosted panes went into the window frames of the laboratory so that no one could look into the place.

It was at Cooper Procter's orders that such secrecy was maintained. Secrecy about what? The laboratory researchers refused even to hint. They kept to themselves in a kind of self-imposed isolation, working endless hours, endless days, with their new machinery. The only thing a few outsiders learned was that the strange equipment had been developed by a Pennsylvania company; its purpose—to remove paraffin from petroleum oil. Procter & Gamble had purchased the exclusive rights to use it in the manufacture of a new product.

Eventually word spread around Ivorydale that the researchers had developed what they called "winter oil." Most employees probably did not know what this meant. Yet its significance was clear enough. Winter oil was so named simply because it remained limpid at severe winter temperatures. (Cottonseed oil, containing stearine, started to crystallize when the thermometer sank to 65° F. The winterizing process developed in the laboratory removed the stearine; thus the refined oil was unaffected by cold.)

At the outset its principal sales potential appeared to be that of the major component in salad oil. Judging by market tests, hotels, restaurants, hospitals, and other bulk buyers would purchase it in large quantities. But should P&G attempt to sell a salad oil directly to American consumers?

Some members of management opposed the idea. "We're in the soap business and not in foods," they contended. In addition, they felt the household market for salad oil might not be big enough to justify the cost of new installations, equipment, advertising, sampling, and all the other expenses involved in introducing a new product.

James N. Gamble had his own ethical reason for not wishing to sell salad oil to the public. The company, he said, should not offer anything to American consumers without first testing it thoroughly in conditions of home use nor without first learning everything there was to know about it. He did not oppose bulk sales to institutions. Their buyers were experts who could rely on their own tests and judgment. But America's housewives were without the scientific background to test new products; they had to rely on the integrity of P&G's claims. He urged that the company get a few years of experience in the production of institutional foods before selling vegetable oil products for home use. Though for a time Procter & Gamble did sell its salad oil only to institutions, it became a profitable business.

In April, 1905, the need for additional office space once more made it necessary to move the P&G offices. This time they went to the Citizens National Bank Building at Fourth and Main Streets, two blocks from the original Cincinnati shop established by the founders.

Hardly a month later, on May 4, 1905, the Procter & Gamble Company was reincorporated in Ohio, a change made possible by the liberalization of Ohio's laws. Also, though its results could not be foreseen, that year a young man named Richard R. Deupree joined P&G as an office boy.

*   *   *   *   *

In 1907 the company sustained a tragic shock. William Alexander Procter took his own life in suburban Glendale.

His death came on the fourth anniversary of the death of his wife. A Cincinnati newspaper speculated that the suicide "was brought about by Mr. Procter's constant grieving over the loss of his wife . . . Other members of the family would attempt to divert his mind from the sad occurrence, but their efforts were always futile."

Noting his many gifts to institutions and individuals, the newspaper added:

He had for half a century been active and prominent in every good work . . . No man could have been purer in his private or business life, and he enjoyed the confidence and entire respect of all who knew him.

The same newspaper published a previously unknown insight into William A. Procter's character:

A few years ago several charities were receiving substantial sums from an unknown source, the donor using the name of "Sunshine." When it was announced that Sunshine was William A. Procter, the contributions ceased, so sensitive was Mr. Procter about the disclosure of his good deeds.

On April 16, 1907, the Procter & Gamble board of directors met in special solemn session to name William Alexander Procter's successor. There was only one choice, 44-year-old William Cooper

Procter. He was elected president and chief executive of the Procter & Gamble Company.

* * * * *

Company milestones seemed always to come at times of national crisis. When the business was founded, the Panic of 1837 had caused banks to fail amid economic hysteria. After Procter & Gamble was incorporated in 1890, a general business depression undermined the economy. Now, shortly after William Cooper Procter took office, the Panic of 1907 brought still another crisis.

This one began with a run on the Knickerbocker Trust Company, New York, causing that leading bank to close its doors. Like the proverbial fall of dominoes, other banks across the country were immediately subjected to runs and forced to close. Led by J.P. Morgan, a group of New York financiers finally brought the panic to an end by combining their resources to import $100 million in gold from Europe. Nonetheless, a wave of unemployment spread across the nation.

During this national ordeal William Cooper Procter focused his attention on the affairs of Procter & Gamble. His problems were many. There were start-up difficulties at the Kansas City soap plant and in the preparations for opening the new Staten Island factory, Port Ivory. And though P&G White Naphtha was a success, the company was still having trouble with its manufacturing process, while an ever-increasing need for cottonseed oil constantly required additional cottonseed crushing capacity in the form of building or purchasing more mills.

At Ivorydale, the growing research staff was engaged in a new project. Commercial laundries in the United States now had washing machines which were becoming large users of soaps. Procter & Gamble had been selling soap chips to these laundries, but with mediocre results. (The chips were exactly that: bar soaps like Lenox and Ivory reduced to wafers in a cutting machine, then dried to prevent them from sticking together.)

The research people, seeking improvements, worked to develop very thin, quick-dissolving flakes. Data had been accumulated by the sales force to suggest a wide potential market for these.

In the midst of such activity the company received a letter from a German chemical engineer, E.C. Kayser, dated October 18, 1907. It described research he had been conducting on "hydrogenation of unsaturated fats in the liquid state." He asked if P&G was interested in knowing about his findings.

During the development of winter oil P&G researchers had become absorbed in the possibility of converting cottonseed oil into solid form for shortening. They hoped this could compete in quality and price with lard, butter, and the many compounds already on the market. Kayser's letter indicated he might have answers to some questions which had baffled the P&G staff. He was invited to visit Cincinnati with samples of the hydrogenated or "hardened" vegetable oils his letter mentioned.

The German chemist arrived within a month. He brought samples of a solid white substance which he handled as if it were a tennis ball. "This is cottonseed oil," he assured the fascinated Cooper Procter. "I turned liquid cottonseed oil into a solid with my hydrogenation process."

Cooper was so astonished and excited by what he saw that Procter & Gamble immediately entered into an agreement with Kayser to purchase the U.S. rights for his method. Also, it employed him as a consultant while the company experimented with his process. Dr. M.B. Graff, a senior member of P&G's research staff, was assigned to work with Dr. Kayser. Later Dr. Graff wrote with wry humor about those early days:

> I remember one particular thought that Kayser had was to force steam through hot coke and centrifuge it to separate the hydrogen and carbon monoxide. So we got a tank of gas and rigged up a couple of barrels hooked up with perforated pipe. All of this material was in an old shed. I had started the gas and then went out of doors for something or other. I had just gotten outside when the mixture exploded. It seemed we had not done quite the proper thing.

Although Dr. Kayser's predilection for keeping "gentlemen's hours" (9 A.M. to 3 P.M.) frustrated Graff, their experiments ultimately resulted in the development of a solid product that was described as being "hard enough to drive tacks with." Since this hardened oil could not itself be used as a shortening, the next step was to produce a softer mixture by blending the solid substance with liquid cottonseed oil (somewhat like adding water to dry clay to make it pliable enough for modeling).

Construction of a hydrogenation plant began at Ivorydale in 1908. The unit was ready by February, 1909. It was expected to enable Procter & Gamble to introduce a new shortening, principally formulated from cottonseed oil, that could compete with the lard compounds being sold by the meat packing companies. Principal outlets for the lard compounds were bakeries, restaurants, and other food establishments. (Simple lard and butter were still the preferred cooking fats in American homes.)

Fortuitously, Wallace E. McCaw, owner of the McCaw Manufacturing Company of Macon, Georgia, approached Procter & Gamble at this time with an offer to sell his business. McCaw's principal product was a shortening called Flake White. Cooper Procter saw an opportunity to acquire a complete shortening factory as a pilot plant for concepts which might emerge from P&G's hydrogenation research. He recommended that the company buy the McCaw business for $1.4 million. The board of directors approved, and the purchase was made on January 2, 1909.

After that, with equipment available, P&G's experiments were accelerated. A small department for continuing the manufacture of Flake White was installed at Ivorydale. The Macon plant, meanwhile, was used to test an intriguing result of the hydrogenation research: By combining liquid cottonseed oil with hardened cottonseed oil, P&G could indeed make a very satisfactory, soft, all-vegetable shortening.

Would consumers like it? Initial tests were disappointing. The new Flake White did not have the "keeping qualities" consumers desired. It dried in its container. So the research force sought a new approach. This time they tried only partial hardening of the oil. And this proved to be the answer. The partially hardened product did not require refrigeration and held up well for long periods.

On November 10, 1910, Procter & Gamble applied for a U.S. patent on its new vegetable shortening. "This invention is a food product," the patent application said, "consisting of a vegetable oil, preferably cottonseed oil, partially hydrogenized, and hardened to a homogenous white or yellowish semi-solid closely resembling lard. The special object of the invention is to provide a new food product for a shortening in cooking . . ."

The specifications continued in highly technical language. Basically, however, P&G was patenting an all-vegetable shortening that had properties superior to all shortenings then on the market. It was white (although the patent allowed P&G the option of making it yellow) and it was bland. Creamy in consistency, it was easy for homemakers to blend.

Under federal law, edible products containing animal fats had to be stamped with a government inspection label. As a strategic move to prevent competitors from realizing how much progress P&G was making with hydrogenation, the company continued to use a tiny amount of oleo-stearine in Flake White. Thus, Flake White still carried the government inspection label. The materials used were identified as cottonseed oil, stearine from cottonseed oil, and oleo-stearine. Not a word suggested hydrogenation.

Now the new product needed a brand name. "Krispo," P&G first decided. But trademark complications in Washington made it impossible to use that name. The search turned to an earlier candidate, "Cryst." Many members of P&G management objected to that name. It could suggest a religious connotation. Finally, at a meeting in Cooper Procter's office, someone suggested that the two names be combined. A vote was taken. The new product was named Crisco, suggestive of something fresh, firm, clear.

By 1912 it was being widely advertised as "An absolutely new product—a scientific discovery which will affect every kitchen in America." This was no overstatement. Crisco was truly on its way to capturing the kitchens of America.

7

"WAR MAKES SOLDIERS OF US ALL"

Save-

We want no person in the United States to eat less than is required for good health and full strength, for in this emergency America requires every atom of the productive power of our people. While many can eat less, all of our population can substitute other food stuffs for the few that are vitally needed for export.

—Herbert Hoover.

THE shield of the National Food Administration in over ten million American homes is the seal of a sacred covenant made with their country by patriotic housewives, pledged to help win the war by the conservation of food.

Use other cereal flours and save wheat. Give corn meal and oat meal a larger place in your menus. Use no butter in cooking. Use vegetable fats. Use less sugar.

★ CRISCO
*For Frying—For Shortening
For Cake Making*

Economy and conservation both result from the use of Crisco. It gives completely satisfactory results for minimum expenditure. It is so rich less is required.

Crisco is the solid cream of wholesome, edible oil. It is always of the same dependable quality. It has no taste, no odor, and gives only richness to foods.

All war-time recipes are made richer by the use of Crisco. Its delicacy improves these additions to your menus. Crisco easily blends with barley, graham, rye and other flours necessary to save wheat. It successfully takes the place of butter. Experience with Crisco has taught millions that to use butter in cooking is both unnecessary and wasteful.

The next time you buy a cooking fat, try Crisco. You can get it in one pound, air tight, sanitary tins, free from all the impurities to which fats sold in bulk are exposed.

A Cook Book for Today

Have you ever seen "Balanced Daily Diet"? Every progressive housewife should own a copy. In this book, illustrated in color, Janet McKenzie Hill, of the Boston Cooking School, tells how to prepare over 150 new and palatable foods for physical strength and mental activity. Your hot weather problems of serving will be solved by the suggestions for well balanced summer meals. Contains the interesting story of Crisco. Published to sell for 25 cents, we will send a copy for 10 cents in stamps. Address Department H-7, The Procter & Gamble Company, Cincinnati, O.

Food Will Win the War Don't Waste It

World War I patriotic Crisco Advertisement.

"The business is growing, and the outlook so far as this company is concerned is satisfactory," William Cooper Procter wrote in 1913 in a letter to stockholders. "We shall take pleasure in furnishing further information to any accredited stockholder who is interested and who will apply, in person, at the company's office in Cincinnati." (If any stockholder did come for further information, no record of such curiosity exists. The annual letters remained terse until 1920 when the company began putting the report in a pamphlet which included a "condensed general balance sheet.")

If stockholders had not been upset about the absence of annual reports during William Cooper Procter's first six years as president, it was because a regular $12 dividend on common stock was declared every year. A new issue of 15,000 shares in 1910 enabled stockholders to purchase one share for each seven shares held. Though the cost to P&G stockholders was $200 per share, the stock had a market value of about $400. Nobody complained.

The common stock continued to rise. By 1913 it was selling for $555 to $570 per share. Also in 1913, the company declared the first of twelve consecutive annual stock dividends of 4%. For each twenty-five shares held, a stockholder received one new share free.

Still, not all the years between 1907 and 1913 were so bright. In 1911, for instance, P&G's earnings dropped by more than 50% from the previous year. The precipitous decline was caused by drastically increased operating costs. The boll weevil's devastating impact on the southern cotton crop reduced the available supply of cottonseed just at the time Procter & Gamble had become the world's largest consumer of the oil. Cottonseed prices soared. And there were other expenditures. Apart from investing heavily in expanded plants for soap and edible products, the company organized a bulk sales department which introduced a new soap, Amber Flakes, for commercial laundries. In 1913 P&G could tell its shareholders that Amber Flakes and a companion product, White Crown soap chips, comprised a "very satisfactory business ... both in regard to volume and profit." That report also contained these comments about other products:

> *Ivory soap—this is the best known brand of soap in the country, and has been advertised more extensively than any other article on the market ... The success of Ivory soap, however, would not have been possible through advertising*

alone. It is made of the purest materials which can be obtained, and its manufacture today is as carefully watched in every respect as when it was first marketed in 1879.

Lenox soap—second in importance to Ivory ... the largest selling brand of laundry soap in the country. It is a good, dependable, inexpensive piece of laundry soap that gives the consumer more for the money than any other brand, which is the reason for its success.

P&G White Naphtha—a high-grade laundry soap retailing for five cents and particularly satisfactory for laundry and household use to the woman who does her own work ... It gives satisfaction to all who use it.

Star soap—a fine yellow laundry soap for consumers who desire to receive premiums for their soap wrappers. The premiums are selected with care and give satisfaction to the consumer, and the soap is worth the money for which it sells.

Star Naphtha washing powder—made to use for all manner of rough cleansing, pots, pans, wood floors, etc. It has been a remarkably successful brand from the time it was put on the market, and it has had a steady and gratifying growth ever since.

Flake White—a cooking fat made from cottonseed oil sold very extensively, particularly in the South. It offers a satisfactory outlet for the surplus production of cottonseed oil and constitutes a profitable branch of the business.

Yet of all P&G consumer products advertised in 1913, only Ivory and Crisco were to survive the demands of technological change.

*   *   *   *   *

There was no mention to shareholders, however, of a serious business problem Procter & Gamble was facing in the New York area. This had begun to manifest itself when local wholesale grocers harassed P&G sales people with demands for preferential prices because of critical market conditions. "I walked into a wholesaler's office," one salesman reported, "and first thing I knew he was shaking a finger under my nose and practically insisting I cut prices for him."

Strangely enough, this situation had arisen out of a Supreme Court ruling. Procter & Gamble had long required wholesale grocers to honor P&G's policy of treating all customers on an

75

equal basis. This did not preclude the normal custom of granting discounts for exceptionally large orders or prompt payments. But it forbade favoritism. The same discounts had to be available to all whose orders merited the special consideration.

In 1910 the Supreme Court of the United States had invalidated such strictures as a trend toward price fixing. The result was that wholesalers could make all kinds of deals with their retail customers. Within two years prices were being slashed in a wild price-cutting war. So far, this was limited to the New York area, but it could easily spread across the nation. The wholesalers, pressured by retailers, clamored for special prices not only from Procter & Gamble, but from Lever Bros., from Colgate-Palmolive, from all grocery products manufacturers. This necessitated emergency meetings of top executives in Cooper Procter's office.

Procter recognized that "The only way to maintain a decent public respect for our prices and products is for us to take over the job of dealing with the retailers. Once these retailers become convinced that we insist on quoting the same price to every store, that we will not haggle or play favorites, then common sense may return to the New York market. They'll stop trying to cut our throat—and each other's."

In the matter of selling directly to retailers, somebody asked, "How will the wholesalers feel about our bypassing them?" And another added, "Won't we need a much larger sales force in the New York area? There are thousands of stores to be covered." Cooper Procter conceded that the task would be difficult. "But I think it's worth doing," he decided.

To manage direct selling to retailers in the New York area, Cooper Procter appointed Stockton Buzby. Buzby had joined P&G's sales organization after having worked as a retail salesman for a Procter & Gamble agent in Baltimore since the early 1890s. When P&G announced plans to sell directly to New York's retail grocers, the major wholesalers in the area promptly declared that they would no longer handle P&G brands. The head of P&G's sales office in New York vividly recalled those days:

"The big wholesale grocers did their level best to blacken our name with the retail trade. They originated the battle cry that P&G now meant 'Passed and Gone.' As far as they were concerned, they said, we had already passed out of the picture. They even got a nearby small soapmaker to make a cake of white floating soap called Tusk with which they were going to run us out of the New York market. The wrapper of Tusk was artfully designed so that when you saw it across the store it looked for all the world like an Ivory soap wrapper . . . Tusk was supposed to be the knockout blow. Actually, it backfired. The cake was of very inferior quality and not advertised, and after a few weeks on the shelf, it curled and powdered and was unsalable."

The New York sales force quickly expanded from a dozen employees to more than seventy-five. "After we started selling direct," Buzby recalled, "we had to set up warehouses in Brooklyn and in the Bronx and make our own delivery and payment arrangements. It took about three years to get things straightened out. During that time the wholesale grocers gradually returned to handling our goods, although we did find several smaller jobbers who were willing to stock P&G brands and 'help us out' right from the start."

* * * * *

An intensely interested observer of P&G's struggles with the direct selling problem was Richard Redwood Deupree. By this time he was manager of the Western Sales Division for Consumer Products. He had no responsibility for what was happening in New York; nevertheless, Deupree felt obligated to stay abreast of developments. He wanted to be able to help his sales people explain to their customers why Procter & Gamble was taking such an unusual step in the East.

The career of Richard R. Deupree was unquestionably the most notable result of Cooper Procter's efforts to develop top management people from within the company. At age 12 Deupree had left school in Covington, Kentucky, to work as an insurance agency's office boy at $1 per week. He did this out of economic necessity and moved on to a couple of other jobs before applying for work at Procter & Gamble. Hired in 1905 as an office boy in P&G's Treasury Department at $4.50 per week, he soon was promoted to a cashier's cage. It was there that he caught the attention of Thomas H. Beck, head of what was then P&G's newly organized Bulk Soap Sales Division. Beck was struck by Deupree's pleasant nature. "You're the first cashier I've known who ever smiled when paying out money," he said.

Beck remembered the amiable young man in 1909 when his division needed another salesman. He offered the job to Deupree, who accepted somewhat reluctantly. Nonetheless, put on the road to sell to laundries, hotels, textile mills, and other bulk soap users,

Richard R. Deupree

Deupree built an impressive sales record. (He always insisted that he was not a natural salesman. In his later years he vividly recalled standing outside a buyer's office door trying to calm "the panic in my stomach" before making a sales presentation.)

Within two years, by 1911, he was manager of the Bulk Soap Sales Division. And in 1912 he became manager of P&G's western sales for all consumer products. He now reported directly to Cooper Procter. In the course of their frequent meetings Cooper came to admire the younger man as a manager and as an individual. Despite the disparity in their ages, the two became close friends.

In 1917 Cooper Procter appointed the 32-year-old Deupree P&G's general sales manager. The lives of the two were to intertwine during the next seventeen years in ways neither could possibly envision.

* * * * *

When the Archduke Francis Ferdinand of Austria was assassinated at Sarajevo in 1914 it seemed incredible that such an event could plunge the entire Western world into warfare, yet it happened. Though the United States was not immediately involved, all National Guard officers were ordered to Plattsburgh, N.Y., for special wartime training.

Cooper Procter had long ago joined the Ohio National Guard. Now in his fifties, he had attained the rank of Lieutenant Colonel. (P&G employees were calling him "Colonel.") He packed his belongings, embraced his wife Jean as if he were starting for battle, and left for the Plattsburgh training camp. His business responsibilities fell to associates, most going to his longtime assistant, John J. Burchenal.

The commanding officer at Plattsburgh, General Leonard Wood, had once commanded the Ohio National Guard. A general strike—one not involving any P&G employees—which threatened to paralyze Cincinnati had brought him to the city. There he had met Cooper Procter and, working together, they had become friends.

In Plattsburgh Procter ranked only as a private (as did all officers during their training period). Still, within a few days he was able to write to his wife: "Tonight I am to have the pleasure of dining with General Wood." That dinner led to other meetings; within weeks he was appointed an aide to the general. It strengthened what was to become a lifelong friendship. Also, it was the beginning of an association that later would take Cooper Procter away from Procter & Gamble for many months during a critical point in the company's history.

When his training period ended, he returned to Cincinnati to confront an unexpected business problem. Procter & Gamble had long been exporting soap to Canada, where Lever Bros. was its principal competitor. Now Lever was consolidating several Canadian companies into a single entity in which it held controlling interest.

How could P&G meet such strengthening Canadian competition? Cooper Procter found that his management colleagues had

79

agreed there was only one effective answer: Build a Procter & Gamble plant in Canada. In that way P&G would avail itself of lower Canadian labor costs as well as exemption from the country's import duties. It seemed the only logical means to meet the Lever challenge.

Would the Canadian government welcome the arrival of Procter & Gamble? Would there be any objections, political or otherwise? Cooper Procter was assured that all preliminary investigations had indicated no serious governmental problems existed.

Despite the war in Europe, construction of the Hamilton, Ontario, plant began in 1914. Opening in 1915 with seventy-five employees, it focused on the production of Ivory soap and Crisco.

That year, 1915, a German submarine sank the *Lusitania*. Among the 1,198 people who lost their lives were 124 Americans. The United States found itself being sucked inescapably into the vortex of war. "If it should come," Cooper Procter wrote to his niece, "and if there is a call for troops, I will undertake to raise a new regiment at once."

His age among other things prevented him from enacting that Teddy Roosevelt-like recruitment plan, but other wartime activities soon were thrust upon him. Governor James M. Cox of Ohio made him a member of the State Council of National Defense. The Red Cross called on him to head a fund-raising drive. So did the YMCA, the Council of Social Agencies, and a number of Cincinnati organizations. The energy Cooper devoted to these causes was illustrated by an incident Merle Crowell recorded in *The American Magazine*:

> *Governor James M. Cox of Ohio sent out a call for all members of the State Council of National Defense to meet in Columbus. Right on the heels of the governor's summons came one of the worst storms of the winter, a blizzard that drifted roads and tied up all railway traffic. When the hour for the conference came around there were only two members present from the whole state—the chairman who lived nearby and William Cooper Procter of Cincinnati, 100 miles away.*
>
> *"How did you make it?" the governor asked. Procter pointed to his open, topless automobile which had snow and ice caked in every crevice. "I drove up," he said. It was after midnight when they finished, and the temperature had dropped far below zero.*

"The last I saw of Mr. Procter," the governor said, "he was getting into his car for the 100-mile drive home."

At 7:40 the next morning Cooper Procter walked into his office, rubbing half-frozen hands, ready for the day's work. Wartime production had to be maintained, not only of soap but of that highly important ingredient of munitions, glycerin.

On April 6, 1917, the United States, now the victim of unrestricted submarine attacks by the German Navy, declared war on Germany. American materials, including Procter & Gamble products, already had been speeding across the Atlantic to nations aligned against the Kaiser's forces. In fact, goods were being shipped in such quantities that shortages of raw materials were throttling many American firms.

How, then, could P&G continue to produce at maximum capacity? The circumstance that the company fared better than most was attributable largely to foresight. Recalling the lessons of past wars, it had bought enough raw materials to see all plants through a full year of production. This plenitude of supplies brought an historic note from Cooper to a relative who was a stockholder: "Procter & Gamble," he wrote,

> are very fortunate and have enough raw material to last them a year and could make a great deal of money out of their position, but I am going to try not to do so. We are practically not going to advance prices at all, but base our selling prices upon our cost prices of raw materials and not upon their present value which I think is about $8 million more than what they cost. I don't want to make any money out of the war, and I don't want the company to do so. I am afraid we will have trouble holding our prices down as our orders will be more than we can fill, but I have already told the Procter & Gamble office to notify our trade that we would regulate our shipments as we thought fair and not on the basis of what a man had ordered.

This pricing posture was made all the more difficult by the rising costs of machinery, labor, and those raw materials which the company still had to buy. To meet higher expenses, Procter & Gamble was compelled in 1917 to raise added capital by selling $25 million in bonds. The bonds were retired within five years.

With labor unrest prevalent across the United States, the company did not remain untouched. Word reached Cooper Procter in

81

September, 1917, that P&G's Kansas City plant had been forced to close because of a labor disturbance. He caught the next available train. Arriving at the Kansas City plant, he found pickets but no disorder. He sought out the plant manager. "What's going on here?" he asked. "Those pickets don't look like P&G employees to me."

"They're mostly not our people," the plant manager explained. "What happened was that the workers at the local packing houses went on strike. They wanted help from our people, so they threw picket lines around our plant. They threatened anybody who crossed that picket line. About a hundred of our people were so frightened that they went home. It looked as if there might be real trouble, with maybe a lot of P&G people getting hurt, so I shut the plant to avoid violence. I don't know what's going to happen next."

The P&G plant manager showed Cooper Procter a list of demands being made by the leaders of the strike. The list made Procter shudder. Compulsory union membership was one demand, and he was unswervably opposed to all forms of compulsory unionism. Strike leaders were also insisting that no promotions, merit pay, or discharges be made without union consent. Further, the union leaders were calling for the abandonment of insurance, pension, sick-benefit funds, and even the elimination of profit sharing.

Procter could not believe that a majority of P&G's 800 employees at the Kansas City factory agreed with such demands. At his instructions the plant manager climbed to a loading platform and loudly announced that "Colonel" Procter would be glad to meet with a committee of Procter & Gamble employees. He had come to Kansas City for that purpose and hoped a committee would call upon him that afternoon.

A committee did arrive. The meeting set a notable precedent in P&G's management-employee relations. Cooper Procter listened attentively to an explanation of what P&G employees wanted. He learned quickly that the only issue of major concern was the length of the workday. "We're satisfied with our wages," the committee said. "We know P&G already pays the highest in Kansas City. What we want is an eight-hour day with the present ten hours' pay."

Procter had actually been considering putting an eight-hour day into effect in all P&G plants. "All right, we'll agree to an eight-hour day as a matter of principle," he told the committee. "But our nation is at war, and we all have a wartime duty to do our utmost to keep production as high as possible. Therefore I ask you to agree to continue to work ten or even eleven hours a day until the war is over. In turn, the company will pay you time-and-a-half for all time over eight hours. After the war, we will institute an eight-hour day. You have my word on that."

How could workers argue against a patriotic plea during a war? All America was alive with the excitement of the conflict. In Kansas City, as in Cincinnati, New York, Washington, Chicago, and everywhere else, people were "doing their bit." Even children were lustily singing "Over There!" and "K-K-K-Katy," "Oh, How I Hate to Get Up in the Morning," and "Pack Up Your Troubles in Your Old Kit Bag and Smile, Smile, Smile!"

An eight-hour day had been the major demand of the P&G employees, and, because Cooper Procter's offer seemed both patriotic and reasonable, the workers were satisfied. The Kansas City plant immediately reopened.

Back in his Cincinnati office, Cooper reflected on the meeting. He decided to establish employees' conference committees as a means of two-way communications between management and employees. The Employees' Conference Plan, as it came to be called, was established early in 1918. Two months after World War I ended this new communications mechanism was put to use when Cooper Procter told the conference committees that the company was ready to institute the eight-hour day. At the same time employees were told that P&G planned to eliminate overtime. This meant that they would receive less take-home pay unless wages were increased.

In a letter to the Ivorydale plant's conference committee, Cooper Procter wrote: "I want you to call meetings in all the departments and thrash this out. Decide for yourselves what you think you ought to have . . . and report your decision in ten days."

Exactly ten days later he received this answer from the Ivorydale committee: "We want the eight-hour day, but it is our unanimous decision that we don't want to say what you shall pay us. You know as well as we that the cost of living has gone up, and you will take this into account. You have always treated us right and we know you are going to keep on doing it."

Such a response, probably unique in employee-management relations, must have brought pride to Cooper. Soon thereafter employees learned that P&G had instituted a new wage scale which would enable workers to receive, on average, the same pay for eight hours that they had been receiving for ten.

Cooper found as much gratification in the Employees' Conference Plan as they did. He made that clear after the war in an interview with a Cincinnati journalist. Always incisive in speech, he leaned across his desk and told the visitor: "The plan is, I believe, the first move of its kind in business history. Certainly it is one of the first. We worked out the idea of having the employees elect by secret ballot a conference committee to meet monthly with management in order to bring to our attention matters that seemed to need correction or to make any suggestions for the general betterment. Each department with not more than fifty workers chooses a representative, and there is one representative for every fifty persons in the larger departments.

"Up to the present," he added, "no suggestion by the employees, and they made many, has been turned down unless we were able to show them it was impracticable. I always feel that if I talk with our people and cannot convince them that they are wrong, the chances are they are right.

"The chief problem of big business today is to shape its policies so that each worker, whether in office or factory, will feel he is a vital part of his company with a personal responsibility for its success and a chance to share in that success. To bring this about, the employing company must take its people into its confidence. They should know why they are doing things, the relation of their work to other departments, and, as far as practicable, to the business as a whole."

The Employees' Conference Plan remained a major communications medium for P&G management and plant workers until 1937. That year the U.S. Supreme Court ruled that the National Labor Relations Act of 1935—the Wagner Act—was constitutional. To comply with that legislation, Procter & Gamble had to abolish the conference committees. By that time, however, its plant employees were so accustomed to direct communications with management on labor policy matters that they chose to organize independent unions at each plant.

* * * * *

Before and even during World War I, Procter & Gamble's competitors in the soap industry had been developing new products designed to take business away from Ivory, P&G White Naphtha, and Lenox. Lever Bros. invaded the U.S. with Lux Flakes; later it launched Lux, a hard-milled white soap. Colgate improved its Cashmere Bouquet, a product actually seven years older than Ivory, and also introduced Palmolive soap.

In the face of such competition many questions confronted P&G's management. Had Procter & Gamble grown too smug? Was it relying too much on the prestige of its products? Was Ivory soap being advertised as vigorously as it should be?

Other business problems were also looming. The most serious was called to Cooper's attention by sales manager Richard R. Deupree. Wholesale grocers across the country were now demanding more and more discounts. The discontent that had erupted in New York in 1913, impelling Procter & Gamble to sell directly to retailers, was spreading to other parts of the country. "Let's extend direct selling, starting with the New England area," Deupree proposed.

Though Cooper Procter agreed, he was thinking beyond the problem of the moment. And Deupree knew what was on his mind. It was something that had repeatedly shattered the well-being of P&G's factory employees—the agony of being laid off from time to time because of the wild up-and-down nature of purchases by wholesale grocers.

The cause lay in the fluctuating prices of commodities. Wholesalers who supplied the retail grocery trade were shrewd businessmen. They watched the commodity markets. If the cost of raw materials showed the possibility of an upward trend due to drought on farms, wartime demands, or other critical developments, they at once bought heavily, stocking their warehouses to capacity before prices rose.

A veteran worker at the Ivorydale plant, remembering those occasions with a sad shake of his head, said: "Sometimes we'd get orders for forty carloads of soap from one part of the country, fifty from another, and so on, all at the same time. We'd work ourselves to the bone to get the orders filled. And then, after those goods were shipped, there would be no orders at all for a spell. We knew we couldn't expect any business until the wholesalers' warehouses were almost empty, and this could take months. If the company felt it had to lay people off or sometimes even order a factory shutdown, who could blame them? Better to lay people off and keep P&G alive than go bankrupt by paying men wages to do nothing."

The fact that most workers understood the situation did not make them any happier. No one enjoyed losing income by being laid off. Employees with families to support had to seek jobs elsewhere when such layoffs occurred. When orders once more began to come in, many of these former employees were no longer available. That meant new people had to be hired and trained, and training could be an expensive, time-consuming process. (At the Ivorydale plant, for example, personnel turnover due to such bleak periods rose as high as 11½% per month in 1919.) Beyond the severe hardship it imposed on employees, the matter of losing hundreds of employees every month and the cost of training replacements was a financial drain on the company.

How could the intermittent purchases of wholesale grocers, causing peaks and valleys of production, be corrected? Could Procter & Gamble continue to operate profitably unless it found an answer to this growing problem?

8
STRAIGHT PATH TO RETAILERS

P&G Sales Representative, mid-1920s, calls on an account. Note sample case on the counter.

Early in 1919 Cooper Procter called a meeting of his management colleagues. "We must make a decision," he told them, "on whether a plan for Procter & Gamble to sell direct to retailers throughout the U.S. makes good business sense. Mr. Deupree and I have been talking about this for quite some time. We think the company has learned a lot about how to sell directly to retailers through our experience in the New York area. We think it's about time to extend direct selling to the rest of the country."

Cooper was now surrounded by an able, experienced top management team. There were men like John J. Burchenal, vice-president and general manager; Herbert Greer French, vice-president and chief financial officer; Ralph F. Rogan, who had been advertising manager since 1914; and, of course, Richard R. Deupree, general sales manager.

Under what Cooper Procter described as "a true definition of the plan," the company would sell directly to any dealer handling soaps and cooking fats. The price would be based on the quantity purchased. There would be a five-box price, a twenty-five-box price, a carload price. Any dealer—wholesaler or retailer—could buy P&G products on that basis.

Everyone present knew that the key question was P&G's ability to deliver five boxes of soap to any grocer in the U.S. All also knew, from the New York experience, how harsh would be the reaction of wholesale grocers to any move to bypass them. Overcoming all doubts, Richard Deupree made a point he was to repeat on many occasions:

"Steady employment for our people, if it can be attained, will be economical for Procter & Gamble and good for its people. And the means to steady employment is this: We must produce to a selling and consumption line [the retailer and consumer] rather than a buying line [the wholesale grocer]."

"We do not face this problem alone," he added. "In all industry that I know anything about there come periods when either because of rising material prices or a plain scare the buyers become alarmed and want to buy heavily. The result is, as we have seen, a tremendous wave of buying. But—and how well we know this—simply because those purchases are being made doesn't mean that the goods are being consumed."

Cooper Procter expressed his agreement. "Consumers buy soaps, Crisco, and so on as they need them, and their needs are constant," he said. "If we supplied the retailer with what he needs on a week-to-week basis, the outflow from our plants would likewise be a steady week-to-week flow. If we are to avoid periodic layoffs, the solution seems to be to sell so that we will be filling retail shelves as they are emptied. In that way, our outflow will be as steady as the retailer's. And we can stabilize our employment year-round to match the retailer's year-round sales.

"Therefore, the first thing we have to do," Procter pointed out, "is make up our minds whether or not we should produce to the line of consumption or whether we are going to follow the old practice of catering to the buying habits of the wholesalers. The only way we can get control of our own production schedule is to produce to the consumption line."

Herbert French was among the few who were dubious. "Seems to me if there is real merit in the idea others would have tried it," he observed.

Deupree pointed out that, as far as he knew, nobody else had tried it because nobody had thought of it. Besides, it could be discontinued if it failed.

There were other questions from the accountants. "We now have about 20,000 accounts on our books. If we go straight to the retailers, we could have well over 400,000 accounts overnight. Do you realize what it would mean in accounting and billing costs? We'd have to quadruple the size of the office staff."

Such an investment, Deupree answered, would be justified by results. It would probably not amount to as much as the annual cost for training new personnel to replace those laid off.

Several others had their own doubts: "How are we going to service stores all over the country? We'd have to open hundreds of warehouses. We'd have to hire trucking companies all over the United States to deliver to the retail stores."

"Will the wholesalers become so furious when their P&G business is taken away that they'll start a boycott and refuse to sell anything to stores that deal directly with P&G? Then where would we be? That could ruin us."

"How can P&G possibly build a sales staff large enough to visit every little grocery store in America? The sales division would have to be bigger than the U.S. Army!"

Every such penetrating question, and there were more, had to be dissected, debated. Each was valid in its way. Clearly, if the idea were to be acted upon, its details required profound advance planning. Yet Cooper Procter was confident that the system could be made to succeed. So was Deupree.

The decision was made. Starting with the New England area, the direct selling practice that had been in effect in New York for the past six years would be extended to the entire United States.

* * * * *

Implementation began in September, 1919, from a P&G sales office in Boston. Word quickly spread throughout the U.S. that "Procter's going national with this plan." Immediately, nationwide antagonism rose against the company.

Hurried management consultations were called in Cincinnati. Could Procter & Gamble afford to proceed at a leisurely pace to extend direct selling to the remainder of the country? Would delays give the wholesale grocers too much time for an organized counterattack? Early in 1920, responding to Deupree's warnings that "the company has to move very fast before this thing gets out of hand," Cooper Procter approved a greatly accelerated program of direct selling. Within ninety days district sales offices were set up in nineteen cities ranging from Philadelphia to Chicago to Minneapolis to Denver to Dallas to Atlanta to Baltimore.

William G. Werner, who had joined P&G as a salesman in 1911, recalled those hectic days: "I was part of a team that went from office to office, staying one week at each city. While others were actually employing salesmen, our team had to set up district offices for the salesmen to work out of. The team consisted of a man responsible for breaking in an office manager, a credit and traffic manager, a bulk products clerk, and an accounting-treasury manager.

"The week before each office opened, the salesmen had been told to tell all the trade [retail grocers] to start sending their orders to the district office. As a result, on the very morning when the new personnel were being broken in, orders started to come in. The result was real 'on-the-job training.' It was a very difficult period because the new people knew nothing about the company or its products and had to be instructed from the ground up. At the end of a week, the team would have to move on to the next district office where an advance office manager had already hired the personnel to report on a Monday morning for instructions in their new jobs."

(Top) Sampling crews, like this one for Chipso, canvassed the country in 1931.
(Below) P&G's leading consumer products of 1913.

The furious pace of organization continued. Almost overnight the sales force was increased from 150 to 600 people. About 125 local warehouses were established by rental or purchase; almost 2,000 contracts for truck deliveries were signed; the company's accounting department was geared to handle more than 450,000 accounts.

As all these pieces came together during the first half of 1920, although not as neatly as P&G's normal penchant for thoroughness demanded, Cooper Procter decided it was time for a detailed public declaration of the company's intentions. Notices went out to wholesalers and retailers. They announced that Procter & Gamble would begin marketing direct to stores throughout the United States as of July 1, 1920. The notice to wholesalers said in part:

> *The increasing importance of our cooking fat business, combined with the large volume of our soap and soap powder business, makes it necessary that we be in closer contact with the distribution of our products and that we market them at the lowest cost, in order that we may render the greatest value possible to the consumer. Our experience in the Metropolitan district [New York] and the New England states where we have been operating on the direct basis, has influenced us greatly in making this decision to extend direct selling.*

> *We want you [the wholesaler] to know that this change is made with genuine regret on our part, because it necessarily affects the close business relations which have existed between this company and the wholesale grocers of the United States for so many years.*

Procter & Gamble was doing its best to mollify the wholesalers. A price list enclosed with the announcement showed the favorable terms available to them (and to retailers, of course) on quantity purchases.

The effort was wasted. Acrimony and antagonism continued. Among the many new sales representatives hired in late 1919 was Thomas J. (Jeff) Wood. He too recalled those early times: "These were the days before the supermarket. Independent grocers and the wholesalers who supplied them controlled about 95% of the business. They were firmly entrenched and convinced that no one could stay in business without them. No manufacturer had tried to sell direct on a nationwide basis.

"The wholesale grocery trade accepted P&G's direct selling policy as a challenge to their power, their system, their economy —in fact their commercial lines. The number of wholesale grocers, their assets, their personnel in the aggregate were very much greater than P&G's. Their sales personnel alone, plus industry competitive salesmen at that time, were at least ten or fifteen to one as against Procter & Gamble ... To lick P&G was the objective. The battle lines were drawn on July 1, 1920. Millions of spoken words, thousands of printed words in newspapers, trade publications, and sales bulletins kept the battle at white heat, since it was one lone manufacturer determined to prove to the world the economy, wisdom, and practicality of its move."

Wood went on to point out that "the word-barrage on the other side produced a big, bitter noise," and he presented a couple of examples from wholesale grocery trade publications. "We have known for a long time that Procter & Gamble were as rotten as their soap grease, but we couldn't figure out whether they were dead or a living pile of pollution walking around to save funeral expenses."

"We hope the retailers will resent this dastardly act on the part of P&G to confiscate their business. We know every grocer with guts will resent it. The man who doesn't strike back in defense of his business is a lousy cur, unfit to call himself a merchant and unworthy to wear the name of man."

On July 31, 1920, the eminent *Journal of Commerce* published a long article which asserted, "Every passing day piles up further evidence that the expected reaction of protest on the part of wholesale grocers to the P&G sales policy is assuming large and effective proportions."

The bitter complaints of wholesalers resolved themselves in a flood of cancellations of orders previously placed. In an attempt to mollify the brokers, Procter & Gamble responded with a form letter:

> *We have for attention your favor of [date] asking that we cancel your orders governing the carload of soap which you have on file with us. We beg to say that while we have instructed our factory to withhold shipment of this car to you, we are not actually canceling same until our representative has had a chance to call on you personally, it being our feeling that possibly at that time you may decide that you prefer to have this car come forward ...*

As for retailers, they also protested. Their practice, observed for generations, of dealing with wholesalers—many of them their personal friends—created a situation hard to change. Besides, they saw little reason to accommodate Procter & Gamble. Some even became resentful. A P&G representative would tell them that in order to make direct deliveries to their stores economically practical they would have to order at least five cases of soap or Crisco at a time. Quite a few of these small shopkeepers were accustomed to ordering one case at a time. They had no desire to invest heavily in inventory, especially with all the evidence of a new depression now menacing the nation.

Across the country the derisive description of Procter & Gamble became common language in the grocery trade. When a Procter & Gamble sales representative identified himself by saying, "I'm with P&G," a response came swiftly: "Yes, P&G—Passed and Gone." So Procter & Gamble faced difficult times indeed. But the real dimensions of those difficulties had not yet come into focus.

*   *   *   *   *

For perhaps the only time in his career, Cooper Procter allowed one of his many outside activities to divert his primary interest from the affairs of the company. He turned to national politics. He did this on behalf of his friend, General Leonard Wood. The general had agreed to seek the Republican nomination for president of the United States in 1920, an ambition in which he was opposed by Governor Frank Lowden of Illinois. Cooper Procter became the general's campaign manager. For months he traveled across the United States, whipping up support and funds for his candidate, making numerous speeches, enlisting the help of leading citizens.

It was more than personal friendship that motivated him. He had an impassioned desire to save the country from the philosophy which had characterized the administration of Woodrow Wilson. Cooper Procter and Woodrow Wilson had clashed in the past. In 1909, Procter had offered a multi-million dollar contribution to Princeton University, his alma mater, for the building of a graduate college but with a condition that it be built off the campus with ample space for expansion. Woodrow Wilson, then president of Princeton, said the graduate unit would have to be built on the present campus. The inner circle of trustees of Princeton knew that Wilson was using Procter's offer as a tactic in his private fight to oust Princeton's graduate dean, Andrew Fleming West. It had been Dean West who had persuaded Procter to make the gift in the first place. Wilson lost the struggle and later resigned the Princeton presidency after gaining the Democratic gubernatorial nomination in New Jersey. After the graduate college was built in keeping with Cooper Procter's terms, a student publication at Princeton printed this clerihew:

> Here's to Andrew Fleming West,
> A Latin scholar, self-confessed,
> He lived to see his life long hope
> Constructed out of Ivory soap.

Though Wilson himself was now desperately ill, the philosophy of his regime might well be continued by Ohio's Governor James N. Cox, slated to be the Democratic choice for president. "I feel," Cooper said, "that the Republican party represents many of the best elements of the American people, and that probably never before was its success more necessary for the good of the nation."

One of the keenest disappointments of his life occurred in June, 1920, when the deadlocked Republican convention in Chicago, after nine unsuccessful ballots, turned wearily from both General Wood and Governor Lowden and gave its nomination to Ohio-born Senator Warren Gamaliel Harding. Exhausted and dispirited after the campaign, Cooper went off to rest. And resting, he had time to think. His conscience obviously troubled him because of the time he had taken away from Procter & Gamble, for he wrote: "I sometimes wonder if I am right in allowing so many outside things to depend upon me. . . ."

His sense of guilt deepened after his vacation when he returned to Cincinnati and studied P&G's sales figures. They clearly showed the grocery trade's negative response to the company's direct selling efforts. Some P&G people were doubtful that it cculd ever succeed. To make matters worse, still another national business recession was affecting Procter & Gamble.

"It was an awkward coincidence," Deupree later said, "that the changes, the difficulties, brought about by direct selling came during this time of financial crisis in the United States."

The shock of the recession in the early 1920s was all the more severe because its arrival was unexpected. On the strength of orders received after the First World War, manufacturers had

95

built up large inventories of raw materials, purchased at inflated prices. Then, without warning, the market broke and an extensive liquidation occurred. Orders that had seemed dependable were abruptly canceled.

Although better off than many other companies, Procter & Gamble shared in the difficulties, particularly because of its own large inventory of high-priced raw materials. By the time business was back to "normalcy," as Harding termed it, the company had written off a loss of more than $30 million. That approximated P&G's total earnings for the previous five years.

Would things have turned out differently if Cooper Procter had been in Cincinnati instead of stumping the country for General Leonard Wood? Probably not. Nevertheless, he sank for some months into the bitterness of self-censure. Still in this mood he wrote to his niece, Mary E. Johnston, one of the most disheartened letters of his life:

> The question of the stock dividend has to be answered. It cannot be continued, but I cannot decide the best thing to do or how to announce it. Of course, it is going to adversely affect the value of the stock . . . My own judgment and prestige will suffer. I cannot help it . . . In the long run the present plan [direct selling] will work for the advantage of the average stockholder who held his stock as an investment and not as speculation . . . Notwithstanding all this, I know I am going to have a tough time . . . I wish I could decide on the best thing to do and the best way to put it to the stockholders . . . [In fact, P&G did pay a dividend on its stock in 1921.]

What eventually happened, in spite of Cooper Procter's self-censure, was due largely to the persistence of Richard Deupree.

Procter's long absence from Cincinnati had served a valuable if unintended purpose. By throwing many executive responsibilities on Deupree, it had helped prepare him for the day he himself would head the company. It also gave Deupree a degree of freedom in trying to make direct selling to retailers a success.

"In time, wholesale grocers began to change their attitude," Jeff Wood wrote in his recapitulation of those days. "Within a reasonable period and after much effort on the part of the field sales force, practically all wholesalers began to realize that direct selling was going to be a success, that it need not interfere with their own growth and development, and that rather than fight, the right procedure was to cooperate and grow together."

As a matter of business practicality, Procter & Gamble too had to change its attitude somewhat. It simply was not economical for P&G to deliver to retail stores in less than five-case lots, as a great many small stores—especially in rural areas and in many parts of the West—were accustomed to buying. The task of trying to service them directly was proving highly uneconomical. Therefore P&G found it advantageous for a few years to switch back to jobbing arrangements in parts of the West and South.

The practical results of the company's more moderate attitude were later outlined by Deupree in a talk to company employees: "When we started this plan five and one-half years ago," he said, "we had 50% more salesmen than we have today. We had three times the office force to handle the details of our business than we have now. We had double the number of warehouses and double the number of trucking arrangements. The reduction in expense to sell has been very great. As a matter of fact, it was costing us about twice as much to sell a box of soap during the first year of this plan [1920] than it is today [1926]."

Deupree also pointed out that direct selling had proved to be "of tremendous value in maintaining an even flow of business from our plants." That, of course, had been the key objective all along. P&G had inaugurated the process on a national basis only because Cooper Procter had concluded that the move would be good for the company and for its employees.

By 1923, after a long, difficult period of gestation, the direct selling program was on such firm footing that Cooper concluded the company was finally in a position to guarantee stable year-round employment to its workers. Procter & Gamble's sales and manufacturing curves had previously looked like a series of waves. Now the manufacturing and employment graph was starting to look like a straight line.

P&G's announcement that it would guarantee steady work at least forty-eight weeks of the year to the employees of its Ivorydale, Kansas City, and Port Ivory plants made industrial history. Letters of inquiry by the hundreds began to arrive. Other companies wished to know how they might benefit from such a plan. In response to the queries, a pamphlet was distributed. It was largely a reprint from a newspaper article which had said:

97

On August 1, 1923, a statement of more than usual interest to the world of labor and industry was issued by Procter & Gamble Company. This was a guarantee of steady employment to the employees of the company in plants and offices located in thirty cities in the United States.

This epoch-making announcement meant that for the first time in American industry the thousands of employees of one of the country's largest corporations were assured of steady employment the year round; regardless of seasonal depressions in business which occur in every industry and which, in the past, have necessitated retrenchment and the subsequent closing down of the factories for extended periods.

The substance of the plan is that all employees who are participating in the profit sharing plan, in return for conscientious services, are given a guarantee of full pay for full-time work for not less than forty-eight weeks in each calendar year, less only time lost by reason of the customary holiday closing or through fire, flood, national strikes, or other extreme emergency. The requirements of the plan are broad and liberal and the details have been worked out in a manner that will insure equal benefits to all.

Once, at the nadir of the company's struggle with the wholesalers, Richard Deupree was asked kiddingly by a newspaperman if P&G wasn't perhaps clinging to a lost cause. He answered in the same facetious mood: "We like to try the impractical and impossible and prove it to be both practical and possible —if it's the right thing to do in the first place." Though Deupree intended it as a joke, his comment was in a sense enunciating fundamental P&G philosophy.

And that philosophy certainly had been put to stern tests during those first years of the 1920s as the company held to its convictions about the "rightness" of the direct selling plan. For three years Procter & Gamble had persisted in spite of continuing difficulties and financial losses, some of which had sorely threatened the very viability of the company.

9
P&G AGAINST P&G?

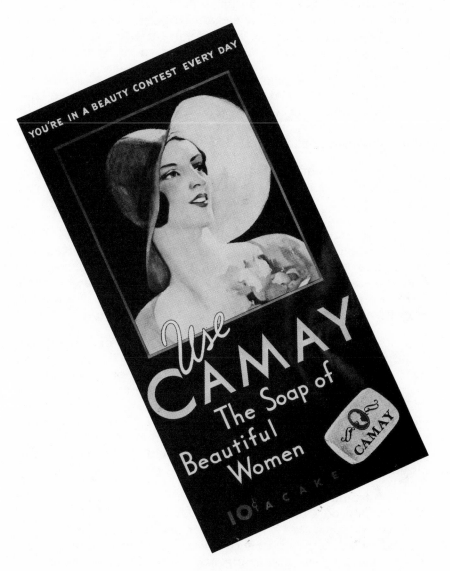

Camay 1929 advertisement.

It was not until 1919 that the company produced its first new brand of consumer soap since the introduction in 1902 of P&G White Naphtha. This was Ivory Flakes. It was made of tissue-thin shavings of Ivory soap, and a cynic might have said it was the old Ivory served in a new form, nothing more.

Nevertheless advertisements ("Safe suds in a second!") described Ivory Flakes in the elegant language of the day as "the most advantageous form of Ivory for those uses which require that soap be completely dissolved before it is applied to the articles to be cleaned."

Admittedly, Ivory Flakes was a response to competitive challenges like those of Lever's Lux Flakes. Both were primarily meant for light duty; designed mostly for washing dishes and the hand laundering of fabrics such as silks and wools.

Yet the heavy-duty field was where the large volume lay. Procter & Gamble's brands in that category continued to do well. P&G White Naphtha was still the largest selling bar soap in the world; Lenox and Star were competing effectively with the lower-priced soaps; and Star Naphtha powder went on winning its own consumer favor. All in all, Procter & Gamble had little reason to rush to market with new products. However, by introducing soap flaked at the factory, ready for instant use, the research people were preparing for *future* changes in home laundering equipment.

For the government itself, discussing the future of self-powered washing machines, noted in a pamphlet that there were five types, all of which could be operated by hand or by gasoline or electric motors. With the expectation that mass production of such equipment, plus the spreading electrification of U.S. homes, would change laundering methods, Procter & Gamble accelerated its research to develop a general purpose flaked soap for machines. If the old laundry bars would have to meet this internal competition, that could not be helped.

The outcome of the intensive research effort was that in 1921 P&G introduced Chipso, "a white flaked soap for all cleaning purposes . . . particularly adapted for washing clothes by any method, whether the housewife boils or scalds the clothes, merely soaks them, or uses a washing machine." Chipso won what a P&G sales manual described as "the most spontaneously favorable reception of any product ever introduced by the company." (By 1926 P&G advertisements boldly described Chipso as "the most amazing success in the history of household soap.")

Yet that "amazing success" was to be short lived. Soap flakes, despite their initial popularity, were cumbersome to produce. They would occasionally clump together. That shortcoming had been on the mind of a laboratory chemist early in 1924 when, in one of many experiments, he scraped a bar of soap with a pocket comb, letting the tiny particles fall onto a hot plate. The particles immediately puffed up into little granules. They were irregular in size, slow to dissolve, but the granular form of soap was intriguing. Would it work better than flakes?

A few weeks later another P&G researcher suggested a different experiment: What about spraying liquid soap into a heated tower,

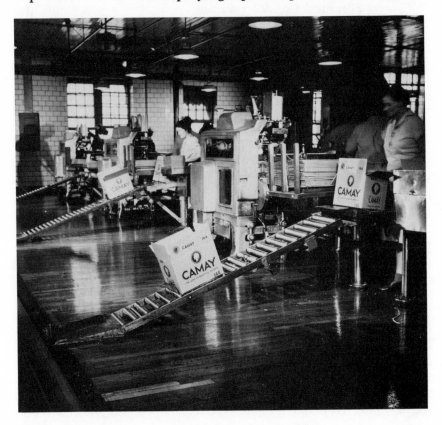

P&G's packing lines were models of shiny, clean precision.

letting the droplets dry out as they fell to the bottom? Spraying wasn't new. Certain food products, like milk and fruit juices, had been spray-dried since the 1900s. However, these food products were more like dust than granules.

Though spray drying of soap seemed good in theory, the technicians faced some difficult chemical and engineering problems. After two years of trial and error they contrived a new kind of drying tower. It was converted from a dust separator an engineer had rescued from the scrap yard. And it worked.

The resultant spray-dried granulated soap was called Selox. It was introduced in 1927. But somehow its "puffiness" didn't altogether please consumers. And the big packages of Selox didn't last long enough. So, with further refinements, P&G succeeded in producing soap granules of a greater density and longer lasting power. This led in 1929 to changes in Oxydol, a brand acquired in 1927; and although Oxydol was not immediately successful, its introduction did launch the move from soap flakes to granules.

*   *   *   *   *

Another new product destined for a long, successful life was Camay. Camay would compete directly with Ivory, especially with Guest Ivory, the small size designed for the bathroom washstand. Camay was launched with heavy advertising fanfare in 1923.

Its birth, it must be admitted, came after considerable intramural wrangling. At the outset Cooper Procter remained remote from the argument. The principal protagonists, pro and con, were Richard Deupree, by now a P&G director, and Herbert French.

Deupree felt that consumer preferences for hard-milled, perfumed toilet soaps would continue to grow. He argued that competitors' Lux, Palmolive, and Cashmere Bouquet were eroding Ivory's business.

The basic question was a matter of logic: Did it make any business sense for P&G to bring out a new product that would have as its principal competitor Ivory soap—the company's oldest and most successful brand? Might Camay mortally wound Ivory as it waged its own campaign in the toilet soap field? Moreover, Camay was a dainty perfumed soap, and Ivory advertising recently had been disdainfully dismissing "heavenly smelling" soaps. Could Ivory advertising talk that way about another P&G brand?

Cooper Procter could no longer remain silent. As chief executive he had to make a decision. When he approved the test marketing of Camay, he once more affirmed P&G's historic willingness to compete with itself. Some thirty years later, Deupree voiced his emotional attachment to Ivory in responding to a question at a Los Angeles press conference about a new soap, Zest, that P&G was introducing nationally. "Oh, I suppose Zest is a good product," Deupree said, "but I'm going to continue to use Ivory."

Promotion of Camay included sampling. Householders were invited, after trying a sample, to write letters of comment to the company. Did they like it? Would they buy it? If not, why not? Had they any suggestions for improvements? Was there a similar article on the market which they preferred? Why?

House-to-house distributors of samples, hired locally, sometimes caused odd problems. A P&G supervisor, traveling with a truckload of samples and a couple of assistants, would employ twenty or so local people to carry his wares from door to door. Once a week he would receive a check from Cincinnati to cover everybody's wages.

One veteran of the sampling service said, "Did you ever try to cash a check for $600 or so in a little town where nobody knew you? The ingenuity with which we managed it had a real bearing on our chances for promotion. It indicated how clever and self-reliant we were."

"How did you do it?" he was asked.

"We had a couple of favorite ways. For instance, we could urge the local banker to telephone the Cincinnati office for authentication. But some local bankers shied away from that sort of thing. I guess they figured if I was a crook I'd have an accomplice at the office who'd swear for me. Generally it was more effective to go to the largest P&G customer in town and ask him to vouch for me at the local bank. To make sure he'd do it, we'd get our local sales representative—somebody the grocer knew—to tell the storekeeper in advance that we were coming and that we were there to help his future sales by distributing samples. One way or another, our distributors never went without pay. The only time they had to wait for their money, as far as I can recall, was when my check arrived too late to be cashed on Thursday and Friday started a three-day holiday when the banks were closed."

* * * * *

Among the employees who heard about the internal differences regarding Camay was a young man named Neil Hosler McElroy. He had joined the company in 1925, fresh out of Harvard. Tall and sandy-haired, extraordinarily extroverted, McElroy started work as an advertising department mail clerk at a salary of $100 a month. As part of his duties, he read incoming mail in order to direct it to the proper offices. Some of his colleagues probably pitied him for the dullness of so static an assignment. Sitting at a desk reading letters hour after hour seemed uninspiring. In fact, McElroy himself had expected the job to be dull. "I figured I'd do it for about a year," he once said, "just so I could save enough money to go back to Harvard Business School."

Within months he gave up that idea. He found he had a job which, far from being dull, afforded an exciting education about practically every aspect of the Procter & Gamble operation. The more McElroy learned, the more absorbing his job became. His enthusiasm soon caught the attention of Cooper Procter and Richard Deupree.

A profile of McElroy written by William J. Miller for *Cincinnati Magazine* years later (in 1968) drew this picture of the six-foot, four-inch man:

> *McElroy moved fast after graduating in 1921 from Withrow High School in Cincinnati. He entered Harvard at 16 on a scholarship provided by the Cincinnati Harvard Club, the third of the McElroy boys to be so honored ... Strict Methodists, both father and mother taught Sunday school and saw that the boys did their chores, including lawn mowing, leaf raking, and delivering copies of the throwaway* Madisonville Weekly Bulletin. *Neil also wrapped bundles in a laundry and worked in a can factory. By the time he graduated from high school he had saved $1,000.*

> *"Without question," says McElroy, "our parents gave us our basic start in terms of work habits and study habits, as well as standards of conduct. We probably haven't lived up to them, but we came a lot closer than if they hadn't done so."*

> *At Harvard, McElroy found two ways to make money. One was poker. The father asked that he not do this any longer. Neil said he wouldn't, and he played bridge.*

The second money-maker was to follow in his brothers' footsteps and to organize pay-as-you-enter dances at Wellesley College. The Wellesley girls had sharp restrictions on their rights to leave campus, so the McElroy boys brought the willing Harvards to them, at a profit. Neil's contribution to it was to charge, in addition to admission, a transportation fee to and from Wellesley.

"We sort of made it coming and going," he says.

* * * * *

By the mid-1920s Cooper Procter could write, "The business has been turned from going downhill and is starting uphill. I think we have started on the way to greater earnings and volume than ever before."

In another letter, a private note to his niece, he revealed an inner turmoil:

Some day I will get credit for the past few years. It has been harder work than you realize. I had the burden of protecting the livelihood of many people and was always conscious of it. I had no personal benefit or interest to gain; my outside investments being ample even if P&G met disaster. And I gave consideration to interests and feelings of others longer than I should have done, as I jeopardized the interest of the company in doing so. It hurt more than you have any idea during the past few years, but thank heavens, it is behind me, and the other side, I believe, will gradually appear. But I am not yet quite through with the job, and when I get through, I want to put it in shape where it won't easily go upon the rocks.

During the last half of the 1920s, with Richard R. Deupree already viewed as heir apparent to the P&G presidency, Procter and Deupree were constantly acting to put the company "in shape where it won't easily go upon the rocks." They did this at a time when neither could possibly envision the rocky times that the firm would again face, as would the United States itself, just a few years later.

* * * * *

In 1923 Procter & Gamble did something no other company of its kind had ever done. It established an economic research department whose chief assignment was to help anticipate fluctuations in the commodity markets. One of the early economists

105

was Dr. D. Paul Smelser. But Smelser was less interested in studying commodity prices than asking questions about what consumers thought about P&G products.

In conferences with Deupree or Cooper Procter, Smelser would ask questions like, "What percentage of Ivory soap is used for face and hands and what percentage for dishwashing?" In some embarrassment, both Deupree and Cooper had to admit that they did not know.

Before long Smelser was back with other queries: What kind of people use Ivory, young or old? What kind of family incomes do they have? Do people really break the large size Ivory into two bars, and if so why do they do it? Deupree, like Cooper Procter, probably became mildly exasperated by having to repeat, "I don't know. I don't know." He finally told Smelser to "go out and find the answers to those damn questions yourself."

Smelser did. In doing so he launched a consumer research operation that was thereafter to serve Procter & Gamble as a permanent major marketing tool. Under his direction, P&G's market research department grew in size and importance and earned a reputation for unprejudiced, unbiased reporting.

One of his associates said of him, "Doc Smelser hated to have other people tell him what to think. He put the same philosophy into practice when writing reports. He believed strongly that his research should contain facts, not editorial matter; that the person who requested the study should be able to read the report free of any bias and come to his own conclusions as to what action was called for."

Every new assignment seemed to broaden Smelser's knowledge and methods. For example, when his department was asked to determine which perfume would be most effective for Camay soap, his first procedure was to ask women to smell this or that scent. Their reactions proved useless; a perfume is hardly the same in a bottle as when it is diluted to become part of a soap. Moreover, its strength may change day after day as the soap is melted down. What Smelser learned from the experience was that all such tests had to be made on products in actual use. That eventually became a principal tenet of his work: to test soaps, toothpastes, and everything else in use.

Also, in interviewing the public he had to develop the art of asking the right questions in terms everybody could understand. (Once, when an advertising agency used the word "bland" in its

Oxydol (left) as it first appeared as a P&G brand (1930), and (right) before being sold by The Waltke Company (1928).

copy for Ivory, Smelser discovered that a great many people believed the word meant "to scorch." The term was instantly dropped.)

His market research did not confine itself to products. It tested even the effectiveness of advertising—especially that of radio broadcasts. By such devices as offering "Ma Perkins flower seeds for an Oxydol box top plus ten cents" he was able to gauge the extent of public attention to a program. In the early days, probably no one in P&G's advertising departments or in its agencies did more to ascertain an advertisement's CPM (cost per thousand) as a guide for the efficient use of company funds. In short, Smelser and his associates, thirty-four of them by 1934, produced the basic data on which production, advertising, and other operating decisions were made.

"Looking back, all this seems quite simple and obvious," a former P&G advertising manager said. "But in those days there was a touch of genius to it. People were forever wondering how Procter & Gamble managed to make so many brilliant moves. Much of that brilliance rose out of the market studies made by Smelser's group."

As far as new P&G products were concerned, none were distributed nationally before being subjected to regional market tests. If some failed to win public acceptance—and quite a few did —they were discontinued. Their early withdrawal probably saved the company millions of dollars in what could have been futile promotions.

Was Smelser a pioneer in his work? He denied it. "Pioneers generally knew their destinations before they set out on their trips," he said. "I just stumbled into mine." Smelser's expertise, however, was widely acclaimed. A 1952 story about him by a nationally syndicated newspaper columnist reported: "There is a man in these United States who knows more about the habits of the opposite, or female, sex than the irreverent Dr. Kinsey, even if he doesn't ask the same questions."

"Doc" Smelser felt that the ultimate responsibility of P&G's market research staff was to help the company's management anticipate changes in the marketplace and continually to improve its products and marketing programs to capitalize on those changes.

As the company's current chairman, Edward G. Harness, once put it: "In our business we are forever trying to see what lies around the corner. We study the ever changing consumer and try to identify new trends in tastes, needs, environment, and living habits ... The successful company is the one which is the first to identify emerging consumer needs and offer product improvements which satisfy those needs. The successful marketer spots a new trend early and then leads it."

* * * * *

Cooper Procter had severe personal problems to think about by 1927 at age 65. Arthritis, a wrenched back, asthma, and other painful ailments were forcing him to take frequent vacations. Whenever he felt strong enough, he went hunting, especially quail hunting. In these trips he often persuaded Deupree to join him. "Nothing more relaxing," he insisted. "Sends you back to work with renewed vigor." Procter succeeded in making a bird-hunting enthusiast of his business associate and personal friend, although in later years after a visit to Canada, Deupree told acquaintances he would never shoot at Canadian geese. "I was told that when they mate it's a lifelong union," he explained. "I wouldn't want to end a 'marriage' like that."

Possibly in their relationship both men had long since forgotten a memorandum Deupree had sent to Cooper ten years earlier:

I would much rather be in a position with responsibility of my own [he had written] than a bigger position as an assistant. I appreciate it could do one good to be an assistant for a short period of time, but I think it would be bad if continued over a period of more than approximately two years.

I think a man who sits alongside an executive for any great length of time is bound to lose a great deal of his initiative. He will lean upon the bigger man. I think I can say he will almost think as the other man thinks rather than use his own mind. I will admit that occasionally an assistant of long standing finally "comes through," but where you find this you will likely find that the assistant was a stronger man than his immediate supervisor. He simply forced his way through.

When he wrote that memo in 1917, Deupree was arguing for the necessity of giving sales employees broader responsibilities, thereby helping them to develop all their abilities. He probably didn't realize that he was arguing for what would become broad P&G policy: that of subjecting people to every kind of responsibility they could handle in a wide variety of posts. Only this operating practice could make "promotion from within" effective by assuring future executives the broadest possible understanding of the company's ways, problems, objectives.

Cooper Procter decided in 1927 to give Deupree the responsibility of general manager. A year later, on Procter's recommendation, P&G's directors elected Deupree vice-president. In effect, Deupree became the chief operating executive of Procter & Gamble. And with Procter's full blessing, he increasingly assumed the responsibilities of the chief executive.

Both must have been emotionally affected by the knowledge of the great change that would soon come. The day Cooper Procter stepped aside as president, as he now spoke of doing, there would for the first time be neither a Procter nor a Gamble among the company's top executives.*   This realization placed a heavy burden on Deupree's sense of responsibility. In fact, it brought a feeling of uneasiness which, in candor, he confessed to Cooper Procter. Cooper waved it aside. "Always try to do about what's right," he advised. "If you do that, nobody can really find fault." (That rule of conduct, simple and straightforward, has been passed on to every head of Procter & Gamble since Cooper's day.)

On October 14, 1930, William Cooper Procter, now 68, became the company's first chairman, a position created for him. And Richard Redwood Deupree, aged 45, was elected president of Procter & Gamble.

---

* Though James Norris Gamble remained a vice-president and a director of the company until his death in 1932 at the age of 96, he had long been inactive. He was the last member of either founding family—with the exception of William Cooper Procter—to serve as a P&G officer. His brother, David B. Gamble, had left the company's ranks in 1905, though he continued to sit on the board of directors until 1920. His son, David B., succeeded him on the board, serving until 1956, when he was in turn followed by his son, David G., who sat on the board until 1970. As for the Procters (other than William Cooper), the last of their family to be on the board was William, son of Harley T. Procter. He held his seat for thirty years, from 1920 to 1950.

10
"A LIFE OF NOBLE SIMPLICITY"

The Ivorydale memorial to William Cooper Procter, purchased through the contributions of P&G employees.

Under Cooper Procter's leadership Procter & Gamble experienced a truly astounding surge of growth; much of it was achieved through the purchase of other firms' plants and brands.

As examples, in 1927 P&G had bought the William Waltke Company of St. Louis, a veteran in the soap business whose history dated back to 1854. Among the products which came with the purchase was Lava, a soap based on vegetable oils and pumice. More important—indeed, of outstanding importance— was its Oxydol brand. Once known as Ozonite, it had won a considerable market. Yet P&G immediately asked its chemists to widen Oxydol's uses to adapt it to swiftly changing laundry methods.

Within a month of making this acquisition the company purchased one of its neighbors, the Globe Soap Company in St. Bernard. Globe had two principal products, Pearl soap and Grandma's washing powder. It was not these brands that Procter & Gamble wanted; it wanted the firm's manufacturing facilities. In fact, it soon dropped the brands and used the plant's equipment to manufacture its own products.

Deupree himself had of course been part of this expansionist record, yet as he contemplated it now in his new position as president he must have marveled at its extent. The Waltke and Globe purchases had been only a beginning.

Next came the acquisition of Duz, a sodium perborate bleaching powder for light laundry use. Procter & Gamble had to buy the entire firm (a New York manufacturer) in order to get the brand. Cooper Procter must have had remarkable foresight in purchasing Duz and asking his chemists to try converting it into a granulated, heavy-duty soap. By 1939, that foresight was to launch the famous slogan, "Duz does everything."

Meanwhile, in Chicago, P&G had been competing vigorously with James M. Kirk & Company, manufacturers of American Family brands, a company it finally bought. Concurrent with all these acquisitions was the increase of plants, by purchase or construction, for crushing cottonseed. By 1930 the company was operating fourteen such mills through its Buckeye subsidiary. They were scattered throughout the Cotton Belt.

And a wholly new industry was beginning to flourish. P&G's scientists had found a way of converting cotton linters—the short cotton fibers which had to be removed from cottonseeds before crushing—into sheets of pulp which were sold to producers of paper. In fact, the company had built a $1 million plant for this purpose in Memphis and was beginning to sell this by-product for countless other uses (eventually for rayon, photographic film, plastics, and many other products).

There was also growth overseas. Though the company had been exporting Ivory soap to England, Lever Bros. had dominated the British market. Their company, Unilever, had begun a campaign of mergers to strengthen their position throughout Europe, and Cooper Procter must have realized that it was impossible to compete successfully in England without having an English plant.

He learned that a comparatively small English firm, Thomas Hedley & Co., Ltd., was having a difficult time. Though it was selling seventy brands of soap, including its leader, Fairy soap, it needed financial bolstering. And it had a ready-made soap factory at Newcastle upon Tyne.

Could this be bought? Cooper Procter sent Deupree overseas to investigate. Deupree did more than investigate. He finalized the purchase. Returning to Cincinnati, he told Cooper, "We've got to send someone over there to get a solid marketing program organized. Somebody who can do it diplomatically, without offending the British."

Who would this emissary be? "I've gone over the list," he said. "There are several possibilities, but I like best that young fellow working on Camay. He seems able, bright, and persuasive [he might have added handsome], and he's learned a great deal about advertising in the past five years. I mean Neil McElroy." Cooper Procter nodded. "Fine. Send him."

So it was that McElroy went abroad. He remained in England only a year but he fulfilled his mission and learned a great deal which was to enrich his own abilities in the years ahead. In the process he gave Procter & Gamble a firm footing in the British Isles.

*　*　*　*　*

All things considered, Richard Redwood Deupree did indeed face a formidable challenge in trying to emulate the success of his predecessor. He stepped into the presidency at a time when the country was on the brink of the Great Depression. It was becoming increasingly clear that Procter & Gamble, like every other company, would be plunged into difficult times. Yet when he delivered his first address as president of P&G, Deupree talked

113

with confidence of the future—confidence based on the record of Procter & Gamble in past periods of trial and on the able men who surrounded him in the managerial ranks.

* * * * *

Sales, earnings, physical expansion of plants and products are, of course, a facile way to assess the efficacy of a corporate leader like Cooper Procter. A more penetrating appraisal requires an analysis of *how* he applied his talents. Richard R. Deupree once said of him:

> *He was a wise executive. He delegated authority; he selected and trained subordinates, then gave them freedom commensurate with their responsibilities. Although he often surprised his associates by his familiarity with specific details, he never lost his perspective through preoccupation with matters belonging to a particular department.*
>
> *He insisted first upon quality products perfected by scientific research and kept standard by laboratory controls, and next, upon technical equipment and procedures that would insure efficiency in their manufacture. The story of quality in the product, presented convincingly to dealers and the public, brought increased sales, and these, in turn, called for closely figured manufacturing quotas. To keep all these activities in harmonious adjustment was an administrative task to challenge any man's resourcefulness.*

Although Deupree noted that Cooper delegated authority to others, there was one notable exception. Because of his long-held convictions about the "inseparability of interests" of the company and its employees, Procter never ceased giving his own personal attention to employee relations. It was 1933, for example, when he encouraged Deupree to install a five-day, 40-hour workweek at all P&G's plants—a historic social decision.

In April of the following year, learning that Port Ivory employees were threatening to strike, Procter told Deupree that he himself would go to Staten Island to meet with the workers.

He did not make the trip. For a long time his health had been failing. Now he was more than ever tormented by arthritis, asthma, lumbago, and other ailments. Weakness and pain sent him to bed. His wife sat beside him for days. (They were childless, having lost their only baby at birth.) And on May 2, 1934, at the age of 71, William Cooper Procter died.

INDUSTRIAL CRISES

The day a cake of Ivory sank at Procter & Gamble's

New Yorker cartoon of 1928 reprinted with the permission of New Yorker Magazine, Inc.

An editorial in the *Cincinnati Enquirer* said of him:

A Courageous Champion Of Worthy Causes

William Cooper Procter achieved a greatness of mind that enabled him to build a colossal industry of unshakable strength. He achieved a greatness of spirit that spread through a hundred charitable and educational and civic enterprises, and brought happiness into the lives of countless men and women and children who never saw him. The whole nation pays homage to his memory because his restless intellect and driving energy brought about, in our industrial fabric, startling innovations which set the pace for a growing nation.

It can be said of William Cooper Procter that a multitude of men and women and a host of little children are happier because he lived. What other epitaph could be so fine?

Monuments to distinguished soldiers and politicians are not uncommon in the state of Ohio. After all, seven Ohioans have become president of the United States. It is unusual, however, to find a life-size statue memorializing a deceased business leader (in Ohio or any other state), especially a statue primarily financed by contributions from his employees and former employees.

The life-size marble sculpture honoring William Cooper Procter stands on a grassy plot overlooking the Ivorydale plant where he conceived the idea of profit sharing in 1887. Procter's figure, head forward, foot advanced, emerges from a block of marble whose sides bear reliefs of groups representing employees. Inscribed on that memorial sculpture are these words: "He lived a life of noble simplicity, believing in God and the inherent worthiness of his fellow men."

Too many businessmen are forgotten after their deaths. This was not true in the case of Cooper Procter. Forty-two years later *Fortune Magazine* elected him to its Hall of Fame For Business Leadership. In that exclusive category he joined Henry Ford, Alfred P. Sloane Jr., John D. Rockefeller, J.P. Morgan, George Eastman, Andrew Carnegie, Cyrus H. McCormick, and Thomas A. Edison, as distinguished an industrial group as America has ever produced.

11
THE START OF BROADCASTING

Soap Operas ruled the radio airwaves, reigned over by programs such as "The Goldbergs."

As he assumed his presidential duties, Richard Deupree could look back over the twenty-three years in which his predecessor had headed the firm, a time in which P&G's sales had risen from $20 million (in 1907) to over $200 million (in 1930). Net earnings had increased in the same proportion, and annual dividend payments had never been interrupted. Could that record be continued?

The optimism with which Deupree discussed the company's future was hardly justified by the Great Depression. Within two years 86,000 American firms collapsed; the country's gross national product dropped from $104 billion to $41 billion; 28 million American families were reduced to a state of deprivation. Procter & Gamble could not escape the misery. The market price of its common shares sank from their 1930 high of $70 to an all-time low of $20.

In this country-wide debacle people simply could not afford to buy household commodities at their former prices. Cheaper soaps were eroding P&G's sales. For the first time in its history, to meet public needs and to avoid surrender to competition, the company was forced into manufacturing what it called "price brands." Of these the best selling were Clean Quick soap chips and OK laundry soap. "They were good enough products for the money involved," a sales manager of the depression era recalled, "but we couldn't sell them with the same enthusiasm because they were nowhere close to being as good as our regular brands. You might say we offered them as a public service to meet a national need."

In this trying depression Deupree had no choice but to order drastic curtailments of expenses throughout the business. All wages and salaries were reduced by 10%. "We must save every pin and paper clip," he said. Despite all such economies, P&G's gross sales for the 1933 fiscal year were down 28% from 1932.

Then in 1933, Franklin Delano Roosevelt entered the White House. His declaration of a "bank holiday" on March 5, 1933, the day after his inauguration, could be described as the nadir of the Great Depression. At the same time, it was also the turning point destined to lead to a stronger economy.

* * * * *

As Richard Deupree sat at his desk in the Gwynne Building, he could look across the nation at some strange contradictions. The United States Steel Company was functioning at only 19% of capacity, but the Fuller Brush door-to-door business was booming. Stocks were down to 11% of their 1929 value (registering a $74 billion loss for American investors). Yet business was good for Atwater Kent who produced radios. The largest manufacturer of locomotives had been able to sell only one in 1932, as compared to 600 in 1931, but many purveyors of low-priced essential goods were prospering.

Such facts made one thing evident: Despite the depression, people were buying what they most wanted and needed. They could not deprive themselves of essential household products. Therefore, though some shareholders argued that P&G ought to reduce its advertising spending because of poor economic conditions, Deupree insisted that the company should continue its advertising. He was convinced that, regardless of whether times were good or bad, Procter & Gamble could not interrupt its communication with consumers.

And a new avenue of communications was opening for the firm. Radio advertising, still in its infancy in 1933, appeared to Deupree and his associates to offer a novel way of reaching the public. But could radio help P&G sell soap? Nobody knew. This was what Deupree decided to test at a time when many other businessmen were viewing radio skeptically.

* * * * *

What was the background of the man who served the company longer than anyone else, for more than half a century? Though economic necessity had forced him to end his formal education at the age of 12, he more than made up for that by becoming a voracious reader. "I never knew of a man with a broader education, even though most of it was self-taught," said a retired P&G officer who worked with him for many years. "I remember walking into his office one day to find him absorbed in an Emerson essay. He handed me the book and pointed to a particular paragraph. 'Read that,' he said. 'It's one of the best lessons I ever had.' The paragraph read: 'Self-development. There is nothing higher than this. Make yourself grow to your full stature. That is the essence of success and morality and happiness. It is the one way to make the best of this world and every other world.'"

Many who knew Deupree casually viewed him as a stern, saturnine man. His thick, black eyebrows added a forbidding seriousness to his countenance, as did the firm set of his lips.

"That impression was misleading," a retired associate said. "Beneath it was an elfish wit that manifested itself in unusual ways. For instance, if Deupree believed you were wrong in some prediction about the business, he'd promptly offer to 'bet a dime' that time would prove you in error. He made a big thing of such bets, neatly recording each in a notebook. Later he would phone, or even march into your office, to tell you whether you had been right or wrong. If you had been right, he promptly gave you a dime. But if you had been wrong, you were expected to go to his office and place that ten-cent piece on his desk. He won far more times than he lost."

There were those among his colleagues who regarded the "bet-a-dime" proclivity as an extension of an urge to gamble; Deupree became, in fact, an inveterate devotee of horse racing in his later years. But he had his own explanation of the ten-cent wagers.

"People often urge a course of action," he said, "when they have nothing to lose should they be wrong. In most cases, this is merely idle talk and does no harm, but when the habit becomes fixed and uninformed opinions are given to someone who might act on them, it can be dangerous. You'd be surprised how the prospects of putting up even a small sum on a clear win or lose proposition stimulates careful study."

As another idiosyncracy, Deupree strongly disliked any memorandum more than one typewritten page in length. He often would return a long memo with an injunction: "Boil it down to something I can grasp." If the memo involved a complex situation, he sometimes would add, "I don't understand complicated problems. I only understand simple ones." When an interviewer once queried him about this, he explained, "Part of my job is to train people to break down an involved question into a series of simple matters. Then we can all act intelligently."

Deupree had been breaking the question of radio advertising into a series of simple matters at least seven years before he became P&G president. Far back in 1923 the pioneering station WEAF in New York had let it be known that it would accept a limited amount of advertising (the word "commercial" was yet to be coined). Deupree and advertising manager Ralph Rogan investigated. First they wanted to know how many homes a radio broadcast was likely to reach. In the New York area, they learned, there were about 50,000 sets, and the number was rising at a

(Above) The Queen of the Soap Opera, "Ma Perkins," in one of the photographs she sent to loyal listeners. (Below) Camay's "This is Hollywood" gathered stars such as Anne Baxter, Otto Kreuger, Hedda Hopper and Paul Muni.

remarkable rate. Within a year or two the figure might well exceed a million.

Only wild-eyed optimists would have believed such a prediction, but P&G decided that 50,000 sets presented a fair basis for tests. The Blackman Company, a New York advertising agency, was brought in for consultation.* Headed by J. K. Fraser, Blackman had been involved in newspaper and magazine advertisements for Ivory and Crisco. Radio presented a different challenge.

"We want to test radio for Crisco," Deupree and Rogan told Fraser. "The problem is what kind of broadcast will bring the best response?"

"Recipes," Fraser suggested. "Tell women how they can use Crisco to best advantage. I think it ought to be done on a morning program before the woman of the house plans what she's going to cook that day." Would women bother listening to radio programs while they were busy with morning chores? Nobody knew. The only way to get an answer was through experience.

Of the several ideas the Blackman people submitted in 1923, P&G chose a program called "Crisco Cooking Talks." WEAF announcer Graham McNamee introduced the various speakers who read recipes that called for the use of Crisco. Soon there was a "Radio Homemaker's Club" hosted by Ida Bailey Allen; she offered Crisco recipes with an appealing mixture of homespun simplicity and dignity.

Seven years later, in 1930, radio networks covering dozens of cities had been formed by both the National Broadcasting Company and the Columbia Broadcasting System. And P&G was riding the radio waves with a variety of daytime programs: Emily Post's etiquette chats and Helen Chase's "Beauty Forums" for Camay; Mrs. Reilly's discussions of the uses of Ivory soap; Ruth Turner's "Washing Talks" on behalf of Chipso; and the popular "Sisters of the Skillet," another Crisco cooking program. Though each of these attracted its own sizable audience, P&G still wasn't sure it had found the best way to sell its product on radio.

---

* P&G had turned Ivory and Crisco advertising over to Blackman in late 1922. It became the company's first full-service advertising agency. Before that (ever since 1900) P&G had funneled its advertising through the Procter & Collier Company, a Cincinnati printing business which did advertising placement as a sideline.

George, the Lava soap man, a singer, became the first P&G sponsored radio entertainer. His evening program in 1930 seemed to build sales for Lava, so Procter & Gamble decided on further tests of evening programs. They launched three that won large audiences. One featured the singing of the Mills Brothers; the second was a comedy show, "Stoopnagle and Budd," whose popularity brought on scores of other comedy teams; and third was the dance music of the B. A. Rolfe Orchestra.

Despite all such experiments, daytime and nighttime, over a period of ten years, Richard Deupree, Ralph Rogan, and Neil McElroy (then in advertising) felt that the company had not yet found the most effective kind of program. Deupree himself had become much too busy to devote a great deal of attention to where P&G should go next with its radio efforts. He delegated these responsibilities to Rogan and McElroy. They, in turn, leaned heavily on William Ramsey, who was appointed director of radio in the advertising department.

Their thoughts turned next to some effective advertising in Sunday rotogravures. The Blackman people had created a cartoon family of Ivory devotees, "The Jollyco Family." Every family member and their very closest friends used Ivory. But there was a villainess, one Mrs. Percival Folderol, who dared to use another brand. Questions for an executive conference: Could the "Jollyco" concept be extended from rotogravures to radio? Would people be interested in listening to the foibles of a fictitious group?

The market researchers had been finding a great deal of evidence to show that homemakers liked radio to entertain, not instruct. And they preferred entertainment that involved the activities of recognizable characters. It was against this background that P&G decided to try a new type of daytime radio entertainment, a decision that brought a lasting phrase into the English language: the soap opera.

Describing the first experimental efforts to win public attention through broadcasts, Alfred Lief wrote:

> It started with Oxydol. The agency handling the account developed a comic-strip type of story with continuing action, "The Puddle Family." It was tried out on station WLW in Cincinnati at the end of 1932 ... and not deemed good enough to go on a network.
>
> But the serial idea possessed fundamental appeal. A suggestion was offered by another agency [which had Lava and

*was given Oxydol] to run "Ma Perkins," conceived by one of
its men, Larry Milligan. It dealt with a self-reliant widow
and her business problems . . . The new program was strong
enough by December to let the show go national [NBC
network, Chicago]. When the situations began to diminish in
interest, a new writer was hired to do the script. He was Orin
Tovrov, a former newspaperman whose gift for stretching
out drama was inexhaustible . . .*

How many people were actually listening? How many to each
station? An offering of flower seeds for ten cents and an Oxydol
box top brought the answer. The audience was tremendous.

"Satisfied that daytime radio could sell," Lief wrote, "the company used it for all its brands. 'Vic and Sade,' a husband-and-wife
comedy team, worked for Crisco. Their scripts, by Paul Rhymer,
provided complete episodes each day and were so deftly done
that Hendrik Willem van Loon, a well-known author, dropped in
at Cincinnati just to tell P&G that they were 'the greatest folks
writing in America today.' Most of the programs, however, used
the serial story technique: 'Home Sweet Home' for Chipso,
'O'Neills' for Ivory, 'Pepper Young's Family' for Camay, and a
little later 'The Guiding Light' for White Naphtha and 'Forever
Young' for Camay—together forming a solid block of afternoon
listening. P&G virtually built daytime radio for the networks and
became the leading radio advertiser measured by the number of
periods of time on the air."

And its use of network radio continued to expand. It moved
into evening time when research revealed that some shows (such
as those of singers Morton Downey and Rudy Vallee) brought
gratifying results. Yet the company's principal emphasis
remained on its daytime programs.

It became clear that the most important ingredient of daytime
serials was emotion. The anxieties and agonies, sometimes the
joys of familiar radio characters enthralled audiences. Women
listened while they did their housework. According to the letters
they sent, they sometimes wept for the characters. When they
went to their grocery stores they remembered what they had
heard in commercial messages, and for Procter & Gamble business boomed.

* * * * *

The wisdom of Richard Deupree's determination to continue advertising during the Great Depression was amply demonstrated when the crisis passed. At the end of the decade the public was as familiar with P&G products as it had ever been. Ivory, Crisco, P&G White Naphtha—these were not new, upstart brands; they were veterans whose quality had long been established and advertised.

Between 1933 and 1939 shipments of Ivory soap nearly doubled; sales of Ivory Flakes more than doubled; Crisco's shipments almost tripled. As for P&G White Naphtha, despite tremendous competition in the field of granulated laundry products, its volume of sales increased 45%. In 1933 the company's soap brands had accounted for only 36% of its total shipments. By 1939 the figure had risen to 60%.

Such progress was certainly attributable to the effectiveness of P&G's advertising, its heavy sales promotion, and of course to improving economic conditions. And even though practically all of the company's brands had experienced bad times in the early part of the depression there was one notable exception. Camay shipments actually increased by 65% from 1931 through 1933, then gained another 40% by 1939.

Meanwhile, Oxydol was helping to create a new format for print advertisements: the "slice-of-life" situation. For example, a housewife learns from her grocer that she need no longer suffer from backaches after laundering. He tells her, "Oxydol makes everything easier." The scene shifts to the dinner table and her husband says, "A big meal like this on wash day? And we're going to the movies? Say, where's that old backache?" His wife responds with a happy smile, "I've found a new soap called Oxydol, dear. No more backaches for me!"

In a Crisco advertisement, a gentle, elderly Mrs. Paul comes into a distraught woman's kitchen, a can of Crisco in her hand, to show the housewife how to make "a light and digestible pie" that will delight her husband's boss when he comes to dinner.

Oxydol's growth spectacularly outdid most other P&G products. From 1933 to 1939 its shipments increased nearly sevenfold and it became the nation's leading packaged soap.

Chipso, however, began losing popularity. Its decline was attributable to the proliferation of washing machines. In them, Chipso flakes were far from efficient. They could hardly compete with granulated soaps like P&G's Oxydol, Lever's Rinso, and

125

Colgate's Super Suds. Chipso was the victim of changing technology.

In truth, the development of granulated soaps like Oxydol was actually helping to make washing machines popular. And, in turn, the popularity of washing machines stimulated the sales of granulated soaps. It was a hand-in-hand situation; and many of those involved in it prospered.

12
CENTENNIAL!

Roll of Ivory Soap wrappers being placed on packing line — 1937.

"This too shall pass" optimists had said during the Great Depression. They were right. By 1935, despite the constricting regulations of the New Deal, Richard Deupree could report, "The condition of the company is healthy, and we see no reason why it should not so continue." Net earnings in 1934 totaled $14.4 million, a 33% increase over 1933. Then came another 33% increase in 1935.

"During the depression years," Deupree said, "many consumers of household commodities abandoned the use of standard brands in favor of poorer grade products. Now there is a positive indication that these consumers are returning to the brands of superior quality."

The recruiting of managerial prospects never ceased. A number of outstanding people joined P&G during these years, many who were bound for high positions in Procter & Gamble, though no one was destined to rise as high, or have such impact on the company, as Howard Joseph Morgens.

Morgens grew up in St. Louis where he went to Washington University to earn an A.B. degree in 1931. From there he went to the Harvard Graduate School of Business Administration. ("I had saved some money and figured I could scrape up the rest," he recalled years later. "Harvard seemed the best place to go to get a good start in the business world.") From Harvard he sent an application to Procter & Gamble.

The application eventually reached Neil McElroy. He probably read the detailed resume with amusement. It was a description of a young man with an incredibly diversified background. During his undergraduate years his extracurricular activities ranged from singing with the Municipal Opera to working for the local phone company. While president of an amateur theatrical organization at Washington University he had helped produce musical comedies which played in downtown St. Louis theaters. And he had added to his savings by adapting plays for broadcast on a St. Louis radio station. Later, at Harvard, the resume showed he had amplified his resources by waiting on tables and taking a variety of part-time jobs off campus.

When P&G invited Morgens to Cincinnati for an employment interview, McElroy probably expected a brash young fellow with a multifaceted personality matching the diversities in his resume. Instead, he saw a quiet, reserved man of 22, soft-spoken, with

128

remarkably vivid blue eyes and an air of calmness and confidence.

During the interview McElroy learned that Morgens had for years sat late into the night writing short stories—dozens of them, enough to fill several books. What the efforts got him was a large file of rejection slips. Still, the fact that he had written and kept writing gave testimony of perseverance as well as a creative, inventive mind.

McElroy liked what he saw. So did Bill Werner and Ralph Rogan. "We'd like you to join us as a junior salesman," Werner told him. "We'll pay you $150 a month." Morgens accepted.

When he reported for his first job in late June, 1933, he was assigned to a P&G sales territory in New Mexico and Arizona. He found in that territory wild terrain, violent snowstorms, isolated trading posts, and many Spanish-speaking storekeepers whose customers included nomadic Indians with unpredictable buying habits.

In those days a Procter & Gamble salesman not only wrote orders but, in some territories, personally delivered merchandise in a Model A Ford supplied by the company. There was a decal of P&G's Moon and Stars trademark on the car's door. Morgens discovered that this emblem served as a calling card, assuring him of ready recognition wherever he stopped. On the car's back seat he carried samples of Ivory soap, Crisco, Camay, Ivory Flakes, Lava, Chipso, P&G White Naphtha, and other popular items, as well as a few brands destined for early oblivion, such as OK, Quick Chips, Lenox, and Star; in effect, he carried a traveling exhibit of P&G wares.

Morgens did something beyond sending in orders. Studying Procter & Gamble advertising wherever he drove, he thought of ways it could be made more effective. He forwarded his suggestions to Cincinnati. There his initiative attracted even more notice than his sales reports.

As a result of this enterprise he was summoned to headquarters in 1934 and given a position in the advertising department. Now he was in a highly stimulating milieu which afforded endless opportunities for creative thinking—the very qualities of imagination he had once tried to infuse into the writing of short stories. Given this chance to turn ideas into realities, Morgens thrived.

*　*　*　*　*

The 100th anniversary of Procter & Gamble, 1937, began with calamity. The Ohio and its tributaries rose to flood heights. In early January the waters overflowed the banks, their threat made all the worse by torrential rains which continued day after day. Mill Creek near Ivorydale and St. Bernard overran nearby roads and raged higher and higher toward the Procter & Gamble buildings.

Hundreds of P&G employees worked desperately in the downpour to fill 20,000 sacks with sand to be stacked around the factory walls. The precaution proved futile. The waters, soon ten feet deep, swirled over and around the sandbags. Abandoning the useless levees, the workers rushed indoors to carry whatever valuable equipment they could from the lower floors of the plant to upper levels.

In the warehouse at one end of Ivorydale thousands of cases of soap and Crisco would have been washed away. But the employees formed a kind of bucket brigade, passing boxes from hand to hand to higher storage space. With all regular work suspended, practically every employee who could reach the plant came to help in the labor of salvage. A temporary kitchen was established on high ground, and hot coffee, soup, and sandwiches were delivered to workers from rowboats and rafts.

Richard Deupree himself could not at once reach Ivorydale. All direct roads were under water. He finally managed the trip by a circuitous route over nearby hills, arriving at a high spot from which he could survey the damage below.

He saw the hastily recruited rowboats and rafts, the latter floating on empty glycerine drums. Some of them were transporting cases of soap and Crisco to be loaded on trucks waiting on higher ground. He had been assured by General Superintendent H. C. Knowles that the trucks would try as best they could to keep up with delivery schedules. Considering the devastating power of the flood, Deupree had already wired other Procter & Gamble plants to ship soap to Ivorydale's customers.

Looking southward, he could see clouds of black smoke a few miles away. Fires were raging and nothing much could be done to control them. All water and electric power lines had ceased to function. Deupree could only hope the distant flames would not be windswept toward Ivorydale. (Fortunately they never crossed the flooded land.)

(Above) P&G's quality control laboratory at Ivorydale, 1948. (Below) P&G's Long Beach Plant built in 1931.

By January 24, a day recorded in Ohio's history as Black Sunday, the Ohio River had risen nearly eighty feet above its normal level, something unmatched in years past. Cincinnati's city manager declared an emergency during which all businesses, theaters, and schools were closed. It was hardly necessary for him to do so. There were few activities anyone could undertake in the flood.

Following that Black Sunday climax, the waters began to recede. National Guard troops appeared to prevent looting of abandoned homes. The Red Cross initiated a $4 million relief program for those who had been forced to seek shelter on higher ground.

A few days earlier, on January 20, Franklin Delano Roosevelt, taking the oath of office for his second term, had bewailed the fact that he still saw "one-third of the nation ill-housed, ill-clothed, and ill-fed." In Cincinnati, men of grim humor, seeing the wreckage of the flood, were paraphrasing Al Jolson, "He ain't seen nothin' yet!"

But then, the president of the United States was facing problems that had no relation to the flood. Confronted with the intractable problems of the economy and watching the rise of Hitler's power in Europe, Roosevelt was preparing for confrontation. For counsel he summoned some of the nation's leading industrialists to Washington. Deupree was among them. Roosevelt asked him to serve on the White House Business Advisory Council whose mission was to formulate national policies encouraging steady employment.

Despite immediate concerns with the aftermath of the flood, Deupree felt a strong commitment to assist the nation's economic recovery and continued to shuttle between Cincinnati and Washington. The company's ever increasing advertising expenditures were proving their value in steadily increasing sales ($230 million, with net earnings in 1937 of $26.8 million). Another thing that was proving its value was the policy of giving able employees widely diversified experience.

In addition to financial growth at the time of this 100th anniversary, the company had a recent record of physical expansion. Its acquisitions included the Portsmouth, Virginia, Cotton Oil Refining Company (1931); Sabates, S.A., a soap company in Havana (1931); the Hewitt Soap Company, Dayton (1933); and the

Philippine Manufacturing Company, Manila (1935). While making these acquisitions P&G had continued to construct additional plants of its own: one in Baltimore (1930) and another in Long Beach (1931).

Yet physical growth was not the only measure of Procter & Gamble as it reached its centennial. The spiritual qualities inherited from the founders had never been abandoned. Historian Edward Hungerford wrote:

> *If there is any one thing that the hundred-year-old company had demonstrated through the course of its successful career, it is that a concern may make money for itself and still maintain a labor relationship that is clean-cut, generous, and fair; that it may retain the full regard of its workers as well as its own self-respect. This Procter & Gamble has done. The spirit of its founders, reflected and repeated through their sons and their grandsons, has been retained. And even though the three generations of the two outstanding families that gave their names and their ability to the company are now almost gone from active service, the company, in new hands and with other names on its executive roles, sails its course serenely and faces the future with hope and optimism.*

Much of its physical growth was leading P&G into new ventures. As an example, the Portsmouth firm was producing shortenings and cooking and salad oils for bulk sales. It crushed soybeans as well as cottonseed. So here Procter & Gamble gained sound experience in refining soybean oil.

As for the Philippine acquisition, it brought with it an existing business in soap and vegetable oil products. It also gave P&G a coconut oil processor near the source of this basic raw material. (P&G's list of raw materials, which had grown steadily, now included coconut, soybean, fish, peanut, and palm oils.)

Observing the 100th anniversary of the company's founding, Deupree stressed the continuance of age-old policies. "First," he said, "the company has placed foremost in its efforts the building of a strong organization. Second, it has concentrated on the uniform production of goods of high quality. Third, it has maintained at all times the highest efficiency in its manufacturing plants . . . In addition, our company recognizes the importance and value of research in its sales, manufacturing, and advertising departments, as well as in its personnel.

133

"In referring to *research*, I realize that the word has been so generally used that its significance may not be entirely clear. With us, research means an extensive study of all the problems which are involved in this business, both of the present and as they may be anticipated for the future. Research has more than paid for itself.

"In my opinion, this constant effort to better what we have and to anticipate the trends of the future has been an important factor in keeping the company in its strong position."

Even as he spoke at this meeting, he was looking ahead to the next century. Construction was underway on a five-story building adjacent to the Ivorydale plant. It would house the growing number of personnel involved with constructing P&G's plants. It would also house research people. In keeping with the responsibilities of its occupants, the new structure was named the Manufacturing Administration & Research Building. (Later renamed the Ivorydale Technical Center, it became one of eight P&G technical centers in the U.S. and abroad.)

All such activities seemed more important than any formal celebration of the anniversary year. Yet there was much to celebrate. After 100 years of growth the company now owned eleven manufacturing plants in the United States and five plants in four other countries—Canada, England, Cuba, and the Philippines. It was operating twelve mills for the crushing of cottonseed. Also, for the processing of cellulose it had in Memphis what was described as "the largest such mill in the world." The founders would have been astounded.

13
AND NOW
SYNTHETIC DETERGENTS

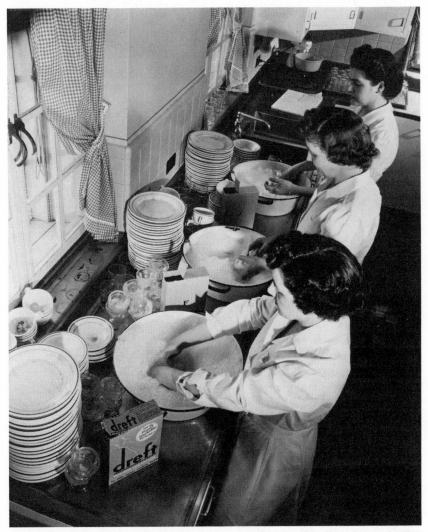

The dishpan test compared Dreft Detergent to other unnamed products of 1934.

Procter & Gamble's research organization had grown rapidly, but it had been a subordinate part of manufacturing. This had seemed a puzzling relationship even to employees. To end confusion, a directive in 1921 stipulated that the manufacturing and research organizations would henceforth be separated.

The new plan hinged on the establishment of a Manufacturing Department which would have two divisions: a Factory Division that operated plants and mills and a Development Division (later renamed the Chemical Division) whose principal function was research.

P&G research people soon justified the increased emphasis on their importance. They perfected the spray-drying process for making granulated laundry soaps like Oxydol.* And Oxydol was but one of the new and improved products to emerge from P&G's laboratories.

A section was created within the Chemical Division (in 1923) to study ways of satisfying consumers. An energetic young man named Wes Blair was assigned the job of conducting this investigation.

In his new assignment Blair went into the field with advertising crews and sales representatives. He distributed product samples, interviewed homemakers, spent much time in commercial laundries and bakeries talking to people who used P&G's products.

For years there had been a laundry behind the employees' lunchroom at the Ivorydale plant; it was used for washing uniforms. Now, based on Blair's research, it became a laboratory for studying commercial laundry methods and seeking to improve them. To qualify as the manager of this novel laboratory, the first of its kind in American industry, a person had to know a great deal about soap, chemistry, and about washing clothes. A chemist got the assignment.

Later, following the same research principle, a professional baker was employed to operate a laboratory section equipped as a

---

* The spray-drying process led to one of the major patent suits of the 30s and involved P&G's Oxydol, Colgate's Supersuds, and Lever's Rinso. The suit was based on claims by Procter & Gamble and Colgate-Palmolive-Peet that certain steps in the manufacturing process for Lever's Rinso granulated soap trespassed on a process owned jointly by P&G and Colgate. After first winning in a lower court, Lever eventually lost the suit and was forced to pay $2,500,000 to each plaintiff.

commercial bakery. One of the baker's early experiments involved a cake recipe based on pretested proportions of sugar, milk, eggs, shortening, and flour.

Unfortunately, when his new formulas were tried under commercial bakery conditions, with mechanical mixers and in large batches, the resulting cakes were failures. They sank, or "dipped." Though the problem was clear, an answer was hard to find.

Of all the additives tested, one called monoglyceride proved the most successful. When it was added to shortening in proper amounts, bakery cakes turned out lighter and did not quickly dry out. Also, because it was possible to incorporate more sugar, the cakes were sweeter. Thus was born Sweetex, a new bulk shortening that allowed commercial bakeries to make a much tastier product. When P&G introduced the brand in 1933 it was an immediate success.

Naturally, company researchers sought a way to incorporate the benefits of Sweetex into Crisco. But here they met an insurmountable problem. Although Sweetex made excellent cakes, it could not be used in frying. The high temperatures required for deep frying made the monoglyceride smoke.

Experiments continued, but at a moderate pace. Since Crisco was the best selling all-purpose home vegetable shortening, why spend a lot of time and money trying to make a major change in a winner?

But a competitive challenge was looming. In January, 1936, Lever introduced Spry with a $3 million sampling campaign. It was an excellent shortening, and suddenly Crisco no longer had the advantages it had enjoyed for twenty-five years.

Spry's encroachment on Crisco became so serious that P&G research efforts to improve Crisco were intensified. The efforts eventually succeeded. New Sure-Mix Crisco was ready early in 1940. Advertising called the improvement "the biggest shortening discovery in twenty-nine years" (referring, of course, to the original development of Crisco twenty-nine years earlier).

The new formula was based on "molecular rearrangement and an improved process for plasticizing." To consumers that meant a Crisco which creamed easier, blended more quickly with liquid ingredients, and produced higher, lighter, moister cakes than was possible with any other shortening, Spry included.

Now the Engineering Division had to design and install special equipment necessary for processing the improved product. In order to deliver to the consumer a shortening that remained fresh on grocery and pantry shelves, the engineers devised a plan to blanket the product with nitrogen before its metal container was sealed. And an ingenious key-type lid was developed to make it easier for consumers to open the can.

With these formula and package improvements, Crisco regained a commanding position. Spry had challenged; Crisco had responded. And consumers benefited because vegetable shortenings were better than ever. (Although Spry continued as a strong competitor and other new vegetable shortenings entered the arena, continuous Crisco improvements over the years enabled it to maintain its leadership. Entering the 1980s it was still by far the best-selling shortening brand in the United States.)

* * * * *

Research concentration on shortenings in no way lessened laboratory work on soaps. The need for a soap which would serve well in hard water had long been recognized. For years no one had found a workable formulation.

In 1931, a P&G scientist, Robert A. Duncan, was assigned to help the English plant at Newcastle upon Tyne overcome some processing problems. As a secondary assignment, he was asked to survey the state of the soap business in Europe. It was during Duncan's tour of the I.G. Farben Research Laboratories in Germany that he learned of a development considered more of a laboratory oddity than anything having commercial possibilities.

During World War I Germany had experienced its own critical soap shortage. The textile industry had desperately sought a substitute material. One of Farben's employees heard that a small textile plant had used cattle bile with good results. Farben began research to determine what it was in cattle bile that provided its wetting effect. Once it identified the compound, the company began synthesizing it for use in a product sold to the textile trade in paste form. It was described as "a good wetting agent, a fair detergent, not affected by hard water, and resistant to acid."

When Duncan found that a second German firm was about to bring out a similar wetting agent, his interest heightened. He bought 200 pounds of the finished product and shipped it to Cincinnati for analysis.

138

Preliminary studies by Procter & Gamble were so encouraging that the company negotiated for American rights to the product. In 1931, it became a joint licensee with E. I. du Pont de Nemours & Company. P&G received the exclusive right to use the material in the household laundry field. While P&G's Bulk Soap Department sold it to textile mills and laundries, researchers at Ivorydale sought means by which the material might be used in a home laundry product.

Preliminary tests showed it was possible to create a complex, two-part molecule shaped somewhat like a string. One end of the string was attracted to oils and grease; the other end was attracted to water. This two-part characteristic allowed the molecule (known as a surface active agent, or surfactant) to break up oils and grease in fabrics. Once that happened, soiled spots could be washed away.

Before long, researchers learned to spray dry the paste in the same kind of drying towers used for producing Oxydol. Exhaustive tests of the new granules showed them to be highly effective not only for laundering lightly soiled garments but also, to everyone's delight, for washing dishes.

The outcome was that in 1933 P&G introduced Dreft. Dreft was the first synthetic detergent for all-around household use. Its only drawback was that its "miracle molecule" could not handle heavy dirt very well. Further research began at once in hope of finding a formula for a heavy-duty synthetic detergent. The search went on and on for nearly a decade.

There was, however, one quick spin-off from the early efforts. That was the development of Drene liquid shampoo. Before Drene there had been only two ways to wash hair—with soap or with oil. Both methods required energetic lathering by hand and elaborate lemon or vinegar rinses. Both sometimes left a dull film on human hair.

Introduced first to beauty parlors in 1934, Drene soon was sold to retail drugstores. Within two years it reached national distribution, only to stun researchers with the discovery that Drene cleaned hair too well. It removed all natural oils. Consumer complaints quickly led the company to add a conditioning agent to Drene and the fault was corrected.

The development of Drene resulted in a new kind of P&G research laboratory—a beauty parlor. Female employees at the Ivorydale center could have free shampoos and hair waves. For testing purposes they had to be willing to have one side of the head washed with one shampoo and the other side with another shampoo. (Some strange coiffures were seen in Ivorydale corridors.)

Meanwhile Procter & Gamble established a wholly new sales department to sell Drene. The product's success became the foundation for later brands. One of the first of these was likewise a spin-off of the synthetic detergent technology—Teel, a liquid dentifrice.

Not that old-fashioned soap was being neglected. Since 1933 work had been in progress to replace the procedure of making batches of soap in giant kettles. The result, after five years of experimentation, was P&G's first continuous soapmaking process at the Ivorydale plant. There a shiny stainless steel tower (hydrolyzer) 70 feet in height enabled P&G to process soaps from raw fats to finished products in hours rather than days. Of course, this continuous process rendered Ivorydale's giant soap kettles obsolete.

Basically, the method reversed the traditional procedure by removing glycerine from fats via hydrolysis before converting the fats into soap. The overall result was a soap of higher quality and uniformity. In addition, production economies of time and space helped hold down costs. (An added benefit was improved glycerine recovery.)

* * * * *

Since the 1880s the floating soap field had virtually belonged to Ivory. Bulwarked by nearly sixty years of advertising, its purity and mildness were almost exclusive properties.

By the 1940s, Ivory's first strong challenge loomed. This was Swan, a new Lever product. A P&G advertising manager described the situation: "Procter & Gamble's name was uniquely linked with Ivory soap. While most consumers might not be able to say what company made Oxydol or Lux or Octagon, they knew that Procter & Gamble made Ivory. P&G's top executives were fiercely jealous of Ivory's reputation and tradition. There was, in fact, quite an emotional feeling about Ivory, clearly different from the company's attitude toward other brands. Ivory soap was Procter & Gamble's banner, so to speak, and the executives identified their own and the company's fortunes with the success or failure of Ivory soap."

So there was a convulsive reaction when the company learned that Lever was planning to bring out a white floating soap aimed at sinking Ivory. (It was later discovered that, unknown to top management, some overzealous P&G employees had acquired information about Swan from a few disloyal Lever employees.)

Procter & Gamble at once prepared for the Swan challenge. Ivory had to change; it could not rest on its laurels. Six months before Swan went on sale, the company began test marketing a new and distinctly different type of Ivory. New Ivory was the result of research in crystalline structure. It was made possible by the continuous soapmaking process and a new method for freezing and aerating.

When Swan appeared in 1941, Ivory was prepared for the challenge. To the average consumer the advertising claims for Swan and New Ivory were nearly identical—whiter, purer, milder, faster lathering, better suds, and less moisture. Lever advertising billed Swan as ". . . the first really new floating soap since the gay nineties." P&G declared that Ivory was "better than ever."

The marketing battle of the floating soaps began in magazines, newspapers, and medical journals. But it soon moved to the courtroom. Lever brought a patent infringement suit against Procter & Gamble in the Baltimore federal court. Lever claimed that the process used for New Ivory was its own Swan soap process. P&G struck back with a plea in the Cincinnati federal court for an injunction against the sale of Swan, claiming it was an obvious imitation of Ivory. Lever's next legal step was to charge that three lower-level P&G management people had used the mails in a conspiracy to steal trade secrets through several Lever employees. The P&G employees were found guilty and each was fined $6,600.

Though Procter & Gamble had won the patent suit in a lower court, Lever's appeal brought a reversal (1943). P&G's own patent, however, was not invalidated. To settle the litigation, Procter & Gamble dropped its unfair competition suit and paid Lever $5,675,000 in back royalties, full and final.

Despite Lever's monetary victory in the courts, Ivory won in the marketplace. Perhaps Swan tried to copy Ivory too closely. Consumers could not see any marked difference, and there was strong public affection for Ivory. It was a brand people had come to trust. Faced with a new brand they perceived to be no better than Ivory, consumers voted strongly for their old favorite.

All in all, P&G's experiences made it clear that new technology as well as expanding product categories would play an increasingly important role in the growth of the company. As one researcher remarked: "We create the future. The company will go ultimately where we take it."

Also, the competitive situations P&G faced involving its two oldest brands, Ivory and Crisco, made another point clear. "It isn't enough to invent a new product. Through constant improvements we must manage every existing brand so that it can flourish year after year in an ever-changing, intensely competitive marketplace."

14
P&G
GOES TO WAR

Harvey C. Knowles, Lt. Gen. William S. Knudsen, and Richard R. Deupree, after the wartime completion of P&G's shell-loading plant.

Considering the many economic trials the United States has experienced in its history, one must marvel at the fact that Procter & Gamble has consistently been able to double its sales volume in every decade since 1900. This was true despite some years of financial setbacks. For instance, net earnings in 1938 were $17.4 million, a 35% decline from the record earnings of $26.8 million in 1937.

Richard Deupree explained what had happened in a letter to shareholders: "The entire year was characterized by declining markets in raw materials [animal fats and vegetable oils primarily], and it was necessary each month to overcome a market loss on those materials used in the manufacture of our products . . . In addition to this . . . the company, in accordance with good accounting practice, wrote down the book value of its entire inventory on hand in the amount of $3,802,810.93."

Procter & Gamble now took $4 million out of reserves and added it to the amounts available for dividends that year. Toward the end of 1938 economic conditions in the United States were finally improving. Agricultural crops throughout the world were good; the anticipated lower prices for raw materials promised to be a business stimulant. In consequence, net earnings for fiscal 1938-39 jumped to $25.3 million, a whopping 45% increase over the previous twelve-month period.

That year was significant in still another way: Procter & Gamble's guaranteed employment plan was 15 years old.

"In the light of existing conditions," Deupree said, "the importance of steady employment is realized more fully today than ever before. Our plan has been a very real value to employees and to the company. We believe that it has been well worthwhile and the expense fully justified." (Expense included a new provision Procter & Gamble had added for its plant employees in 1936: one week's vacation with pay. This was an extraordinary pioneering step in employee relations for the entire country.)

By the time Procter & Gamble shareholders had their annual meeting in October, 1939, war had broken out in Europe. How would it involve American companies like Procter & Gamble? At the outset no one could say. Deupree himself remained confident of P&G's ability to cope with whatever crisis might develop. "We are most fortunate," he pointed out, "in having a business which furnishes people with certain of the necessities of life. Some of our products are indeed vital essentials."

Nevertheless, with uncertain times looming, Deupree stressed the importance of P&G's organization. "A critical time always emphasizes the great necessity for capable people in key positions. We must have men of such caliber and ability that they can carry the company through any emergency which it may be required to meet. We not only must have such men, but we must see to it that it is worth their while to stay with us.

"In a period such as this, men of real ability are in great demand. In my opinion, that demand will be greater than the supply, so it becomes increasingly important that we continue our policy of maintaining an able and vigorous organization . . . A strong organization is the best protection which the shareholders of this company can have, and is the best security for its employees. I believe our organization is stronger today than it was a year ago, and there will be no letup in our efforts to strengthen it further."

Was it coincidence that shortly after Deupree spoke these words a new management recruit arrived at P&G who would confirm and share these sentiments? History does not tell. But the new recruit was Edward G. Harness, a liberal arts graduate of Marietta College in Marietta, Ohio.

Born in Marietta on December 17, 1918, the son of a newspaperman, Harness had no thoughts of a business career when he entered college. ("I had planned to go to Ohio State and play football, and perhaps go into newspaper work or coaching after graduation," Harness later recalled, "but my father talked me into going to Marietta College. I really didn't understand why he felt so strongly about this until he died in the middle of my sophomore year. Only then did I realize that he had kept secret from me the fact that he had a serious health problem. He was anticipating death and wanted me to be in Marietta to help out when my mother was left widowed.")

Harness played football at Marietta as a 210-pound lineman. ("College football was an awfully important part of my life. However, my closest approach to being a 'hero' was when we beat Denison by one point because I blocked an extra point attempt with my nose. Unfortunately, the football broke my nose.")

During his first two years at college, Harness began to concentrate on two possible careers: newspaper and law. However, he concluded that he couldn't afford to go on to graduate school for a law degree. He would have to go directly to work after graduation. "The next conclusion I reached," Harness recalled, "was that there were jobs in the broad field of communications, such as advertising, that offered better starting salaries than the newspaper field in those days. So I got interested in advertising, and that's how I ended up at Procter & Gamble. The company offered me a job at $130 a month, and I went to work two weeks after graduation in 1940."

145

According to the 1940 census, the United States had a population of 132 million, and some 30 million owned radio sets. Day in and day out radio reported the catastrophes of the European war and the increasing involvement of the United States. This country sent fifty over-age destroyers to Great Britain as part of its lend-lease program.

On October 9, 1940 (as Cincinnatians celebrated the Cincinnati Reds' World Series victory over the Detroit Tigers), Richard Deupree warned Procter & Gamble shareholders and employees that "the company must be ready at all times to meet sudden wartime emergencies . . . No one can possibly foresee what the future may hold, but we have the satisfaction that we have built wisely in preparation for the future and . . . are prepared to meet conditions as they may develop."*

Fourteen days later Deupree received a mysterious telephone call. Immediately after he hung up he summoned Harvey C. Knowles, P&G's general manufacturing manager.

"Harvey," he said, "when the westbound National Limited pulls into Cincinnati tomorrow morning, you're to board the train and go to the fourth car. There you'll find the compartment of Colonel Francis N. Miles, Jr. He's chief of the ammunition division of the Army Ordnance Department. He wants to talk to you."

Knowles, perplexed, asked, "What's it all about? Why this cloak-and-dagger secrecy?"

"They didn't explain. You'll find out on the train."

When the Limited arrived from Washington the next day, the puzzled Knowles boarded the train as instructed and located Colonel Miles' compartment. As the train pulled out of Union Terminal, the colonel locked the compartment door and began to talk.

Ever since Germany's invasion of Poland in 1939, he said, it had become increasingly, even drastically, urgent for the United States to launch a massive expansion of production facilities for

---

* Despite threats of war, three new plants were completed in 1940: a soap plant at Quincy, Massachusetts; a third plant for the English subsidiary in London; and a soap plant at Surabaja, Java (Indonesia), to operate in conjunction with the Manila plant. Also in 1940, a soap production unit was being added to the shortenings and oils plant in Dallas.

all types of ordnance and munitions. "Nobody knows how soon we must be prepared," Colonel Miles said. "Our best intelligence indicates we haven't much time. Starting immediately, we have to have outside help, the best we can get, and I'm here to ask for Procter & Gamble's help."

Knowles asked what a soap and shortening company could possibly provide in munitions.

"Let me give you more background," the colonel said. "The explosives industry has been working with us, but the 'Big Three' —Atlas, DuPont, and Hercules—simply cannot provide all the facilities we need. There is a pressing need for new shell-loading capacity. We've been purchasing plant sites during the past six months. Now we're ready to go ahead with several new plants and we want Procter & Gamble to build and operate one of them."

Knowles pointed out that Procter & Gamble had no experience in shell loading or any other kind of ordnance work. Colonel Miles said the Ordnance Department knew that, but saw no reason why P&G's expertise in putting powdered and granulated soaps into paper packages could not be applied to putting powdered and granulated explosives into steel packages.

"That's why Procter & Gamble is the first company outside the explosives industry that we have contacted," he said. "We think P&G, even without any direct experience in handling explosives, is ideally suited to help the Army."

Showing how thoroughly the Ordnance Department had studied the company before approaching it, Colonel Miles got down to details: "P&G has personnel trained and experienced in training others in applying scientific and technical methods to large-scale, high-speed manufacturing. You also have experience in designing and building large plants. You've developed manufacturing systems and specialized equipment for packaging products under high quality control standards. All those skills are important in shell loading.

"Also, Procter & Gamble has a fine reputation for good relations with its employees. That, too, is important, considering the scope of the operation we have in mind and the thousands of employees who will be involved."

As Knowles listened he knew that Richard Deupree and other top P&G managers would feel the company was obligated to accept the assignment.

147

"Colonel, we'll try to work it out," he said. Knowles left the train at the next stop and hurried back to report.

In less than a week a P&G team was in Washington for the first in a series of meetings to develop a plan for Procter & Gamble's involvement in the defense effort. Scarcely more than two months after the club car conference, a formal contract was ready on December 27, 1940.

Designated W-ORD-494, the document was signed for the government by Under Secretary of War Robert P. Patterson and for the Army by Brigadier General L. H. Campbell, Jr. Richard R. Deupree signed as president of the Procter & Gamble Defense Corporation, a newly formed P&G subsidiary. According to the financial terms, P&G would incur no losses and would make no profit. The government would finance the operation.

In short, with Harvey Knowles put in command, P&G assumed complete responsibility for designing, building, staffing, and operating an immense shell-loading installation. Every month, according to the contract, the plant was expected to ship 1,000,000 rounds of 20mm or 625,000 rounds of 37mm ammunition; 175,000 rounds of 155mm; 1,000,000 rounds of 60mm, or its equivalent in hand grenades; and the fuzes and boosters necessary for all these rounds.

Weeks before the contract signing, P&G had begun developing its own plan of action. The first step was to select a team of about a dozen P&G technical men who would comprise an initial group to analyze the job of shell loading. Its various elements were parceled out among the team members. Each was instructed to learn all he could about his part of the operation.

Most members of the team went to the Army's Picatinny Arsenal in Dover, New Jersey, to study the shell-loading operations. They worked beside regular employees, handling explosives and shells manually, and paid very special attention to safety measures. (Wanting to take movies of the work for subsequent training purposes, the P&G people were stopped when told that artificial lighting couldn't be used for safety reasons. One ingenious P&G manager solved that problem. He procured large mirrors to reflect sunlight into the arsenal interior while the cameras rolled. Eventually, P&G accumulated about 25,000 feet of 16mm motion picture film which it later used with great effectiveness in training employees.)

148

The site for the plant P&G was to build and operate lay in western Tennessee, a few miles east of the small town of Milan. It covered about 18,000 acres of rolling farmland spread over two counties. Through the site twisted a muddy stream known as Wolf Creek. That creek provided the official name of the installation: the Wolf Creek Ordnance Plant.

As an awed group of P&G engineers viewed the site from a high hill, their Army guide waved his arm to encompass the huge empty tract. "You'll have to build roads, of course, and railroad spurs," he said. "We estimate there will have to be more than 400 separate buildings, including living quarters for some of the 9,000 or so employees you will have to hire and train."

The P&G people were stunned by the immensity of their task. They were expected to build and put into operation within one year what was an entire city rather than a manufacturing plant.

By January, 1941, bulldozers swarmed over the site. An army of workers labored day and night. From twilight until dawn floodlights glared over the operations. Heavy rains during the winter and early spring turned much of the area into a quagmire. Despite clinging mud and all else, the $36 million project proceeded at an ever accelerated pace.

By early summer about 100 P&G employees had come to Milan from throughout the company's U.S. organization to become the managers and supervisors of the Wolf Creek Ordnance Plant. From surrounding areas thousands of persons, most of whom had never been inside a factory, were hired and trained. These employees who would handle explosive materials were taught to load shells with brown sugar before actually handling gunpowder.

In August of 1941, fully three months ahead of schedule, the first production line was ready for operation. It turned out 60mm trench mortar shells. During ensuing weeks, additional production lines came into service. And well before the Japanese attack on Pearl Harbor, Wolf Creek was producing in excess of its contractual commitments.

The production records were so spectacular that the Army asked P&G early in 1942 to build and operate a second shell-loading facility—the Gulf Ordnance Plant at Aberdeen, Mississippi. This also was completed in record time, although it was much smaller. Both were eventually given several Army-Navy "E" awards signifying government approval of jobs "well done."

During the early planning for the Wolf Creek project, Harvey Knowles had told the P&G team that "the principles of good management can be applied to problems in almost any field." He was right. With more than 150 P&G managers eventually assigned to the Wolf Creek and Gulf Ordnance Plants, both installations were outstanding examples of construction and manufacturing efficiency.

P&G's principal contribution was perhaps the application of machine methods, including the design of new equipment, to speed what previously had been essentially a manual operation. For example, the old ways for loading 20mm shell cases at government arsenals required fifteen people to load about seventy shells per minute. P&G engineers devised an automatic filling machine that turned out 110 shells per minute with a three-person crew. Thus manpower was conserved and valuable manufacturing space was freed for other work, while explosion hazards were materially reduced.

Impressed with P&G's achievements, the Ordnance Department asked the company in 1943 to consolidate the Wolf Creek plant with the adjacent Milan Ordnance Depot and operate both as the Milan Ordnance Center. At peak production in 1944, the center had about 11,200 workers. The total employment at both Milan and Gulf rose in 1944 to about 14,500. That was approximately the number of people then employed by Procter & Gamble at all of its other plants in the U.S. and abroad.

Together, the Milan and Gulf operations produced some 25% of all the shells, fuses, and bombs used by U.S. forces during World War II. But in August, 1945, one week after the first atomic bomb exploded at Hiroshima, all production lines stopped. Both plants were put on standby. A unique chapter in the history of the country and of Procter & Gamble ended.

(There was, however, an epilogue. Years later the Korean War brought on reactivation of the Milan Ordnance Center. The Procter & Gamble Defense Corporation again managed its operations. In addition, for about five years in the 1950s the P&G Defense Corporation worked under contract with the Atomic Energy Commission to manage the Pantex Ordnance Plant at Amarillo, Texas. That activity, kept secret at the time, still is mentioned in P&G's files merely as "a manufacturing center for important components of atomic and hydrogen bombs.")

15

AFTERMATH OF BATTLE

Despite all their spectacular achievements, the munitions plants were only one facet of Procter & Gamble's involvement in World War II. Deupree said, "Whatever is right to do in order to win this war we are willing to do." It pertained equally to the company's home-front activities.

That this many-faceted man could retain an impish sense of humor even while dealing with momentous problems was evident only to those who knew him well. His wit could flash at the most unexpected times. Once, boarding a plane for a meeting in Atlanta, he carried—of all things—a small dog in a box. Neil McElroy, who was accompanying him, asked in surprise why the dog was coming along.

"A hunting dog I promised to give to the chairman of Coca-Cola," Deupree answered. "Very valuable. Cost $5,000."

McElroy was stunned. "You mean to say you actually paid $5,000 for that pup?"

"Well, not exactly," Deupree admitted. "I swapped two $2,500 cats for him."

It was hardly the kind of quip one expected from a man with so forbidding a countenance, but it revealed an unsuspected facet of Deupree's character.

As for his home-front concerns, from the start the government had declared Procter & Gamble an essential industry. Each of its twenty-nine plants was in effect an arsenal. Each had to be staffed adequately. Though many young employees had enlisted at the outbreak of hostilities, P&G obtained draft exemptions for others. These continued to work with the women and the older men.

"What we were turning out," a home-front veteran asserted, "did not sound as dramatic as bullets and shells, but it was just as essential."

One of the most important wartime requisites produced by P&G domestic plants was glycerin, something the company had been producing for eighty years. P&G had in fact become the largest processor of glycerin in the world. Not only did it provide the military forces with its own output, it processed large amounts of crude glycerin made by other soap manufacturers who were unable, lacking equipment, to refine it to chemically pure standards. As the basic ingredient of nitroglycerin, dynamite, cordite propellant, and smokeless powder, it became one of America's vital sources of high explosives.

It was no less essential at home. Here it was used to make dynamite for land mines, bridge and road demolition; it helped build dams to supply electric power as well as water for irrigation projects; it cleared the ground for the construction of military bases. Without dynamite the U.S. mining industry would have been unable to meet the tremendous demands for wartime production of coal, iron ore, and other materials.

Simultaneously, glycerin served a healing function as the base for sulfa drugs (sulfanilamide) and great numbers of servicemen, it developed, survived combat wounds only because of prompt treatment with sulfa.

Supplying still another essential material, Procter & Gamble's pulp plant in Memphis operated twenty-four hours a day, seven days a week, throughout the war, producing purified cotton linters. (When treated with nitric and sulphuric acid, linters became nitrocellulose or gun cotton. Just one bale of Tuff-Fluff, as P&G's cotton linter pulp was called, could provide enough smokeless powder to fire 100,000 bullets.)

During those days perhaps the most frequently heard word by the civilian population was "rationing." For most people the concept was new, startling, disturbing. Less than a month after Pearl Harbor, tire rationing decreased the civilian share by 80%. Sugar and coffee rationing followed. So did nationwide gasoline rationing. Soon canned goods, meats, fats, and cheeses were added. And inescapably the government placed soap on the ration list—for industry at the outset, not for consumers. Would there have to be soap rationing for the homes, too? As one historian described what happened:

> In Chicago one of the meat packers, Thomas B. Wilson, conceived a salvage campaign. His plan became part of the civil defense program. Women were urged to take used fats to

butcher shops, and renderers would gather the waste on a regular schedule . . .

The salvage campaign brought the salvation of the soap industry. About 940 million pounds of used fats were collected and thereby prevented soap rationing.

Scores of patriotic slogans inspired the campaign, but one of them was quickly rejected. This occurred when an overenthusiastic copywriter urged, "Ladies, take your fat cans to your butcher!"

*   *   *   *   *

Obviously, big reductions in advertising peacetime products while there were severe wartime shortages could have brought Procter & Gamble important monetary savings. Deupree, however, rejected this kind of thinking.

"We deem advertising and promotion extra important," he said, "because we must prepare during wartime for the day when restrictions will be removed and when we will enter a period of normal competition." He seemed to relish making these hard, sometimes unpopular, decisions. They added challenge to his job.

So P&G continued its intensive wartime advertising. People were listening to radio more than ever to get war news but also for the relief of entertainment. Radio advertising therefore continued to grow in importance. By 1945 the company was spending twice as much for that medium (about $15 million) as it spent on all other advertising media.

As for television, it had been in its infancy when World War II erupted; the war postponed its growth. P&G's initial experiment with it had occurred in the summer of 1939 with the first telecast of a Major League baseball game. This was a doubleheader between the Cincinnati Reds and the Brooklyn Dodgers at Ebbets Field in New York. Sports commentator "Red" Barber read Ivory soap commercials between innings, a historic innovation. But radio still dominated the air.

How heavily the company relied on radio advertising during those years was revealed by the astonishing number of new programs it sponsored: "FBI in Peace and War," "I Love a Mystery," "Professor Quiz," "What's My Name?" "Perry Mason," "Young Doctor Malone," "Breakfast at Sardi's," "Make-Believe Ballroom," and the very popular "Queen for a Day." Many of these as well as others which had started in the 1930s ultimately made the transition to television.

153

One P&G action, despite the war, was directed at fostering corporate growth. This was its 1945 purchase of a Saginaw, Michigan, firm which sold Spic and Span, a wall-cleaning powder. Although Spic and Span was a good product with substantial sales in the central states, P&G set out to improve its formula. The company felt it could make Spic and Span the nation's top seller as an all-purpose cleaner, which it eventually became.

"But you must bear in mind," said a sales executive, "that the year we acquired Spic and Span, 1945, many of us were in no mood to celebrate the event. Too many things were happening that tore at everybody's emotions. In April, President Roosevelt died—a blow to the entire nation. I remember seeing people weeping in the street as I went home. Nobody talked. It was a day of silence. Four months later, in August, President Truman ordered the bomb dropped on Hiroshima, and three days later another destroyed Nagasaki. With things like that occurring in this last year of the war, the purchase of Spic and Span could hardly be regarded as earthshaking. Nor did it attract much attention."

Also, there was the fate of P&G's foreign installations to be considered.

In spite of the German air raids on England, the company's three English plants survived attacks "in tip-top shape." But the situation in the Philippines was different. There the Japanese had stormed and seized the Manila plant. Some of its personnel were interred in the Santo Tomas prison camp. Others, including plant manager Fred N. Berry, were forced at gunpoint to produce soap for the Japanese. Naturally they did not approach the task with any enthusiasm. The plant's output dropped to barely 10% of prewar levels. The quality of the soap would never have passed muster in Cincinnati. Fortunately for Berry and the other captives, the Japanese commandant remained blissfully ignorant of both deficiencies.

"Berry and his assistants," one postwar report said, "had to comply with the Japanese's orders for two reasons: One was to stay alive. The other was to keep the plant operative so that it might be reclaimed by Procter & Gamble when the war ended."

The Manila plant was indeed reclaimed, though there wasn't much of it left. When American forces recaptured the Philippine Islands, some Japanese troops entrenched themselves in and

154

around the factory. It was virtually destroyed in the ensuing battle.

When the war ended, W. Rowell Chase went to Manila to survey the wreckage. What he saw left him grim. When he met the Americans who had been interred at Santo Tomas, he found them in deplorably weak condition. "All are returning to America," Chase cabled Cincinnati. "All need to recuperate fully . . . The P&G port area was destroyed. The oil mill and copra warehouses are also completely destroyed. The office and laboratory are badly damaged. But part of the soap plant and edible plant are in fairly good condition."

It was clear from all Rowell Chase saw that months of reconstruction would have to precede the resumption of work. This would be expensive, but as one officer put it, "Mark it off to the price of victory."

Wartime effects on the soap factory in Surabaja, Java, were almost the reverse of the Manila experience. Reports filtering back to Cincinnati had led the company to believe the plant had been completely destroyed. After the war P&G found to its relief that the factory had been only slightly damaged.

Of course, there were wartime handicaps in domestic operations. No construction of new plants had been possible. Nor was P&G able to procure badly needed replacement equipment for existing plants. Many temporary make-do repairs had to be undertaken. And raw material shortages continually hampered production.

One veteran said, "When you talk of shortages, don't forget manpower." At the height of the war about 30% of P&G's employees in the United States, Canada, and England had left for military service. That threw a heavy burden on those who remained in the plants.

Also, there were shortages that taxed the ingenuity of packaging experts. For instance, the normal Crisco can prevented the product from deteriorating. Now, cans being unavailable, Crisco had to be packed in glass jars. P&G had to add an opaque paper wrapper to keep light out of the jar so as to retard deterioration. Yet one circumstance helped with this problem: Being in such short supply, Crisco very quickly moved off grocery shelves into frying pans.

Even though a shortage of packaging materials made Drene shampoo temporarily a wartime casualty, its principal competitor,

Colgate's Halo, was even more deeply hurt. Halo's formula was based on a glycerin derivative, and the government ruled that glycerin had more important wartime uses than that of washing hair.

As for Procter & Gamble's new liquid dentifrice, Teel, it suffered from another kind of shortage—a shortage of people who liked it. The company had introduced Teel with heavy advertising and great expectations. It was agreeably flavored, attractively colored, and it had a presumed advantage over other toothpastes in that in contained no abrasives. Teel moved into national distribution. For a while consumers were buying it in such quantities that P&G had sound reason to believe it would be an enduring success.

Then came the shock. More and more users were complaining that Teel brought brown spots to their teeth. The "mouth chemistry" of certain individuals, it seemed, caused a discolored dental plaque to develop. Caught by surprise, the company at once cut back on Teel advertising while researchers tried to remedy the fault. They failed. Finally the company dropped the product.

This first abortive venture into the dentifrice field was an expensive failure. Yet the technical research which explained the reasons for its demise gave the company a solid base for further research. Moreover, the experience reemphasized the necessity for in-use product testing over an extended period of time. Teel's effects had been studied, as one scientist put it, "in people's mouths," but the studies had stopped too soon.

16

THE NEW CONCEPT: BRAND MANAGEMENT

A few weeks after General Douglas MacArthur accepted Japan's surrender, Deupree said, "Although practically every kind of product our company makes has been used in the war effort, instead of being helped by the war, our business was hampered."

This seems surprising because Procter & Gamble's sales increased from $214 million in 1940 to $352 million in 1945. But the increase was largely due to inflated prices. Net earnings declined, dropping from $28.6 million to $19.5 million.

Nonetheless, the number of individuals owning Procter & Gamble common stock reflected investors' confidence in the company. In 1930 there had been only 15,669 shareholders; by 1945 the number had nearly tripled to 44,925. True, this expansion was partly caused by more employees buying stock through the company's profit sharing and stock purchase plans. Deupree was pleased. He felt, as had William Cooper Procter, that employee ownership of stock best exemplified the concept of "inseparability of interests."

One thing that bothered him, however, was that many of the company's salaried people (office workers as distinct from factory employees) were not covered by P&G's profit sharing plan. Acting at his urging, the board of directors approved a way to remedy the problem. Effective July 1, 1944, all salaried employees earning more than $3,000 a year became eligible to participate in an innovative profit sharing trust.

This provided that a portion of P&G's annual profits would be credited to a participant's account each year. The precise amount would be calculated according to the individual's salary and length of service. Trust fund accounts would be invested in Procter & Gamble stock (or other securities) and held in trust until a participant retired (or left the company after fulfilling certain vesting requirements).

Deupree called the new plan "one of the most forward steps"' the company had ever taken. It would help immensely, he said, in P&G's constant efforts to build and maintain "a strong, virile organization."

Meanwhile, as in any other firm, management faced constant attrition. Some of it was tragic. On June 25, 1942, Herbert Greer French suffered a fatal heart attack. His death, after forty-nine years with the company, including twenty-three years as vice-president and chief financial officer, stunned his associates. Tragedy struck again on August 17, 1943, when Clarence J. Huff died. Huff had joined P&G when only 15; he had built a record of fifty-three years of service.

As these executives had to be replaced, others were moved upward. Neil McElroy was put in full charge of advertising and promotion. With P&G now among the top advertisers in the United States, McElroy attained a position of considerable prestige in the American business community. And Richard Deupree had still higher things in mind for the former mail clerk.

* * * * *

As many a retired employee remembers with head-shaking distress, hiring outstanding personnel was not easy during the war years. Many able men and women who might have been employed were in the armed forces. And the company also had to exercise caution in adding people; it had to have jobs awaiting the veterans who returned.

A case in point was Ed Harness who worked at P&G for scarcely a year and then went into the Air Force immediately after Pearl Harbor. By the time he returned to Cincinnati in 1946, there had been a new development in Procter & Gamble's practice of promotion from within. For the first time the advertising people saw one of their own rise to top management responsibility. On October 9, 1946, the board of directors elected Neil McElroy vice-president and general manager of Procter & Gamble.

* * * * *

Every month a group of more than 100 retired P&G employees gather for a luncheon meeting in a suburban restaurant. Over drinks and food they indulge in nostalgic reminiscences about their years with the company. All of them talk about Richard Deupree as they might talk about a personal friend. One certain way to stir conversation at such a gathering is to ask: "What was the most significant development during the years that Deupree headed Procter & Gamble?" *That* question immediately draws a variety of responses: "It was the way he steered the company through the Great Depression and through the problems of World War II." "The most important thing he did was to put ever increasing emphasis on research and development. If he hadn't done that, the company would not have grown the way it did." "It was the way he started diversifying P&G's product line by introducing toilet goods like Drene shampoo."

Some retirees answer the question in a more philosophical vein. They believe the most significant thing was the way Deupree reinforced the principles and practices he had inherited from William Cooper Procter, especially those reflecting the ethics of the founders. At the same time, they add, he originated managerial concepts which rose out of his own convictions.

One Procter & Gamble retiree offered an unusual theory: "Of course, Cooper Procter deserves the credit for recognizing Deupree's talents and bringing him along. But Richard Deupree was no carbon copy of Cooper Procter. He had a style peculiarly his own. Probably the most significant facet of that style was the attitude he held about change. To him, there was never anything in P&G's operations which should not be constantly examined to see if there wasn't a way to change it for the better. He welcomed ideas for improvement. In fact, you could say that he expected P&G people to come up with better ways to do things."

The most significant corporate change under Deupree, according to the retirees, was an innovation directly related to his search for "a better way." The innovation was the extension of the brand management system to P&G's advertising department.

The basic principle of brand management—to operate each brand as a separate business—has, of course, become so fundamental a part of Procter & Gamble operations that few people can imagine the company had ever operated in any other fashion. Yet when Richard Deupree became head of Procter & Gamble, the idea that marketing responsibility for each P&G brand should be lodged in the hands of a specialized manager who would concentrate only on that particular brand was only a vague notion still gestating in the mind of Neil McElroy. More than forty years later

Business Week commented: "The company that started it all, Procter & Gamble, continues to be the model for all other companies that set up brand management systems."

The plan was instituted because it made good sense. Many observers agreed it was the most important of the many contributions McElroy made to P&G's growth. Certainly it provided the primary impetus for his swift climb to top management.

One might argue that the general idea of assigning advertising individuals to work specifically on one brand dated back to the introduction of Crisco in 1911. At that time Procter & Gamble was a soap company which was marketing a food product. It was logical, therefore, to designate a manager to specialize in developing ideas wholly different from soap promotions.

However, it was P&G's introduction of Camay which suggested the brand management approach McElroy proposed. For Camay's performance had become disappointing. In the beginning it was not the great challenger of Ivory. Why? Company executives decided it was being held back by "too much Ivory thinking," particularly in the advertising agency which handled both brands. They felt that Camay's advertising had been weakened because of possible reflections on Ivory. In effect, Camay was not being allowed to compete freely with Ivory. It was the victim of an obvious conflict of interests.

Vice-President Rogan proposed that the company appoint a new advertising agency for Camay. The Blackman Company, New York, then handling both soaps, had been P&G's only advertising agency since 1922. [The Blackman Company subsequently became Compton Advertising, Inc. By the late 70s, Compton still had the Ivory and Crisco accounts. The oldest of P&G's advertising agencies, Compton also had the largest number of P&G brands. The company's second oldest agency, Dancer Fitzgerald Sample, Inc. (whose predecessor was Blackett-Sample-Hummert), began working with P&G in 1930. The average years of affiliation with P&G of the company's ten agencies in the late 70s was thirty years.]

Following Rogan's advice, the new agency selected for Camay was Pedlar & Ryan, New York. They were assured there would be no restrictions on competition. Henceforth Camay and Ivory would have to fight each other for a place in the market. Camay would be free to advertise as vigorously against Ivory as against other companies' Lux, Palmolive, and Cashmere-Bouquet.

Granted that prior to Ivory versus Camay there had been other P&G brands competing for the same market. But past situations had been different. When P&G introduced White Naphtha, for instance, it expected this new soap to supplant Lenox. As for Chipso, a laundry product in a new form, it was expected to take business away from P&G White Naphtha because it too was a new type of product. But neither Ivory nor Camay was a new type. Both aimed at the same market.

Given its own advertising agency, Camay's business quickly improved. It seemed wise that its promotion, including day-to-day contacts with Pedlar & Ryan, ought to be supervised by one person in the advertising department. The job went to Neil McElroy. Soon thereafter, however, McElroy was sent on his special assignment in England. His work there exposed him to internal competition as practiced by Unilever, its benefits as well as its weaknesses. The knowledge served him well.

When McElroy returned to Cincinnati, the advertising staff was still quite small. There weren't enough people for the specialized procedure McElroy had in mind. He discussed the "one man—one brand" idea with Ralph Rogan as it related to advertising, and he was enthusiastic.

Though Rogan reacted favorably, he pointed out that the plan would not be feasible without top management approval to add more people in advertising. Would Deupree be willing to hire a new group of managers? "I think we can convince him that the system will more than pay for itself," McElroy said.

Rogan asked McElroy to prepare a written recommendation. The result was McElroy's historic memorandum of May 13, 1931. (Though McElroy was familiar with Richard Deupree's strong aversion to any memo more than one page long, this one bravely ran to three pages.) The recommendation held a concise, detailed listing of the proposed duties and responsibilities of a brand manager, of an assistant brand manager, of "check-up people" who would spend most of their time in the field evaluating promotions at the retail level. In time, McElroy wrote, brand managers would be able to take from sales managers a large part of their ancillary work, leaving them free to sell.

Rogan initialed his approval of the memo and it went to Deupree. This time Deupree didn't respond with a "boil it down" comment. He read carefully. He agreed that the brand management approach made good sense. On that day Procter & Gamble's marketing philosophies and practices began to change.

When *Time* magazine heard rumors of what McElroy was urging, it sent a reporter to Cincinnati. The magazine summed up the idea in a trenchant phrase: "A free-for-all among P&G brands, with no holds barred." *Time* quoted McElroy as admitting, "At first some of the more conservative members of the company cringed at the idea of having a punch taken at ourselves by ourselves."

There are those who vividly remember stormy executive meetings in which the McElroy issue was debated. Among the objectors a few were apprehensive, others were grim. "It's suicidal," an opponent declared. "We'd be encouraging one brand to kill off another with claims of superiority."

McElroy responded that if the brands of competition like Colgate-Palmolive, Lever Bros., and others had been unable to destroy Procter & Gamble products, why fear homegrown competition?

Another man remonstrated, "It's like starting fights within a family. No good can come of it."

There would be no fights, McElroy insisted. The brands would vie with one another like brothers in a race, not like enemies. Internal competition, he maintained, would bring into play every talent, every ability, every tool possessed by brand managers.

The *Time* story concluded: "Eventually McElroy won his point. He persuaded his elders that the way to keep fast-growing P&G from becoming too clumsy was indeed to have it compete with itself."

It was a concept new to American industry. Never before had any American firm encouraged such competition among its own brands. General Motors might have cars like Chevrolet, Buick, and Cadillac, but these were products in different price categories. One could scarcely argue that a Cadillac, then in the $6,000 class, was direct competition for a Chevrolet, then priced at about $2,500. The differential in soaps, on the other hand, could be measured in pennies; often brands sold for the same price. Among them real competition did exist.

Of course with the institution of the brand management concept, people's duties and obligations changed. Ivory, Camay,

Crisco, Duz, Oxydol, and the other brands became independent entities. Each had its own budget, its own advertising staff, its own loyalties; in short, each had its own responsibilities.

Did the plan, once adopted, delight everybody? A former officer said, "No. There are always people who resist change, even resent it, especially old-timers who have been working under a familiar system for many years. Some of them thought the company was about to be shattered by internal disruption. Others felt their chances for advancement would be destroyed now that the traditional avenue for promotions would be supplanted by this new setup. No, there was not what you might call universal happiness. But time was to prove the doubters and dissenters wrong, for the reorganization of P&G brought it greater strength than ever."

Nowhere is the system more clearly described than in a company brochure intended as a recruiting document.

> *Brand management is the mainspring and moving force behind all our consumer marketing. The brand management concept assures that each brand will have behind it the kind of single-minded drive it needs to succeed ... The brand group is expected to know more about its product and how to increase its consumer acceptance than anyone else in the organization. The brand manager leads the brand group [in] developing the annual marketing plan; developing and executing the advertising copy strategy; planning and selecting media; planning sales promotions; coordinating package design; and analyzing and forecasting business results.*

That was what Neil McElroy's memo had proposed in somewhat different terms.

Another development in managerial procedures concerned the increasing importance of the Administrative Committee. Its primary function as a body of top-level managers was to aid the chief executive in guiding corporate operations and establishing corporate policies. Membership on the committee was by appointment of the chief executive.

Its basic value had been foreseen years earlier by William Cooper Procter. He knew that Procter & Gamble would some day become too large for one-man control. He felt the company should have a group of top managers who would discuss various aspects of the business and "in their united wisdom, knowledge, and experience, determine the policies of the company and, in a broad sense, assume responsibility for the successful administration of the business." (The group was first called the Executive Committee. Its name was changed in 1923.)

Procter & Gamble's corporate regulations state that its chief executive officer is "responsible for the supervision, general control, and management of all the company's business and affairs, subject only to the authority of the board of directors." Yet each of P&G's chief executives, starting with Cooper Procter, has relied heavily for guidance on the "united wisdom, knowledge, and experience" of the members of the Administrative Committee.

The Committee's specific functions have varied in minor ways over the years, depending on the wishes of different chief executives. But two details have remained unchanged: The committee always meets weekly (Tuesdays at 10 A.M.), and it always serves as a deliberative body, not as a decision-making group.

If there are no bitter debates in its sessions, the reason is simple. Before any matter is brought to the committee for approval, it has been thoroughly discussed and even agreed to by the appropriate members of top management. The Administrative Committee as a whole either approves a proposal or raises a valid question causing the proposal to be returned to its source for further development. Such referrals are very rare since serious questions are resolved before a proposal appears on the agenda.

One of the great advantages of having such a committee is its communications function. In the course of deliberations all members gather information about the overall direction of the business; they receive a constant update of the major activities of each P&G division.

"Without the Administrative Committee," it has been said, "it is hard to see how our organization could function as it does. That committee brings together the ablest and most experienced people in the company. No chief executive could ask for a better source of business advice."

PART II: 1946–1980
Author's Note

World War II marked a turning point in the history of Procter & Gamble. Before the death of William Cooper Procter, a member of the founding families had always headed the company. Richard R. Deupree, though not a descendant of those families, had been so close to Procter that in many ways he had continued his predecessor's style of leadership. It involved an intimate relationship between management and employees. Cooper Procter had repeatedly had face-to-face discussions with those who worked for him, and Deupree followed the practice to a considerable degree.

But the company's explosive postwar growth, with the number of employees rising into the tens of thousands—a third of them in foreign lands—made such personal contacts impossible. Annual convocations of managers from around the world, meeting with senior executives in Cincinnati, offered the best approximation of the old practice.

And there were even greater changes brought about by postwar growth. What had once been essentially a soap and laundry products company with a few ventures into edible oils and toiletries expanded into many other fields: foods, drugs, paper, cellulose, soft drinks, plus a $1.5 billion stake in industrial and institutional business. At the same time its market reached out from Cincinnati to encompass the world.

In short, Procter & Gamble became a different kind of company, one with an almost incredible multiplicity of interests, products, and problems. No longer could its history be recounted in the simple, chronological terms of an American soap manufacturer vending its wares only in the United States. A new perspective was needed: It would have to view its operations as a leading international corporation.

Did this mean that everything changed after 1945? Not at all. One thing remained constant: This was the character of Procter & Gamble. It remained solidly based on the principles, the ethics, the morals so often pronounced by the founders. Their spirit has become a lasting heritage. It has endured through the company's expansion into other countries and through its growth into new fields of production.

And so after 1945 the P&G saga involves countless new areas of productivity, as well as scores of penetrations into other lands. All these necessitate a broader focus on the company's operations. Instead of being recorded year by year, its operations are best viewed in the growth of its many product categories. And the first of these concerns detergents.

O. S.

17

DETERGENTS COME OF AGE

Tide's introductory store poster, 1946.

The surrender of the Japanese marked the end of the years during which Procter & Gamble's participation in the war effort had to take precedence over every other consideration. Now that the war was over and the future of the nation was secure, it was possible once more to plan for the future of the company.

Also in the fall of 1945 there were endless economic as well as supply imponderables. No one could predict what would happen to prices of raw materials once wartime controls were removed. Even the availability of those materials was unpredictable since suppliers would be having their own problems. For example, how long would it take to restore copra crushing operations in the Philippines so as to provide a normal supply of coconut oil?

And how much tallow would be available? At what price? There were no answers.

Though soaps had not been legally rationed during the war, they had been in extremely short supply. Every package that reached a grocery store had quickly been sold. Brand loyalty and brand preference had for the time been set aside; people bought whatever they could find. As a matter of fact, some P&G products like White Naphtha, Chipso, and Dreft had been temporarily taken out of production because of the diversion of raw materials to the war effort.

And there was the question of Spic and Span's future. When this business had been acquired in 1945, it could easily be sold as a supplement or substitute for other cleaning products. But would it continue to sell on its own merits when the shortages ended? And how strong would be the demand for Crisco when lard was again plentiful?

Like most business executives in the aftermath of the war, Richard Deupree had to reorient his thinking. For four years, busy with government duties, he had spent much of his time in Washington. By presidential appointment he had served as chief of the Agricultural and Forest Products Division of the War Production Board. In addition he had sat on the National Advisory Council and on the War Labor Board. Now he had to focus his thoughts and his energies on the peacetime problems of Procter & Gamble.

Peacetime? The shooting may have ended overseas, but things were hardly quiet at home. Facing a disruptive inflation, 400,000 coal miners were threatening to paralyze the nation with a strike for more pay. Workers in other industries soon joined the outcry. And abroad, in Paris, off-duty American soldiers were marching four abreast along the Champs-Elysees, chanting "We wanna go home! We wanna go home!" Yes, there was a cessation of gunfire in the world, but peace was bringing problems of its own.

What did the future hold for Procter & Gamble? Deupree reasoned that as long as the company had able people and better products than its competitors it would continue to grow. He reasoned that the first order of business should be to strengthen the organization for the future, and he sought to build on the concept established by Cooper Procter that the interests of the company and the employee were inseparable.

He need not have worried about the return of outstanding employees who had joined the armed forces. Many came straight back to their P&G careers, among them Edward G. Harness, Edgar Lotspeich, Dean P. Fite, R. B. Shetterly, Donald I. Lowry, and many more. "Our normal lives lay with Procter & Gamble," one of them said. "It was as natural to come back to the company as to our families."

Then there were newcomers who joined Procter & Gamble after leaving Army and Navy service. Among these were Owen B. Butler and, later, after obtaining his M.B.A. from Harvard Business School, William Gurganus. Still others postponed their return to jobs while they took advantage of the G.I. Bill to enter college. Deupree welcomed this as a trend which would later enrich the human resources available to the company. He defined the kind of people the company wanted as "not geniuses or boy wonders, but smarter than average, hard working, and honest young people who wanted opportunity more than they wanted security."

He returned to that point when he made his last talk as chief executive at the annual meeting of P&G shareholders on October 13, 1948: "We have emphasized time and again the value of a strong organization as it relates to the soundness and progress of our company. With an expanding business, it has been necessary to have a slightly larger group of executives operating the various departments and divisions of our company. Younger men, but men with years of training in the company, and of proven ability, have been advanced to these new positions in traditional company fashion."

As he spoke, Deupree knew what was on the agenda for the meeting of the board of directors to follow that afternoon. He knew that four men, each relatively young but with many years of P&G experience, would be advanced to higher positions "in traditional company fashion."

At the meeting, Procter & Gamble directors reluctantly accepted Deupree's resignation as president and chief executive officer, and elected him chairman of the board. And on Deupree's nomination, the board elected Neil McElroy to succeed him. McElroy's forty-fourth birthday was still more than two weeks away, but he already had more than twenty-three years of P&G experience, including those two valuable years as the company's general manager.

169

Neil McElroy shared more than Deupree's business acumen; he also shared the view that people were the company's most important resource. On his trips around the country he met often with managers in the manufacturing plants and the sales districts, and his first question was seldom "Tell me about your business" or "Tell me about your plant." It was invariably "Tell me about your people."

And it seemed to work. The quest for able people brought all of the top management talent needed for a worldwide, diversified company. At no time during the next quarter-century did Procter & Gamble have to go outside its own ranks to find senior management to operate the business.

* * * * *

A young recruit who had some prior business experience before joining Procter & Gamble in 1952 was John G. Smale. Born in Canada but brought up in the United States, Smale attended Miami University at Oxford, Ohio, for one semester before enlisting in the U.S. Navy in 1945 at age 17. (It was during the course of enlisting in the Navy that Smale declared U.S. citizenship. By birth, he could have become a Canadian citizen.) After his military service, Smale returned to Miami University and, in 1949, got his bachelor of science degree in business.

"I interviewed for a job with Procter & Gamble as a sales representative when I was a senior at Miami," Smale recalls, "but nothing ever came of it. Obviously, somebody decided that I wasn't a good candidate for sales management development, and I think they were right."

Following graduation from Miami, Smale took a job with a New York-headquartered proprietary drug company. Subsequently, he worked for a short time with a small private firm which was introducing a patented nasal spray in the upper Midwest. Largely financed by one man who also had several other entrepreneurial projects going, the new firm got into financial difficulties. Suddenly, and concurrently with the birth of his first child, Smale found himself with "bouncing paychecks." Fortunately, he saw and responded to a Procter & Gamble ad for advertising personnel, in a Chicago newspaper.

"They invited me to Cincinnati for interviews on a Friday," Smale said, "where I learned that they were considering me for a job on the brand management team that was getting ready to put Gleem toothpaste into test markets. I got a job offer by telephone the following Monday, and they wanted to know how long it would be before I could make arrangements to start work. My immediate response was 'How about Wednesday?' "

Recalling that incident, he chuckled and added, "My principal interest in 1952 was how long it would take for me to get a paycheck that didn't bounce!"

As for the other postwar priority—the building of a research and development capability which would assure a flow of new and improved products—the Technical Center at Ivorydale, constructed shortly before the war, underwent major expansion in 1947. The search for improvements in the formulas and processes for soapmaking were intensified.

Washing products prior to the war had two general classes: Brands like Oxydol, Rinso, and Super Suds were formulated for strong cleaning power. Products like Lux Flakes and Ivory Snow were mild to hands and gentle to colors and fabrics.

Shortly before the war P&G had introduced Duz granulated soap with a formula which had both qualities. It cleaned heavily soiled clothes and yet had improved mildness. The advertising theme, "Duz does everything," had helped Duz grow rapidly until wartime shortages began. Now its popularity again grew as shortages ended.

Much of the research effort went toward finding more effective ways to combine cleaning power with mildness. One group, in fact, had been working for a decade on a project that would revolutionize the industry, though nobody was aware of it then. It began with the synthetic detergent Dreft.

In spite of its early success, Dreft had its limitations. Effective as it was for dishwashing and light laundry, it failed at heavy-duty tasks. Market researchers talking to women on their doorsteps were being told, "You ought to see my children's clothes when they come in from play or my husband's jeans when he finishes tinkering with the car. We really need a heavy-duty product for our laundry."

Every major soap company in the United States was trying to develop such a detergent. None had succeeded.

"Hundreds of formulations were tried and not one was satisfactory," said researcher Robert A. Duncan. Practically all of the experiments centered around the old fundamentals of soapmaking. A technological breakthrough came almost by accident.

171

"For years," Duncan explained, "the company had been selling bulk quantities of detergent to commercial users of washing machines. We'd had no complaints. Suddenly, reports started coming in that lime scale was building up in the machines, deposits that clogged the equipment." Seeking a remedy, P&G scientists focused on the chemical family of phosphates. Tests showed that one of these, sodium tripolyphosphate, would stop lime scale buildup in institutional dishwashing machines. So it was added to the formula and users reported the improved product worked very well.

As so often happens, researchers finally made progress in household detergents when they questioned a basic assumption carried over from soapmaking. They began testing formulations with far greater concentrations of tripoly and were excited by the possibilities.

"The results of further tests," said Bob Duncan, "were truly remarkable. Here was a new synthetic detergent formula that could wash clothes visibly cleaner, leave colors brighter, produce better suds, make white clothes look whiter, and even eliminate the major problems of washing in hard water. The company applied for the basic patent in 1944. But it could not begin manufacturing for more than two years. During the war, there was no practical way to build the necessary new plants and equipment or to secure an adequate supply of raw materials."

Even after the war there was considerable hesitation among P&G executives in the matter of launching this new technology for household use. The company had suffered years of wartime shortages and depressed earnings. Just before the war it had begun building the equipment for a continuous soapmaking process which would render all the old kettles obsolete; the interrupted work had still to be completed at heavy expense. Harnessing this new detergent technology would require at least $10 million in capital outlays. Moreover, it too would make a great deal of present equipment obsolete. Was it wise to go ahead at this time?

The answer was that *someone* would surely introduce a synthetic detergent with an effective phosphate builder. Procter & Gamble had a head start with its knowledge. It had the opportunity to be first. There was only one thing to do—forge ahead.

As the war ended, the company assembled a new brand management team which would be ready to market what was to be advertised as "The Washday Miracle." The product's brand name, everyone finally agreed, would be the simple word *Tide*.

Throughout 1946 the team tested Tide in six cities: Springfield, Massachusetts, and Albany, New York, for soft water; Evansville, Indiana, and Lima, Ohio, for medium water; Wichita, Kansas, and Sioux Falls, South Dakota, for hard water. So confident were they that consumers would really see an immediate difference in results that they sent crews from door to door giving each householder a regular size package free.

"It's hard to realize," one veteran recounted, "what happened after we started distributing samples. Householders discovered that 'the washday miracle' wasn't just an advertising phrase. It was a fact. Through advertising, sampling, and word of mouth, news of Tide's miracle performance spread. Consumer demand soared. It taxed all our production capacity so that we couldn't go national till 1947."

Early metal coupons gave consumers extra value for trying out a P&G product, 1930s.

Competition was not sleeping. The results of Tide's test marketing were as visible to major competitors as they were to the Tide brand group. Lever Bros. countered with Surf and Colgate-Palmolive brought out Fab. Each sought formula variations that would give superior performance, at least in some water or laundry conditions. Surf advertised that rinsing was unnecessary with this new kind of product, an idea that won a lot of attention for a brief period—particularly in New York which was suffering a water shortage.

Yet Tide held national leadership. One reason was that researchers were constantly improving its quality, and every improvement was widely advertised. Changes came quickly: A tarnish inhibitor was added to permit washing silver-plated tableware; a new ingredient (carboxymethylcellulose) helped prevent soil in water being redeposited on laundry during the washing cycle; sodium silicate eliminated corrosion of aluminum tubs in washing machines; and a delicate perfume was introduced to overcome any hint of chemical odors.

"By the 1950s," said a company executive, "Tide could claim to be the most popular product in America."

18

THE GROWTH OF PERSONAL PRODUCTS

The introduction of Tide and the flood of synthetic granules that followed Tide were not the only revolutionary aspects the company faced in the postwar decade. Its principal retail outlet, the grocery industry, was undergoing a revolution of its own. The supermarket, indeed the entire system of grocery wholesaling, radically changed the channels to consumers.

Within the detergent industry itself dramatic changes continued to present new challenges. The use of new time-saving automatic washing machines expanded from 3% to 33% of U.S. households during those ten years. And front-loading machines emerged. These did not work well with high-sudsing detergents; they demanded changes of their own.

Meanwhile prewar brands like P&G White Naphtha and Chipso returned to the market only to become the victims of the new detergents. Still, there were consumers who considered detergents harsher to the skin than natural soap products. So brands like Ivory Flakes and Ivory Snow clung to their formulas rather than risk damaging Ivory's priceless reputation for mildness. Other soaps like Duz and Oxydol faced a different problem —whether to change to a detergent formula and risk alienating loyal soap users. Oxydol finally made the conversion in 1952 and later incorporated an effective bleach into its formula. It remained an important brand at the beginning of the 1980s, one of the prewar laundry products to survive.

Duz was less successful. It had been introduced shortly before the war and had no long heritage of loyalty. Several attempts were made to rejuvenate the brand, first as a detergent called Blue Dot Duz, and then as Premium Duz with free premiums in the package. But the original Duz brand, like its arch rival Rinso, yielded to changing consumer preferences.

The company's oldest brand, Ivory soap, responded with changes of its own and thrived. Ivory had grown as an all-purpose soap when the bar form was used for everything— laundry, dishes, house cleaning, and bathing. More specialized appeals became necessary. The smallest size of Ivory was renamed Personal Size Ivory. It was advertised to the beauty soap market, competing with the more expensive, perfumed "glamour" soaps in mildness and economy.

Spic and Span, a small specialty product, was sold mostly through hardware stores for cleaning painted wall surfaces. Procter & Gamble chemists improved the product, and with a more attractive package and better advertising, the sales organization began selling it to grocery stores. America was switching from papered to painted walls during these postwar years, and new linoleum and asphalt tiles were widely used on floors. Cleaning such surfaces, Spic and Span became a major brand.

* * * * *

Procter & Gamble was by no means the only company to seize the opportunities of the new detergent age. In 1947, Colgate introduced Ajax, "the foaming cleanser" with its own impressive results. With detergent-based Ajax, Colgate established not only a successful product, but also a brand name which later was to pose some troubling problems for Procter & Gamble.

Now that the basic technology of the soap industry was veering toward much more sophisticated chemistry, it attracted an entirely new type of competitor. One of these, Monsanto Chemical Company, developed a laundry product called All which produced very little suds while providing good cleaning power. P&G, in common with other manufacturers, felt that consumers really preferred suds. It had little interest in marketing a low-suds product. But things were changing. Many new washing machines introduced in the early postwar period were front-loading machines with a different tumbling action. High suds could interfere with their cleaning process. Monsanto decided to sell the All business and, in 1957, it was purchased by Lever Bros. and remained an important brand, into the 1980s. It was nearly ten years after the appearance of All before Procter & Gamble began broadscale sales of Dash, their first low-sudsing laundry detergent. A belated entry, Dash did well enough but it certainly did not emulate Tide in becoming an immediate sensation.

That indicated that P&G did not have the Midas touch on every detergent it developed. Nevertheless, it did remarkably well with quite a few. One example was liquid detergents.

If the advantage of detergents over soaps was apparent anywhere, it was in the dishpan with its heavy concentrations of greasy oil. Although laundry detergents were rapidly being accepted for dishwashing, P&G researchers felt that a better product could be developed specifically designed to cut grease, be mild on hands, and be convenient to use around the kitchen sink. In 1949 it introduced Joy, a concentrated liquid for dishes. Though tough competition soon developed, Joy remained one of the leading brands in its field for thirty years.

However, there was little time for rejoicing. Every company in America was trying to develop a detergent as good as Tide, or better. The question facing Procter & Gamble was: If somebody is going to develop a challenger to Tide, why shouldn't we do it ourselves? The goal was set. Despite the supremacy of Tide, P&G technicians continued to work. By 1950, they had a new formula to be called Cheer.

"I must admit," said one executive, "that the advent of Cheer was not an immediate cause for flag-waving. It was a good detergent, but for a while its sales were nothing to shout about. We felt we had to find some way of making it outstanding, different from all the others. But how? Nobody knew. We fussed over it, getting nowhere for two full years. And then in 1952 somebody came up with an inspiration so simple that we all felt we should have thought of it years earlier.

"It was this. Many housewives were adding blueing to their wash water because they liked the slightly bluish tint it gave their white clothes. So why not add blueing to Cheer and get the same effect? And it worked. We promptly renamed the product Blue Cheer." Commercials across the nation cried, "It's new! It's blue!" And with that simple change Cheer became a major success. The company seldom had a better illustration of the value of sponsoring competing brands within the P&G family.

*　*　*　*　*

In 1948-49, the company had made three key changes in its organization. Neil McElroy had become president with Deupree remaining as chairman; Howard Morgens was made vice-president for advertising and also had overall responsibility for what were then known as drug products; and Walter Lingle became vice-president in charge of overseas operations.

The drug products operations had, of course, begun before the war with the introduction of Drene shampoo (the first application of detergent technology to the shampoo field) and Teel, a liquid dentifrice which had a regrettably short life. In 1946, the company introduced a new concentrated shampoo in a tube. Called Prell, it quickly attained notoriety because of a lawsuit growing out of a radio commercial which closed with the line, "I'm Tallulah the Tube, take me home and squeeze me!" Tallulah Bankhead—"the only person ever named Tallulah"—expressed outrage at the unwarranted use of "her name." The famed actress sued Procter & Gamble for $1 million. Throughout the land, newspapers carried the story. According to one grinning company veteran, "Both Tallulah and Prell got $10 million worth of free publicity." Prell became a familiar name to every American who could read a paper or listen to a radio. In the end, Miss Bankhead's suit was quietly settled for $2,500.

While the lawsuit undoubtedly helped publicize Prell, the fact was that the product was right for the times. Practically all shampoos were soap based, meaning that they didn't lather well in hard water and they left some soap film on the hair. Packaged in glass bottles, breakage was common on the tiles of most bathrooms. American bathing habits were also changing from bathtubs to showers. A concentrated shampoo in an unbreakable tube had a natural appeal.

Howard Morgens took responsibility for the drug products operation when it was practically a stepchild. The company's other consumer products were sold by a 700-man sales force. Prell and Drene were sold by a national force of fewer than twenty. Similar proportions prevailed in research and manufacturing. And yet health and beauty aids were natural companions of the company's basic soap line. Certainly the care and cleaning of hair and teeth were closely allied to the care and cleaning of skin and clothes.

Morgens won agreement to treat the drug products business as though it were an independent company. He appointed managers of sales, advertising, manufacturing and product development. P&G's early work with shampoos had given it a thorough knowledge of human hair. Here was a chance to capitalize on that knowledge by moving into the field of home permanents. (One opportunity materialized in 1947 when the Toni Company, owned by St. Paul entrepreneur R. Neison Harris, was offered for sale. But an $18 million deal with P&G stalled over the question of who would continue to manage Toni if it came under the P&G umbrella. Harris was impatient and sold Toni the next year to the Gillette Safety Razor Company.)

So P&G decided to develop its own home permanent entry. Two years later, after extensive testing, Lilt was ready. It became P&G's first toilet goods product that was strictly cosmetic. A liquid version of Prell was also tested and then expanded.

Then, in 1954, after almost two years of test marketing, the company achieved its first real success in the dentifrice business with Gleem. It was the result of thorough, careful efforts to find an excellent cleaning and whitening product with a flavor which would best please the taste of the public. Launched as the toothpaste "for people who can't brush their teeth after every meal," Gleem was a quick success, soon rivaling Colgate for leadership.

"If you really want to understand the character of our company," one retired executive said, "you have to consider the fact that at the very time Gleem started soaring to success, we were already seeking a better dentifrice. The research people, backed by what they had learned in producing Gleem, used that knowledge as a basis for further experimentation. And we were on the way to Crest."

* * * * *

The importance of the brand management system became more evident as P&G launched new products to compete directly with those it already sold. Thus Prell competed with Drene, and Cheer with Tide.

Howard Morgens explained how this worked: "We are dedicated to the concept that our business is run by brands. By that I mean we regard each brand as a separate business. Each brand is expected to stand on its own feet in the competitive struggle. And each brand is expected to earn money."

Morgens emphasized the fact that the system permitted, even encouraged, vigorous competition among brands, assuring "no one brand will be neglected."

"Don't think this brand competition isn't tough and hazardous," he said. "Some of our brands die out and disappear entirely. Chipso is one; it was once the largest selling packaged soap in the country. Selox is another; it was once a leader in New York City. P&G White soap was once the largest selling brand in the United States. These brands did not die out because we didn't exercise all the ingenuity we had to preserve them.

"One thing we do not do is borrow from one brand to support another. The principle of running each brand as a separate business provides a discipline which prevents such actions in the employment of our funds. This discipline is extremely important to us."

P&G was among the first to manage its business strictly on a brand-by-brand basis. The discipline Morgens described became a hallmark of P&G's worldwide growth in the years ahead.

19

THE LURE OF DISTANT LANDS

An urgent question soon arose: Where should detergents be introduced outside the U.S.? Virtually the whole world seemed an untapped market.

Prior to the war the primary foreign business had been in England and Canada, with lesser operations in Cuba, the Philippines, and Indonesia. In 1948, when Walter Lingle became vice-president, overseas, it was clear to him that his first task should be to strengthen foreign operations.

The new detergent formula was introduced through existing channels in Canada, Great Britain, and Cuba. This done, Lingle looked for other expansion opportunities. A logical area, close to home, was Mexico.

However, penetrating Mexico proved far from easy. Local soap manufacturers bitterly opposed intrusion by a foreign firm. They sought every legal and diplomatic means to keep Procter & Gamble out of their country, unless they themselves were heavily involved in P&G operations. Much of Mexico was still using bars of soap to wash its laundry on the banks of streams. There was no need, it was argued, for a foreign-owned detergent plant.

Yet Lingle persisted. His reports to Cincinnati told of long, exhausting discussions with Mexican businessmen and government officials. Night after night he would return to his hotel, too weary and frustrated to do anything but collapse on his bed. But in the end he won the right to enter Mexico, and Procter & Gamble was permitted to build a detergent manufacturing plant near Mexico City.

In a sense this success served as an opening wedge to other lands south of the United States. Venezuela soon followed, with operating facilities opened in 1952. Since the company had been in Canada and Cuba even before the war, its products were now penetrating a good part of the Western Hemisphere.

This experience taught P&G some valuable lessons. In every country it hoped to enter it would be necessary to acquire the same kind of intensive knowledge of the local consumer that had guided U.S. growth. Washing conditions had to be studied, as well as the language, the customs, the kind of government, and the business practices.

"Exporting," Lingle once said, "is justified only to test a foreign market. If we are to have a volume business in a major country, we must manufacture in that country. It is the only way to get behind high tariff walls. It is the only way to overcome strict import quotas. In many places we are in the same position relative to local competition that competition is relative to us in the United States. There we are the challenger faced with strong, alert, local and international competitors.

"Moreover," he added, "washing habits and edible fat tastes vary widely from country to country. We must tailor products to fit consumer demand in each nation. We cannot simply manufacture and sell products with United States formulas. They won't work. They won't be accepted."

Having made this clear, Lingle turned to a matter of policy.

"We have decided," he said, "that the best way to succeed in other countries is to build in each one as exact a replica of the United States Procter & Gamble organization as it is possible to build. We believe that exactly the same policies and procedures which have given our company success in the United States will be equally successful overseas."

What about expansion in the vast market of continental Europe?

Through a representative of J. P. Morgan & Company, one of P&G's bankers, word reached Cincinnati in 1954 that a detergent plant, fully operative, was for sale in Marseilles. This promised a firm foothold in France, and Lingle hurried to investigate.

The business, owned by the Fournier-Ferrier Company, was attractive enough, but the detergent tower it had built was disappointing. It was too small for the output volume that would interest Procter & Gamble. Nevertheless, Lingle saw it as a quick way to enter the French market. He and his associate, Donald H.

182

Robinson (later to become vice-president of the Overseas Division) negotiated a deal whereby P&G would operate the plant on a thirty-year lease with an option to buy at a future time. P&G at once increased capacity of the detergent tower, began effective advertising, augmented the French sales force. Within four years it developed a sufficient sales volume to justify purchase of the French plant. And expansion into Belgium followed soon thereafter, with a Malines plant opening in 1956.

As Lingle reflected on the problems of entering new countries, he observed: "Under our system of government, we are remarkably free to participate in the image which our country and our government presents to the world at large. That leaves us with a very important responsibility when we venture overseas. I believe that the character of our company is such that we are carrying our part of that responsibility in a very effective manner.

"In every case which I have observed, we are [by applying Procter & Gamble principles in these foreign subsidiaries] automatically exerting leadership in the overseas business communities in which we are operating."

Adherence to these principles was far from easy. Tariff and other trade barriers made it difficult to enter many of the major industrial nations; and some other markets were simply impenetrable without resorting to business practices like bribery. These were contrary to P&G's way of operating. Neither McElroy nor Lingle was about to compromise the company's principles.

* * * * *

Sometimes foreign operations were actually risky. In one case, the company was forced to close its Indonesian operations in 1964. Never a great potential market, Indonesia proved too volatile in those years to justify continued investment.

Cuba, much closer to home, was even more disturbing. This was a time, in the mid-'50s, of mounting political tension in Cuba. Much was being whispered about a revolutionary named Fidel Castro Ruz. Accompanied by a small band of *barbudos*, bearded rebels who demanded "democracy and independence," Castro was hidden in the Sierra Maestro mountains. From his secret headquarters he was organizing Cuban dissidents for a march against the incumbent dictator, Fulgencio Batista y Zaldivar. His cause was popular (even in the United States) and there was little doubt that a clash would occur.

183

This prospect of political upheaval worried P&G. The company had a considerable investment in the Cuban plant it had built for synthetic detergents. Rumors pervaded the American financial community that Cuban holdings were in danger of being seized by the government; and though few people seemed to be reacting to such threats, Morgens flew off to investigate.

From the moment he stepped off the plane in Havana he saw armed men. Batista's troops seemed to be everywhere. They watched incoming passengers. They watched taxis carrying passengers out of the airport. At the hotel where Morgens stopped, armed men peered at him at the front door and in the lobby. Even in the seclusion of his suite he had the feeling of being under surveillance.

When he went to the P&G plant, most of its personnel refused to believe in the possibility of government seizure. For that matter, there were scores of other American businessmen in Havana who minimized the dangers of expropriation. Yet Morgens was not reassured. He could not shake off the uneasiness that rose from being endlessly watched. This was hardly a sign of future normalcy.

Back in Cincinnati, he called a meeting of his associates. He recommended (indeed, urged) the acceptance of an offer which had been made by a Cuban syndicate to buy the Havana plant. "Better to sell and get our money out," he said, "than risk losing our entire investment."

So in 1960 the Cuban plant was sold. More accurately, it was partly sold, partly lost. Havana's industrialists paid $4,500,000 in cash and the balance in notes. But the notes were never honored. When Castro assumed power after Batista's flight from the country, all talk of Cuban democracy somehow subsided. In its place came another one-man dictatorship. The new government refused to recognize notes of indebtedness to Procter & Gamble. The money the paper represented was lost.

"But at least we had retrieved $4,500,000 of our investment, which was more than many other American companies did," said former vice-president and comptroller Dean Fite.

Yet foreign installations, despite their many problems, had some unique advantages for P&G personnel. As Lingle himself pointed out, "The general management of a major overseas subsidiary is a fine development and training spot for any man who has a chance to become a top executive of the parent company. It gives him an opportunity to have many of the same experiences he will have later at the top executive level in the United States; but it permits him to make his decisions, and his mistakes, on a smaller scale."

And by 1955 Lingle was able to say, "These past ten years have been devoted largely to building an overseas organization. We believe this organization is now well prepared to take advantage of the opportunities for growth which we are certain lie ahead."

When he spoke, the total net earnings of the overseas subsidiaries were $8 million. He could hardly have foreseen that within twenty-five years they would leap to earnings of $149 million with over 200 brands being sold in twenty-four nations and almost a third of P&G's 60,000 employees working overseas.

* * * * *

While expansion outside the U. S. was concentrated in detergents, Deupree and McElroy were pondering other opportunities. They had learned from P&G's wartime venture into the munitions business that totally new activities could be managed successfully with the right combination of management skills, technical expertise, and company principles.

Now Deupree and McElroy looked closely at the dissolving cellulose pulp business. This was being carried on by the Buckeye Division, headquartered in Memphis. Demand for rayon, the main use of cellulose, was growing with incredible swiftness. Also clothing, tire cords, photographic film, and plastics were big users of cellulose pulp, all of them demanding more and more. At the same time the country's cotton production was declining, with a corresponding drop in the supply of cotton linters from which cellulose pulp was made.

Buckeye researchers, applying the same approaches as their research colleagues in other parts of the company, discovered that a dissolving pulp of similar quality could be made from southern pine trees. Here was a rare opportunity for originality, but one shadowed by great challenge.

The burgeoning demand for laundry detergents had compelled P&G to invest huge sums in improving its detergent-making capacity, including the construction of a new plant in Sacramento. A new cellulose pulp mill would itself require heavy capital investment just when the money could be used elsewhere for a proven winner. Moreover, management would have to be

185

transferred from existing operations into the new business. Was it wise? Some thought not.

The Korean War, with the government urging expanded cellulose production and offering tax incentives for new construction, prompted quick P&G action. Two tracts, each about 550,000 acres of pine-growing land in northern Florida, were purchased in 1951 to insure a wood supply. And a giant pulp mill was constructed at Foley, Florida. The land and the Foley mill required an outlay of nearly $40 million.

This was in every sense a major undertaking. The Cincinnati soap company had invested the equivalent of 25% of the book value of all its lands and buildings in a venture in which it had only limited experience. The mill itself was big enough to supply 5% of total world demand, and the P&G woodlands around it were half the size of Rhode Island.

Years later, in recounting the successes at Foley, one veteran said, "We showed that the basis on which P&G operated—good people, efficient manufacture, quality control, endless research, ingenuity—all these could be applied as successfully to the pulp business as to other operations."

Another senior executive recalled that it had started with a couple of engineers who knew a great deal about P&G management methods but nothing about growing and harvesting trees. They hired foresters who knew a great deal about pine trees but nothing about P&G techniques. The result of bringing these two groups together was akin to what foresters would call cross-pollination. It created a cadre which talked in terms of "cords per acre per year," using a computer to choose "the optimum rotation cycles for best return on investment." This new forestry technology used radioactive isotopes to study the uptake of herbicides and fertilizers. It also was studying the control of insects by inducing disease among those that destroy trees. And it produced a genetically superior seed orchard. Such detailed knowledge of the source of cellulose pulp clearly had a significant impact on Procter & Gamble's business.

20
P&G
GOES HOLLYWOOD

Kukla, along with Fran and Ollie, were popular spokesmen for Tide in the early 1950s.

During the first postwar decade P&G jumped, as one observer said, "from just one of the soap companies to the leading detergent and cleaning products company in the country and also laid the foundation for its future paper business."

But then, during that decade revolutionary developments were affecting all of American society. Two in particular demonstrated the company's reaction to change. One was the advent of television, the other was a dynamic upheaval in the grocery industry.

The first, the advent of television, changed every previous concept of broadcasting. Also, it presented a dilemma.

On radio, characters had been recognized by their voices, not by their appearance. They had no need to memorize their lines; they simply read them in front of a microphone. Sets were left to the imagination of listeners. Sounds were the province of sound-effects experts. With an engine-like roar they could make an audience feel it was in a fighter plane high above the earth; by the clanging of chains and a creak of metal, they could simulate the opening of a steel vault in Jack Benny's cellar.

Television changed everything. Now actors had to look like the characters they portrayed. Parts had to be memorized as for a stage play. Sets had to be built, not suggested. The source of sounds had to be visible. All this demanded professional stagecraft. And it was expensive.

What added to the expense was that at the outset there were no TV cable connections from city to city. Every show had to be produced live for its local audience or filmed for rebroadcast. Adding to the negative aspects of early television was the relatively small number of sets in the United States.

In short, television was demanding not only a different distribution of advertising funds but also new methods of production—everything from proper casting to stage design. P&G and its advertising agencies had developed real expertise in the preparation of copy for magazine and radio advertising, and they had unquestionably become the country's most expert producers of daytime radio programming. Now television was demanding the reallocation of at least part of the advertising funds away from these media. Deciding how far and how fast to go with the change to television roused endless debate between brand managers and agencies, between advertising and sales executives.

In rural areas, sales managers sought to keep advertising emphasis on print and radio; there were few television sets in their regions. Sales managers in the larger cities, however, were champions of television; city dwellers were buying thousands of TV sets. And though there was considerable discussion, pro and con, there was really no question of whether or not to do it ultimately. Procter & Gamble had always seen change as an opportunity to improve its competitive position, and this was no exception. To Deupree, McElroy, Morgens, and their associates, it was clear that P&G had better learn to use this new medium as soon as possible.

They went into it with every resource at their command. Script writers, musicians, actors, directors, advertising and brand people —everybody concerned gathered at rehearsal after rehearsal.

On July 23, 1948, a memorable date in the annals of P&G, Ivory Snow and Prell jointly brought to home screens the first of a series of programs called "Fashions on Parade." Every weekly episode was to have its own story, and fashion models were to be introduced by commentator Adelaide Hawley. There were actors, singers, comedians, an orchestra, everything to create an eye-filling, ear-filling performance. One publication in reviewing the show said:

"Combining all the advantages of sight, sound, and action, television's triple impact permits many selling approaches that are not possible on radio or in magazines. For example, Ivory Snow might show a lovely model in a snowstorm, dramatizing the copy that her clothes are 'safe in snow.' And Prell employs lovely Conover models to illustrate radiance of hair after dandruff removal. The models can demonstrate every step of a Prell shampoo."

"Fashions on Parade" was televised live. What viewers saw on Friday nights was exactly what was happening in front of studio cameras. Unhappily an actor might occasionally forget a line, another might trip over a prop—little accidents that destroyed the mood of a presentation. And for some, failure in a product demonstration (like a fizzing tablet that refused to fizz when dropped into a glass of water) could evoke more laughter than sales.

So, beginning with commercials, the advertising agencies and Procter & Gamble agreed it was wiser to put them on film in advance and thereby avoid live accidents.

Howard Morgens, now vice-president for advertising, went further. He advocated filming complete programs. There was good reason for this—reason based largely on experience with radio. Radio programs had been distributed to local stations on records. Similarly, Morgens argued, filmed TV shows could have wide distribution and endless reuse.

"Besides," as one of his associates pointed out, "filming was bound to improve quality. It would provide for careful editing and retakes wherever necessary."

Convinced that Procter & Gamble should take the lead in the development of television programs, Morgens urged the formation of a subsidiary to be called Procter & Gamble Productions, Inc. Inaugurated in 1949, its charter specified it would "produce, or acquire and produce, radio, television, and motion picture shows, programs, and other forms of entertainment."

There was a good deal of speculation in the press as to whether P&G might be planning to "go Hollywood" and produce motion pictures for theatrical distribution in competition with such film giants as MGM, Fox, and Paramount. In a sense, the company did indeed "go Hollywood" in 1949. It went there to shoot the first P&G-owned nighttime dramatic program, "Fireside Theater." (Within a few years P&G was producing more footage of filmed entertainment than any major movie studio.)

"Fireside Theater" was the company's first half-hour dramatic show telecast from film. When coast-to-coast transmission became possible in 1951 (first used by President Truman in addressing the Japanese Peace Treaty Conference in San Francisco), "Fireside Theater" went to a network of ninety-four stations. It won the Sylvania Award for its "adult stories and thoroughly professional technique in programs that are outstanding." It was still popular in 1955 when actress Jane Wyman became its hostess. After she had appeared in some twenty productions, the program became known as "The Jane Wyman Show" and continued to flourish as it advertised Ivory, Duz, and Crisco.

Within a year the show was joined by two others. One, starring Ethel Waters, was "Beulah" for Dreft and Oxydol. The other, for Tide and Camay, was "Musical Comedy Time," a one-hour format of Broadway musicals. Yet nothing so vividly indicates P&G's early leadership in TV entertainment as the list of famed personalities it featured: Loretta Young, Lucille Ball, Robert Sterling, Ann Jeffries, Joan Caulfield, Barry Nelson, Leo J. Carroll, Janis Paige, Jackie Cooper—all reigning stars of their day.

(Above) P&G's longest-running daytime TV drama, "Search for Tomorrow," celebrated its 25th Anniversary in 1976. (Below) Filming the first Crisco commercial.

A different type of P&G show was "This Is Your Life," with Ralph Edwards. The format provided a surprise party for a guest, usually well known, whose biography would be created on the air through a series of flashbacks. This involved the appearance of people who had been closely associated with the guest of honor. The program had an emotional appeal which made it an instant and lasting hit. It won high ratings for many seasons.

With passing years there were all kinds of Procter & Gamble programs—westerns, adventures, situation comedies, game shows, children's programs, variety specials. As the 1950s began, all of them, with the exception of children's entertainment, had one common denominator: They were nighttime productions.

Inevitably brand managers and others began to urge the use of daytime television. But that encountered doubts and opposition. Women at home might listen to radio while performing their household chores; listening did not necessarily interfere with work. But would these same women drop whatever they were doing to stare at a television screen? And since most men were away at their jobs, wouldn't the audience be but a fraction of nighttime viewers? Was it worth $125,000 or so, the cost of a fifteen-minute weekly serial?

And the technical problems were frightening. Actors and actresses had to be found who could adapt to this demanding dramatic challenge by quickly memorizing new parts every day. Writers would have to learn to deal with the requirements for visual action as well as dialogue. In such circumstances could daytime serials be successfully adapted to television? "We'll never know unless we try it," production people said.

They tried it in 1950 with "The First Hundred Years," a dramatization of married life. It was quickly apparent that the transition to TV would have all the problems they anticipated. After a month, "Hundred Years" was withdrawn. Yet its shortcomings taught its producers what to avoid; and when they tried again with "Search For Tomorrow," they hit a bonanza. The serial became the longest-running show, day or night, on American network television. Its success encouraged a TV version of radio's "The Guiding Light," and this too set records by running year after year, and was still running in 1981.

Transition to a thirty-minute format came with "As The World Turns" and "The Edge of Night," and Procter & Gamble's reputation was secure as the champion of the soap opera. How dramatic had been the shift from radio to television is best indicated by the following figures (Procter & Gamble does not publish such figures, but these estimates were carefully constructed by an industry publication):

Year	Share of advertising to network TV	Share of advertising to network radio
1950	3%	97%
1951	29%	71%
1952	47%	53%
1953	51%	49%
1954	69%	31%
1955	80%	20%

Broadcast-Television magazine reported in 1955: "The world's most successful seller of household cleaners is now the world's biggest buyer of television time. Once it was radio, now it is television. The story of how P&G uses advertising to move its merchandise into 56 million homes is predominantly a broadcast story."

As it had with the advent of radio, with the advent of washing machines, with the advent of synthetic detergents, Procter & Gamble had seized on change to strengthen its business rather than cling to the old methods which had made it successful in the past. It had quickly taken a leadership role in TV—not only in the level of spending but more importantly in research about the most efficient advertising uses of the medium.

Was Procter & Gamble spending too much on television? "Look at it this way," said a company executive. "By the mid-1970s it was costing us about 0.25 cents each time one of our television commercials reached an American home. Compare that to the 7 cents postage it would have cost just to mail a single postcard."

* * * * *

Along with television a second social upheaval struck America. It was one that affected Procter & Gamble as drastically as it affected many other firms. People were moving out of the cities into the suburbs. The returning veterans were forming families, and as the baby boom of the late '40s began, more and more young families wanted to get away from the crowded cities and have a yard for the children to play in. Aiding this migration was the renewed availability of affordable automobiles. There were more plentiful mortgage loans, such as those backed by the

Veterans Administration, requiring very low down payments. Housing developments seemed to spring up in cornfields overnight. And, almost as quickly, shopping centers appeared, nearly every one featuring a new supermarket. All of this meant change in serving consumer needs.

In the past, small "mom and pop" stores had placed their orders with salesmen who came in every week. Now that era was passing. If a supermarket was part of a chain, its merchandise came through a central buying office. If it was an independent store, it generally bought most of its needs from one wholesaler— a process much simpler than dealing with dozens of suppliers.

There was no less change among the suppliers, including P&G itself. Here, the number of brands and the number of sales promotions handled by the case goods sales group were increasing as competition intensified. No longer was one person taking orders for a handful of products. Instead, sales people represented many products and many promotion opportunities. And because of Prell, Lilt, and Gleem, the drug products sales group was growing. These products were being sold more and more in supermarkets. It was not unusual for a supermarket manager to be called on by two P&G sales representatives in the same day.

Similar duplication existed elsewhere in the company. Transportation of product, accounting, credit and collection, research, and recruiting were overlapping. The existing corporate structure was creaking and groaning under the weight of new business, and serious minds questioned whether it would be able to handle future growth.

21

"MORTGAGE THE FARM AND GO FOR BROKE."

Despite a corporate structure that was becoming ungainly the management team leading the company—Deupree, McElroy, Morgens, and Lingle—had ample reason to be pleased as they surveyed P&G's progress of the past ten years. The organization they had built was maturing. It had a highly competitive spirit and it had acquired the confidence necessary to support aggressive activities.

The technological achievements of the large staff of scientists and technicians were providing a base for worldwide growth. In the U.S. the company had established itself as the undisputed leader in detergents with Tide and Cheer. Liquid detergents for dishwashing were also becoming a vital and profitable area.

And there was progress in other directions. In the transition from radio to television, P&G's people emerged with new skills in advertising and programming. Simultaneously the company had established, at its Foley cellulose pulp mill, the foundation of a sound industrial business.

As a result of all this, in June, 1955, Procter & Gamble reported record sales of $966 million and earnings of over $57 million. The company was approaching the "billion dollar club," a group that then included only twenty-eight American firms.

To continue such remarkable growth it was clear that some structure would be needed by which management could retain the basic methods and principles that had served so successfully for over a hundred years. A rapid series of acquisitions was just ahead, each designed to accelerate entry into a remarkable range of product categories new to the company: peanut butter, cake mixes, household paper products, disposable diapers, bleach, coffee, soft drinks. Obviously, a widely diversified corporation in the

195

billion dollar category could hardly be run with the simple methods of a small, single-interest soap company.

Fortunately, in the Drug Products Division there already existed an organizational concept which could help shape Procter & Gamble's future. Howard Morgens was generally credited for developing the basic plan.

It was important to outline the idea in a manner which would be clearly understood and accepted by people throughout the organization. Without everyone's help the plan had little chance for success. Talking in his quiet way, Morgens explained it at the annual meeting of managers in 1955.

"The company expects to grow naturally and soundly," he said, "by building on its present foundations in those areas where we already have much background and experience."

But this did not rule out the probability of entering other fields. Everyone who listened to him must have realized that Procter & Gamble could not forever expand without venturing into new product areas beyond detergents and cleaning products.

For the immediate future, however, Morgens spoke of "handling our three major areas of U.S. business—soaps, foods, and drug products—through three separate operating divisions." He reminded his audience that Procter & Gamble had been moving in this direction ever since the drug products group had been created in 1943 as an independent operating unit.

"One might say," he continued, "that now we are simply setting up a Food Products Division which will work, within itself and in relation to the soap business, much as the Drug Products Division has done. That in one sense is all that is happening."

Yet the idea was destined to reshape the operations of Procter & Gamble for many years to come. Each of the three divisions of the company would be responsible for its own operations—its volume, its growth, its profits. Each would have to develop its own people. Each would have its own general management.

"The second basic principle," Morgens went on, "is concerned with how the activities of these three divisions are coordinated into an effective overall company effort. It is concerned with what one might call 'staff' or 'corporate' functions as distinct from line or operating functions."

Former Procter & Gamble Board Chairman Neil McElroy shortly before his retirement in 1971.

Among staff or corporate responsibilities, those designed to serve all divisions, he mentioned basic research; relations with advertising agencies, networks, radio and television talent; general supervision of sampling and couponing activities; and engineering. In addition, there were staff functions under the direction of administrative vice-president Kelly Y. Siddall: legal services, recruiting, finance and accounting, employee benefits, corporate affairs and contributions.

Morgens finished his talk by assuring his listeners: "We feel confident that the company's new organization structure is one on which we can build and one which will support a larger and stronger Procter & Gamble business for many years to come." Then Jake Lingle walked forward to describe how the overseas and Buckeye cellulose operations would fit into the new structure as additional divisions.

There can be no doubt that the "divisional concept" outlined that afternoon became a vital tool in the dramatic growth of P&G during the next twenty-five years.

197

By the late '70s, chief executive Ed Harness would be overseeing ten operating divisions worldwide for consumer products and five for industrial products. Each of these would be served by corporate staff groups in the major disciplines of finance, research and development, manufacturing, purchasing, advertising, sales, engineering, and others. "Each operating division," Harness reported, "is established as an umbrella profit and management center. Each division is managed in keeping with basic company-wide policies and practices. Our staff departments are less visible than our operating divisions, but I believe their importance cannot be overstated. Howard Morgens was the principal architect of our current management structure. I remain his disciple on this subject."

There was a time when someone asked Vice-Chairman Brad Butler how these operating and staff groups arrived at important decisions. Butler promptly answered that in the company "the prevailing attitude is that what is right is far more important than who is right. Facts, logic, truth," he said, "have far more authority at Procter & Gamble than any individual.

"When a question exists, and the answer isn't readily apparent," he said, "our management structure ensures that at least two points of view will emerge. The resolution of such differences . . . dramatically increases the probability that the final decision will be made on the basis of wisdom and knowledge rather than on the basis of individual opinion. This kind of organization creates an environment in which it is possible that a good idea may sometimes get lost, but it is one in which bad ideas seldom survive."

In reviewing the progress of business during this period, Howard Morgens reflected on some of the steps that had been required.

"We knew that the kind of growth we visualized would not be possible without some bold moves," Morgens said. "Bold moves were not something new to the company, of course, it could not have grown the way it had over so many years without them. But P&G had grown so large that any substantial new moves would have a new degree of size. Their aim would seem higher and the stakes would seem larger because of that factor."

Another factor which guided P&G's growth during these years became known as the "unifying product concept." Many American corporations were expanding by means of mergers and

Relinquishing the Presidency of P&G, Neil McElroy (left) is sworn in as Secretary of Defense in 1957. President Dwight D. Eisenhower (center) holds the Bible for the oath of office administered by Percy E. Nelson, Administrative Officer for the White House.

acquisitions, some of which were assembled as haphazardly as the squares of a crazy quilt. P&G recognized the pitfalls in this lack of synergy. Growth without careful planning could lead to dire problems. Caution and wisdom dictated that the company focus on household products which had certain common characteristics.

"These are products," one company executive said, "which move through grocery stores and drugstores primarily for use in the home. They are small unit, low priced, packaged products which are purchased frequently and are used up in a relatively short time. They are high quality products which represent a large volume and an attractive profit opportunity." If one studies the acquisitions P&G made over the years, it becomes apparent that these guidelines were never abandoned.

But growth requires capital. For years P&G had been able to finance its undertakings out of its own earnings. This became more and more difficult—indeed impossible—after Congress increased the corporate income tax to 45% of total earnings, then imposed an extra excess profits tax during the Korean War. Procter & Gamble was forced to seek outside capital.

In 1952 the company had issued $30 million in long-term notes to help finance the cellulose pulp mill in Foley, Florida. By September, 1956, P&G again faced the compelling need, in McElroy's words, "to fortify itself with money in order to take advantage of the opportunities for growth and progress" it foresaw. This time it issued debentures in the amount of $70 million.

When some shareholders asked uneasy questions about incurring such indebtedness, Neil McElroy had a straightforward response:

"We believe the use of that working capital should create earnings sufficient to pay the current interest and, through the years, retire the original obligation and still bring us extra net earnings. When Procter & Gamble takes on an obligation of this kind and size, it is because, in the eyes of management, it is essential to have the capital to realize to the fullest the potentialities of strong, vigorous growth that will keep the company in its leading position."

Neil McElroy was expressing the philosophy of Richard Deupree: "You do something you think is right. If it clicks, you give it a ride. If you hit, mortgage the farm and go for broke. But you can't always hit, and when you don't, have sense enough to get out."

* * * * *

In 1955 a significant event occurred at the corner of Sixth and Sycamore Streets in downtown Cincinnati—construction began on a new building which would house the P&G headquarters. In the mid-1950s, America's center cities were considered to be on the way to decay. The "flight to the suburbs" was carrying business with it. Downtown stores were failing; housing near downtown areas was becoming undesirable; neighborhoods were deteriorating; corporation after corporation was following its employees to the suburbs.

In Cincinnati there were dedicated citizens who were determined that this wasn't going to happen to their city. Neil McElroy and Howard Morgens were among the leaders of that group. They laid plans for a modern, thriving downtown, starting with adequate highway and parking facilities to make it convenient for people to drive to work and to shop.

It was in the midst of these civic efforts that Procter & Gamble laid the cornerstone of its new building in the heart of Cincinnati.

22
AND THEN—CREST!

One of a series of 24 Norman Rockwell paintings commissioned by Crest in the late 1950s.

A vigorous, energetic, and spirited man, Neil McElroy spread an enthusiasm that infused not only the business of Procter & Gamble but all those he met. "He instantly caught your attention," recalled one senior executive. "A magnetic man. Years later I heard the same thing said of John F. Kennedy, but in the case of McElroy I myself saw it happen again and again. His personality compelled attention."

Someone else said, "The man lives a forty-hour day." And the *Saturday Review*, commenting on his civic work, observed, "Forward-looking executives [like McElroy] have developed a growing recognition of their responsibility to serve the public interest as an inseparable part of their corporate interest."

Outside of business McElroy's predominant interests lay in the field of education. Both his parents had been teachers, so this was not surprising. He saw the need for a well-educated work force as an integral part of a prosperous, healthy society. In Cincinnati he was a director of the Council for Financial Aid to Education, a trustee of the National Fund for Medical Education, a sponsor of the United Negro Colleges Capital Fund campaign, and chairman of the Advisory Committee of the University of Cincinnati College of Medicine. In 1952 he had co-chaired, with Joseph Hall of Kroger, the reorganization of the Cincinnati United Appeal campaign, which for years was to set a Cincinnati pattern for successful campaigns.

In 1954 President Eisenhower was searching for an outstanding citizen to serve as chairman of a White House Conference on Education. So many of his advisers suggested McElroy that the president telephoned Cincinnati and asked Procter & Gamble's chief executive officer to undertake the task. McElroy did. He became chairman of what one publication later described as "the most massive and searching consultation on U.S. education in history." It brought more than 2,000 educators to Washington.

How profoundly McElroy impressed Eisenhower was made evident when, in 1957, the president once more summoned him to the White House. This time Eisenhower said, "Neil, I want you to become Secretary of Defense."

If McElroy was stunned by the request, he knew he could not refuse. "You just don't turn down the president of the United States," he said. "Not when he asks you to undertake an obligation of citizenship." Nevertheless, he went back to confer with Deupree who promptly agreed that he had no choice. Moreover, the chairman added, the company would be proud to lend its president to the nation. So, in accepting Eisenhower's appointment, McElroy also announced his resignation as president of Procter & Gamble.

The company's directors, hastily summoned to choose his successor, faced an urgent and difficult situation. Since McElroy was only 53, he had been expected to fill his post for at least ten or twelve years more. Now, without warning, the post had quickly to be filled by someone else. The choice before the board lay between two outstanding candidates, Executive Vice-Presidents Howard Morgens and Walter (Jake) Lingle.

The answer came on August 22, 1957, immediately after McElroy's appointment was confirmed by the Senate. The directors elected Howard Joseph Morgens, age 46, to be president and chief executive officer of the Procter & Gamble Company.

Of McElroy's departure Morgens said, "We know McElroy will make a distinguished record as Secretary of Defense. He goes to Washington with the heartfelt good wishes of every member of

Three generations of Procter & Gamble leadership. From left, Howard J. Morgens (led P&G from 1957–1974), Richard Redwood Deupree (led P&G from 1930–1948), and Neil McElroy (led P&G from 1948–1957).

203

the organization. We look forward to the day when he will return to us."

As for the new Secretary of Defense, he declared, "Howard Morgens has grown with the business and will be surrounded and supported by what I believe to be one of the strongest industrial organizations in the country."

* * * * *

"Triumph over tooth decay!" This not-too-modest announcement flared from the pages of *Life* magazine in January, 1956. In introducing Crest toothpaste, it marked a singular scientific achievement for P&G. Heretofore, the company's technology had been based on its extensive knowledge of the chemistry of fats and oils; more recently, its laboratory discoveries had led to synthetic laundry detergents.

Crest appeared some years after the company's entry into the toiletries business. First there had been Drene shampoo in 1933; Teel dentifrice in 1938; Prell Concentrate in 1948; Lilt Home Permanent in 1949; and Gleem toothpaste in 1952.

But it was Crest that proved to be the base on which the toilet goods business was to thrive during the next twenty-five years. Research Vice-President J. G. (Gib) Pleasants called Crest "one of the most exciting things we have ever done from the standpoint of providing something better for the public."

A dramatic review of the Crest story was given by E. A. (Bill) Snow in the early 1960s. In recounting the brand's success, Snow spoke of the thinking behind Crest as "a belief in an idea and a willingness to support that belief with heavy investment for over twenty years."

Dental disease, he said, had become one of the most prevalent health problems in the U.S., second only to the common cold. It was estimated that Americans developed over 700 million cavities each year. Snow described the generally accepted theory of the cause of cavities, that carbohydrates in food are converted to acids by enzymes that are produced by bacteria in the mouth. These acids attack and dissolve the tooth enamel. Could they be counteracted?

P&G researchers faced many alternative directions for approaching the problem. Some argued that they should seek an ingredient which would kill or retard the growth of bacteria. Other theories proposed to attack the enzymes or to neutralize the resulting acids. And attention was being drawn to yet another solution, one provided by nature.

For years children in several western towns were virtually without cavities. The reason was traced to the natural presence of sodium fluoride in local drinking water. Scientists were able to show that tooth enamel became more resistant to acid when treated with this fluoride substance, so P&G began studying this as a possible ingredient in a dentifrice.

But incorporating sodium fluoride in a toothpaste was not the answer; all tests showed negative results. The trouble was that the ingredients which went into making a toothpaste—particularly the abrasives for polishing and the binders for holding the composition together—were incompatible with known fluoride compounds. They actually destroyed the effectiveness of sodium fluoride. It was clear that a fresh start had to be made involving the development of a new fluoride compound or of new toothpaste ingredients.

Over 500 different compounds were tested. The most promising results centered around two, indium and tin or stannous fluoride. By coincidence, Indiana University researchers had come to the same general conclusion that stannous fluoride could provide the key to an effective anti-cavity toothpaste.

A graduate student at Indiana University, Joseph Muhler, had undertaken the research of stannous fluoride, and his early published work came to the attention of Procter & Gamble. In 1950 an arrangement was made with the university and its key researchers (including Dr. Muhler) to work on the development of anti-tooth decay ingredients for a dentifrice. Coordination of the project rested with Verling M. Votaw, director of product research in P&G's Drug Products Division.

The Indiana University researchers worked with P&G scientists in their new Miami Valley laboratories. Muhler's group eventually discovered the combination of ingredients necessary for making an effective anti-cavity toothpaste. P&G researchers designed the process for manufacturing the product in large quantities. These discoveries led to a patent being issued to Indiana University under which P&G paid royalties for an exclusive contract. Other patents were issued to P&G researchers.

Under Dr. Muhler's guidance, the first clinical tests on human subjects began in 1952. Among children aged 6 to 16, one test showed an average 49% reduction in cavities; another test, a 36%

reduction. The program was later expanded to include a total of 4,500 children and 1,100 adults in nine separate studies. All were encouraging.

Test marketing of Crest in three areas began in February, 1955. But early results were disappointing. Consumers were less satisfied than had been expected, in part because they could not immediately see the benefits Crest promised. After an introductory spurt, market share settled at about 12%. Nevertheless, 12% provided sufficient evidence that Crest could establish a solid business in the face of strong competition, including the front-running Colgate dental cream, Lever's Pepsodent, and P&G's own Gleem. It was decided to expand nationally in January, 1956.

At the outset, results were disturbingly similar to the first market test. After achieving a highly respectable initial market share, Crest's popularity waned until it represented just under 10% of all toothpaste sold in the U.S.

Part of the explanation was that competitors were not idle. Although they did not have access to the patented stannous fluoride formula of Crest, they launched numerous compounds containing sodium fluoride. Some promised broad assurance that they were "safe for children under six." Crest, however, was initially required to carry a package warning because clinical tests had not yet been completed with children less than six years of age. (Later tests proved such concerns to be groundless.) Still, the problem helped stimulate a famous Crest advertising campaign using the theme "Look Mom, no cavities!" Drawings by Norman Rockwell were used and the advertising achieved widespread attention.

But the basic problem remained the same. Crest's unique advantage could not be seen by consumers. What was needed was a way to convince them that they were indeed benefiting from the product's decay-preventing quality. Since consumers couldn't see this benefit, they needed to hear it from an authority. And it had to be an authority they would believe.

Early in the development of Crest it was recognized that the American Dental Association could grant such recognition. In fact, the ADA had set up a formal review panel for appraising and recognizing the therapeutic benefits in oral products, both as a guide to the dental profession itself and to help police the truth of advertising which made therapeutic claims.

Beginning in 1954, P&G submitted to the ADA the results of the company's extensive clinical tests. The big problem was that the ADA had never before endorsed a toothpaste. In fact, it had developed an attitude of general suspicion toward dentifrice advertising, partly because of extravagant claims by some toothpaste manufacturers whose products contained ammonia, chlorophyll, and sodium fluoride. P&G's efforts with the ADA continued over the next five years. As the review wore on, the question of how an ADA endorsement would be handled in advertising became almost as important as the approval itself. Marketing people were added to the P&G team working with the ADA, and John Smale, then associate advertising manager, assumed a major role. He devoted tireless years to seeking the approval of the dental association.

To its credit, the ADA maintained an open mind throughout the period. As P&G's clinical evidence mounted, the association evaluated it carefully and asked for more data. Finally, in 1959, the ADA staff felt it had sufficient data for submission to the ADA's Council on Dental Therapeutics, the decision-making body. Within a few months that decision was reached, a triumph for Procter & Gamble and a reward for Smale's persistence. On August 1, 1960, the *Journal of the American Dental Association* reported: "Crest has been shown to be an effective anticaries [decay preventive] that can be of significant value when used in a conscientiously applied program of oral hygiene and regular professional care."

The ADA did not merely recognize Crest's benefits; it went further. For the first time in its history it granted the use of its name in consumer advertising for a commercial product. The response was electric. Within a year, Crest's sales nearly doubled. By 1962 they had nearly tripled, pushing Crest well ahead of Colgate dental cream as the best-selling toothpaste in the U.S.

Given the therapeutic promise of the new product, it was natural for each patient to ask for his dentist's advice. Therefore, it was important for dentists to hear firsthand of Crest's scientifically proven benefits. So a group of specially trained "detailers" was formed to inform the dental profession throughout the country of the roles of fluorides and of Crest in dental health.

As with Tide, Crest had been built on a base of new technology and persistent determination to succeed. The company's other dentifrice, Gleem, eventually added a fluoride formula of its own.

207

And in later years Lever Bros. pioneered a new dentifrice in the form of a gel rather than a paste. But Crest's continued leadership, into the 1970s, demonstrated the wisdom of the early determination to seek a genuine contribution to the dental health of the public.

As Bill Snow summed it up for the P&G management group, "It's been a long road between firm resolve to produce a decay-preventive dentifrice and becoming the No. 1 brand in the United States. Perhaps first among the lessons learned is that on this road there may have been many ruts, but never any detours."

* * * * *

Opportunities in the toiletries business appeared endless. The array of products in department stores and supermarkets seemed to offer unlimited new directions as well as some sharp changes in merchandising techniques.

The growth of the suburbs, resulting in large local shopping centers, brought innovations of its own. Before the war the bulk of all toiletries went through department stores, beauty shops, and full-service drugstores. By the mid-'50s, however, grocery supermarkets had added departments to handle toilet articles and a new type of discount, self-service store had emerged. These large-volume, self-service outlets were beginning to capture a growing portion of toiletry sales (and would handle over 16% of all toiletries by the early '70s).

So the trend, P&G recognized, was away from personal advice and guidance by beauty counselors and druggists. The self-service sections required new attention to packaging, advertising, and merchandising. And the emphasis fell increasingly on large-volume products.

It was in these high-volume areas that P&G concentrated its growing technological ability. Dentifrice was the largest-selling category, followed by shampoos, deodorants, and home permanents. P&G's goal was to make innovative contributions in all these areas.

Shampoos were a case in point. Dandruff control had always been a baffling goal for researchers. As early as 1950 P&G had begun seeking a long-lasting way to control dandruff between shampoos, a way that would be safe enough to use without a prescription. After five years company scientists isolated one possible ingredient—zinc pyrithione, developed by the Olin Chemical Company—and began extensive testing in conjunction

208

with Vanderbilt University. These tests for safety included animal studies for skin absorption, oral toxicity, and dermatological effects. An amazing series of clinical studies, over 1,300 in all, confirmed the effectiveness of zinc pyrithione in P&G's new shampoo, Head & Shoulders.

Head & Shoulders was test marketed in 1960, expanded three years later, and became another leading U.S. product in its field.

The company's investment in long and patient basic research, with clear proof of a consumer benefit, was thus justified again. It applied equally to other P&G drug products. The '50s and '60s saw the introduction of Scope mouthwash, which became a strong if still distant second-ranking brand to Listerine. The company entered the deodorant category with Secret; and later, in the early '70s, with Sure. Although a brief sally into men's hair dressings, called Radar, was tested in 1962, dentifrices, deodorants, and mouthwashes, together with shampoos and home permanents, represented P&G's principal toiletries areas through the 1970s.

Crest's detailers had provided the beginning of the P&G Professional Services Division which now informed dermatologists about Head & Shoulders. By the late '70s Professional Services representatives were making calls on 50,000 dentists annually, on 5,000 hospitals, and on 4,000 dermatologists. In addition, 16,000 physicians were being contacted on behalf of several prescription products the company introduced as an outgrowth of its broadening scientific knowledge.

* * * * *

After serving just over two years as Secretary of Defense, Neil McElroy resigned in 1959 to return to the Procter & Gamble management team. He brought with him a special award, the Medal of Freedom, presented by President Eisenhower in recognition of McElroy's outstanding service.

Just as most P&G people expected, McElroy was elected chairman of the board upon his return. Richard Deupree, who had been chairman since 1948, was elected to the newly created position of honorary chairman of the board.

McElroy and Morgens realized that if they were to stimulate progress, "bold steps" would be needed in new directions. This meant giving their research people time to study, experiment, and investigate without the distractions of existing business. The company's Winton Hill Technical Center on the outskirts of

Cincinnati was mushrooming. A vast campus-style accumulation of laboratories, it was begun in 1959 and steadily expanded. By 1973, a new site at Sharon Woods was also needed to provide space for the expansion of research facilities.

Meanwhile market and consumer studies were yielding new information of their own. For example, it was evident that though the housewife was still a major customer, teenagers bought 50% more shampoo and deodorant than their mothers.

And the company had gained firsthand knowledge of the impact of government controls on manufacturing concerns. Changes in the Food and Drug Act in 1962 brought a number of P&G brands under its supervision. Head & Shoulders lotion took twelve months to obtain FDA clearance, though Head & Shoulders in cream form was already being sold nationally. And clearance for Scope required eighteen months. The message was clear: As regulations increased, greater lead time would be needed to get products to market.

23

AN INDUSTRIAL EPIC

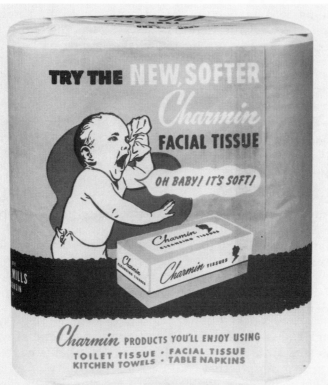

Purchase of the Charmin brand in 1957 brought P&G into the consumer tissue business.

The tremendous success of Crest, plus experience with other toiletries led P&G researchers to increasingly sophisticated applications of industrial chemistry. Now the laboratory technicians were examining the opportunities provided by cellulose and their deepening knowledge of dissolving pulps. This had been gleaned at the giant mill at Foley, Florida, and in the laboratories of P&G's Buckeye subsidiary at Memphis, Tennessee. Knowledge of pulp led inevitably to making paper.

At the executive level, of course, the decision to enter the paper business grew from the pragmatic recognition that disposable paper products were destined for rapid growth. Volume prospects were certainly large enough to justify the effort and expense. Besides, a company with a heavy stake in laundering had to consider the impact which disposable items might have on lessening what went into the washing machine.

Speaking to managers in 1964, Harness outlined some of the reasons for P&G's venture into paper production. He had become manager of the Paper Products Division a year earlier.

"Paper is our kind of business," he said. "It has rapid turnover, products which are 'used up,' move mainly through food stores, and are susceptible to our techniques of advertising and promotion. In addition, our product development people possess a deep understanding of consumer likes and dislikes in products to be used on the skin and in the kitchen, the primary usage areas for tissue products."

Harness reminded his audience that the Buckeye cellulose subsidiary had been gaining valuable experience in basic papermaking chemistry and engineering for many years. Buckeye scientists had in fact responded to an ever-widening range of uses for cellulose. Among them were steering wheels for cars, floor rugs, battery components, tire cords, synthetic sponges, cellophane, rayon fabrics, even frankfurter casings. Each required a distinctly different type of dissolving pulp.

Though the installation at Foley had included the purchase of vast forestry lands, it was vital that the company have control over a timber supply that could assure continuity of mill operations. This required skills. Company foresters led research into tree genetics. They sought ways in which growth could be accelerated through careful grafting of superior tree cuttings onto mature roots; then they harvested the resulting seeds to produce faster growing trees.

P&G was becoming a tree farmer. Each year it harvested a vast acreage of woodlands, promptly replanting the land—as with any crop—for future use. (By the late '70s the woodlands under direct control of P&G were yielding 10 million trees annually, and the company was reseeding or replanting 28 million trees. Managers liked to dramatize the huge acreage represented. They spoke of 4.5 million acres in use as an area equal in size to the states of Connecticut and Delaware.)

This increasing knowledge of tree farming and wood pulp production was of course essential for P&G's growth in the paper business.

At the start the company had no experience in the complex field of paper for household uses. The wood pulp technology Buckeye had developed was not directly applicable. And Foley was making tough, strong pulp, whereas the tissue products P&G planned to develop required pulps for a softer, more pliable paper.

This called for a number of round table discussions. How to venture into an untested field? Wisely it was decided that with so little practical knowledge in the field, a small acquisition would be the best way to proceed with experiments. So in 1957 P&G bought Charmin paper mills of Green Bay, Wisconsin, a regional paper manufacturer which had been in business since 1892.

Charmin had developed a good consumer following in parts of the Midwest for its toilet and facial tissues, paper towels, and paper napkins. More importantly, it had three operational plants. Howard Morgens, who spearheaded the effort for this start in the industry, described Charmin as a "pilot plant and a little pilot marketing area with which to learn the business."

And learn they did. One of the attractions of the new acquisition was its cadre of 1,200 experienced papermaking people familiar with maintaining quality on the high-speed giant machines. "However," one of them recalled, "most of the industry at that time, including Charmin, was in roughly the same state as the soap industry had been years earlier. Quality was subjectively determined by an experienced operator called the 'No. 1 hand' "—much as soapmakers had once judged the quality of a kettle by tasting.

A more aggressive, systematic approach to product development by P&G's scientists and engineers brought fresh vitality into research. Victor Mills, then heading P&G's Exploratory Development Division, saw two immediate tasks. One was to improve the quality of Charmin tissue. The other was to create new products.

Such a program consumed a great deal of time and effort. In fact, chemical engineers at Green Bay worked five years on the problem of upgrading quality. The kind of paper they sought was the result of market research. This indicated that American consumers—thousands of whom were interviewed—would welcome greater softness and absorbency in the tissues and paper towels they bought. So the question was, how do you make a softer, more absorbent paper?

P&G's technicians felt that conventional methods were not adequate. Some entirely new means of production would have to be invented. To develop such a means, the company constructed a small pilot paper plant in connection with its Miami Valley Laboratories.

Here, before any radical changes were instituted, several minor improvements were made. These were mainly the results of formula modifications; yet they did create a new degree of softness which bolstered Charmin sales.

Still the engineers were not satisfied. Basically they were restrained by conventional methods. The system in use throughout the industry relied on soaking pulpwood fibers in a water solution. This immersion was presumed to soften them. But the water had to be squeezed out of the pulp using tremendous pressure, much as laundry is squeezed dry in a wringer. This pressed the fibers into a tight, tough mass which actually reduced their softness and absorbency.

What the engineers ultimately proposed to Cincinnati headquarters was a novel process (called CPF) which would dry the pulp with a stream of hot air. This "fluff dry" method would separate the fibers instead of compressing them. The result, the researchers were confident, would be a much softer paper.

Test operations in the pilot plant proved they were right. Company executives handling the light fiber samples had good reason to be excited. Here was a true P&G innovation, unique in its field. "Many of us," said James M. Edwards, vice-president for paper products, "were ready and eager to push ahead with the project."

But had a gold mine really been opened? The engineers pointed out that adoption of the system would require a good deal of time and heavy expenditures. First, an efficient method of large-scale aeration would have to be devised. The necessary equipment would have to be designed and manufactured. Then a new plant (or plants) would have to be constructed to accommodate the massive machinery. All this would necessitate the expenditure of millions of dollars as well as countless man-hours of work. Was Procter & Gamble prepared to underwrite such great costs? In Deupree's words, the company was ready to "mortgage the farm and go for broke."

214

Charles Carstarphen, left, David S. Swanson, and Charles M. Fullgraf examine P&G's robust Pampers Brand which they helped raise from infancy.

Of course, rumors of P&G's plans at once flew through the paper industry. *Forbes* magazine published an article saying: "Scott Paper Company is betting P&G will abandon these ambitious building plans. 'Do you know how much it will cost them to, say, approach what we've got?' asked Scott's President Dunning. 'It could cost nearly $1 billion to duplicate our physical equipment alone.' " The magazine article added, "Building costs aside, P&G lacks the timber reserves to support a major tissue paper operation."

Procter & Gamble's response to such ominous warnings was typical. It already knew that product improvement would be the key to its growth in the paper business. Consumer research showed that P&G's existing brands, Charmin and White Cloud bathroom tissue and Puffs facial tissue, were already quality leaders in their categories. But it could not afford complacency. Investment was needed to sustain the momentum; so expansions

215

were added to the Green Bay and Cheboygan, Michigan, plants. And, in April, 1965, P&G announced it was building a new paper plant in Pennsylvania. This would be one of the largest in the world, with some fifty-two acres of working area under a single roof.

The Charmin story provided an insight into the interplay between P&G's producing and marketing teams. These groups cooperated to help their advertising agency find an intriguing way to dramatize the product for television. The amazing new softness of Charmin provided just such inspiration. A new campaign was born using the character "Mr. Whipple," a mild-mannered grocery store manager. His plea, "Please don't squeeze the Charmin!" focused attention on the unusual softness which could be confirmed by squeezing. Mr. Whipple's "Don't squeeze" campaign helped lift Charmin to the No. 1 toilet tissue position by the early '70s.

* * * * *

One of P&G's greatest paper breakthroughs, however, began in 1956. Vic Mills, director of exploratory development, had just spent some time caring for his newborn grandchild. He had developed a profound (and understandable) dislike for cleaning diapers. Back at the laboratory, he assigned some of his most talented people to spend part of their time looking into the practicality of disposable diapers.

Months were devoted to studies of existing products (Chux, Drypers, Kleinerts, K.D.'s, and so on) and how consumers felt about them. P&G learned that disposable diapers were used for less than 1% of the billions of diaper changes in the U.S. each year. The disposables were bought mainly by traveling parents when cloth diapers could not be laundered. Mothers simply didn't think they did as good a job. Besides, prices were high.

Nevertheless, the overall social data were impressive: the number of babies born annually in the United States; the average number of diaper changes each infant required each day; the prospects for future growth based on America's increasing population; and the encouraging remarks of many mothers who had been asked if they would like a disposable diaper—all such statistics were enticing. In late 1957 Mills felt encouraged enough to assign Bob Duncan, whose father had been instrumental in the development of detergents, to head a full-time diaper research group.

The initial idea was to develop a highly absorbent, pleated pad that could be inserted in a specially designed plastic panty, similar to a form used in Scandinavia. In six months R&D had a product ready for consumers to try. But the idea nearly died. In testing, Dallas was chosen for parent reaction. The average maximum temperature was 93°F and few mothers used plastic pants in such heat. They made babies too uncomfortable and covered them with heat rashes. Fortunately, the researchers were able to design new samples.

Vic Mills asked Duncan to join him in showing the new types to Gib Pleasants, vice-president of research. At the conclusion of the review, Duncan then demonstrated the neat, new alternative, explaining its advantages. Pleasants looked across the desk and very quietly said, "When you came in, Bob, I was of a mind to stop the project. I can't find it in my heart to stop it now. Test that new diaper."

By March, 1959, an exhausted research staff was ready to have its new version tested. Softer, more absorbent, with an improved "moisture barrier" between the infant and the wet wadding, the new diaper was tested in both a tape-on and pin-on design. The staff had laboriously assembled 37,000 diapers for a test in Rochester, New York. Parents in that city not only said they preferred the pin-on design but nearly two-thirds of them thought the product was as good as or better than cloth diapers. With such encouraging results, P&G engineers were asked to design machinery by which the new diaper could be made efficiently and speedily.

"I think it was the most complex production operation the company had ever faced," said one engineer. "There was no standard equipment. We had to design the entire production line from the ground up. It seemed a simple task to take three sheets of material—plastic back sheet, absorbent wadding, and water repellent top sheet—fold them in a zigzag pattern and glue them together. But glue applicators dripped glue. The wadding generated dust. Together they formed sticky balls and smears which fouled the equipment. The machinery could run only a few minutes before having to be shut down and cleaned." So research continued for better production methods.

For some time the prospective product had no name, although thought was being given to Tads, Solos, and Larks. The name which became the favorite was Pampers. In December, 1961,

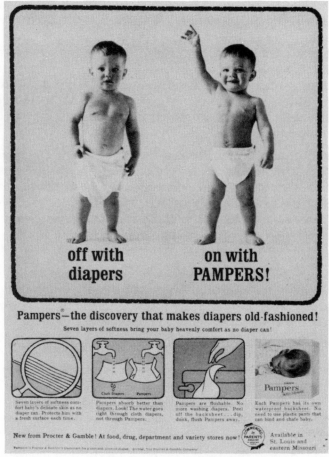

A 1962 Pampers advertisement.

Pampers entered its first full market test in Peoria, Illinois. Within six months it was clear that this test, too, was a failure. Mothers liked Pampers well enough, but the ten cents per diaper price was too much to pay. Costs would have to be reduced, and the only practical way was to increase volume, more than doubling the original plans.

"Do you realize what this entailed?" one engineer asked. For each one-cent retail price reduction, vast increases in volume would be needed. It wasn't practical to test at all price levels. P&G's market research had not always been successful in forecasting consumer reactions to lower prices. And so, largely on judgment that a sharply lower price was needed to obtain broad acceptance, the sales plan was based on a retail price of six cents per diaper. The price was tested and results were highly encouraging. Further tests followed—a total of six markets in all —before consumer response indicated Pampers at six cents each might exceed P&G expectations.

A major reason for Pampers' success lay in its unique three-piece construction. A thin outer sheet of plastic kept moisture in and also eliminated the need for separate plastic pants. Then came a pad of absorbent material that not only helped hold the moisture but worked to spread it evenly so as to avoid soggy spots. Next to the baby's skin was a special porous sheet which allowed fluid to pass through to the absorbent material and prevented most of it from coming back.

In recounting Pampers' success in the late 1960s—after Paper Products had created its own sales force—Ed Harness told an annual meeting, "Pampers is a beautiful example of P&G ability to look into the future and recognize tremendous opportunity. Disposable diapers had been sold in the United States for several generations, yet when the company launched the Pampers development program in the 1950s, less than 1% of the billions of diaper changes which take place in America every year were being made with disposables. Existing products were not good, their prices were too high, and retail distribution was minuscule. Despite these negatives, company people had imagination and foresight enough to recognize that a really good disposable diaper at a reasonable price, backed with marketing know-how, could bring about an enormous change in one of motherhood's oldest chores.

"Today in some of Pampers' longer established markets about 25% of the diaper changes are made with disposables. This has been accomplished almost entirely by Pampers since, with our headstart, good competition is not yet very widespread.

"In this era of what is called consumerism, the critics of American business are quick to say that all products are alike, that advertising is a snare and a delusion, and that the government ought to be given responsibility for guiding consumer wants.

"The company's pulp and paper business seems to give the lie to much of this. Not a single one of the many major forward steps we have taken here has been based on anything but proven ability to offer the public better products than those previously available."

219

Pampers' tremendous popularity did not stop at American shores. Babies are diapered around the world, and Pampers brought a revolution in countries as diverse as France, Japan, Germany, Belgium, Holland, Switzerland, and Greece. Everywhere parents found that Pampers offered greater convenience than all previous diapering habits. By 1980 Pampers was one of the company's most widely distributed brands, being sold in more than seventy-five countries. One publication called its success "an industrial epic."

24

A PLACE CALLED MEHOOPANY

The busiest noon-hour restaurants in Cincinnati are unquestionably the cafeteria and the more formal dining room at Procter & Gamble headquarters. Every working day several thousand meals are served there. If one listens to conversations at table after table, one hears opinions on every local and national event, from the Cincinnati Reds' latest game through the activities of presidential candidates to the most recent developments at P&G as reported in the company magazine, *Moonbeams*. Thus on a day in April, 1965, talk spread that Procter & Gamble, facing an overwhelming demand for its paper products, was about to build a new paper plant in Mehoopany, Pennsylvania.

Mehoopany? Even at Cincinnati headquarters astonished people had to ask, "Where on earth is Mehoopany?" It did no good to look at maps. Few marked the village. Yet the Mehoopany story is an example of what often happens in the construction of a new P&G factory. The problems, the obstacles, the clashes of wills, the disappointments, the struggles—all were illustrated by this Pennsylvania venture.

It began when the company's forestry experts, after inspecting scores of areas in the eastern United States, chose the Mehoopany region as ideal for P&G's purposes. Its surrounding hills were thickly forested. Most of the land was owned by small farmers who seemed willing to sell at reasonable prices. There was a social reason for this: Their children had gone off to work in cities, and the older generations could not forever continue farming. So there would be no resistance, presumably, to the acquisition of a factory site.

Physically the Pennsylvania country around Mehoopany offered many advantages. Good automobile roads and the Lehigh

221

Valley Railroad facilitated transportation. In addition, the entire region had already been electrified. As for the availability of labor, both Scranton and Wilkes-Barre, with their sizable city populations, were close enough to permit workers to drive to the plant.

It soon became evident, however, that Procter & Gamble had social problems to confront. Many of the area's residents, especially those of the summer colony, feared their community would be spoiled by the presence of a factory. They envisioned air black with smoke, a permanent pall overhanging their homes. They spoke of pollutants pouring into their lovely Susquehanna River, of trucks thundering along their quiet roads, of barracks-like housing changing the entire character of the peaceful village. The local newspaper also raised serious questions about big industry coming into the region, and the public began to object. Coping with such a situation was not easy.

"What happened," said a senior plant manager, "was that the company sent representatives to do a kind of ambassadorial job. They talked personally to local landowners, to summer residents, to the editors of the local newspaper. They spoke of how the company would pour $8 million a year in wages into the community by creating some 2,000 jobs. They explained how hundreds of farmers would benefit by selling timber to the company, and how P&G would insist on constant reforestation to protect its own future supplies and to avoid the defoliation of the surrounding country. They told how Procter & Gamble had already spent $30 million on pollution control and planned to spend $45 million more in the next five years. They specifically outlined the environmental control measures that would be built into the proposed Mehoopany plant."

Originally the plant was intended to stand on the banks of the Susquehanna for ready access to water supplies. But Ed Harness, then managing the Paper Products Division, insisted that P&G build its factory away from the river, where buildings and equipment would not mar the beauty of the shoreline.

(Years later this decision won unexpected rewards. When the Susquehanna poured flood waters over nearby fields, the P&G installation, at a safe distance from the river, remained untouched.)

Another step the company took, years before environmental concerns captured the interest of the U.S. public, was to make sure the water quality of the Susquehanna River would not be harmed by the new plant. An internationally known fresh water biologist was commissioned to study the possible toxicity of plant wastes. She and a team of eight scientists conducted a bio-assay of the river, examining the state of fish and plant life above and below the proposed plant site. Then special waste treatment facilities were incorporated into the plant design. (Several years after paper production began, a second survey by the research team showed the river to be in the same healthy condition as before construction, downstream as well as upstream from the plant.)

These early efforts of Procter & Gamble representatives served to change the community's attitude. In time, editorials in the local press began urging readers to welcome the company.

But once land had been bought and construction begun, other problems had to be solved. "If we were to attract some of the hundreds of workers we would need from nearby towns," said the plant manager, "we had to have housing for them. And it had to be decent housing which would not deface Mehoopany. We did this by persuading builders to put up the kind of homes the community would approve of. We would also need a hospital, and toward this Procter & Gamble contributed $100,000. That brought matching funds from the state. The hospital was ready, with four physicians and attending nurses, by the time the factory went into production."

One of the most dramatic challenges was the delivery of enormous machinery components to Mehoopany. The largest component, a "Yankee Dryer," was of such immense proportions that the Lehigh Valley Railroad issued a proud release about its part in the transportation of the great drum-like contrivance. The release said:

> It's so big, so heavy, and so wide that it can't move as any other shipment would on the Valley's main line. It weighs 105 tons and when loaded on a special car it will extend 17 feet 6 inches above top of rail, and 15 feet 4 inches in width.
>
> To get the dryer safely to Mehoopany the Valley started planning, plotting, scheming, and sweating several months ago. The first problem was to provide a special car for this mammoth piece.

223

> *A six-axle depressed-center flat car was taken to the Sayre shops where an 18-inch extension was welded and bolted to one side of the car's floor.*
>
> *Because of this side extension unusual clearance problems were encountered. The Valley ran a clearance car [a car with wide protruding rods] to check every inch of the line to Mehoopany.*
>
> *So that the dryer wouldn't hit anything, the Valley had to move its tracks at eight bridges and four different locations. Also it had to blast out about 600 feet of rock at a cut near Jim Thorpe, Pa.*
>
> *Some of the track changes will be permanent but in other instances the rail will have to be returned to its original position.*
>
> *This dryer will move only in daylight, with top speed of 15 miles an hour on the straightaway, 5 to 10 miles an hour on curves. The adjacent tracks must be clear of trains at all times. When the dryer arrives at the Mehoopany plant, the Lehigh Valley's 250-ton derrick will be on hand to remove it.*

Subsequently, six such giant Yankee Dryers were housed in the plant.

In time a constant parade of trucks brought logs to one side of the building. Another line, at the far end, took away loads of toilet tissue, Bounty, and Pampers. More than 125 local timber growers were selling wood to the Mehoopany plant. The factory was operating three shifts a day, seven days a week, 365 days a year, and providing steady jobs for 2,500 people.

"One of the best results of it all," said a local resident, "is that the availability of local jobs has brought a lot of young people back home. Families that were split are together again. That's one of the happiest things that could have happened in Mehoopany."

Years later, Charles M. Fullgraf, group vice-president, was to recall, "The investment at Mehoopany represented a major gamble. In 1963, the cost was huge, about $150 million. When the decision was made, the ability of this new process to meet production goals was still unproved. But we had enough experience to be reasonably certain of success."

Hardly had the Mehoopany plant been opened in 1966 than its production, enormous as it was, proved insufficient to meet the demand. Three years later the company had to build still another paper plant at Cape Girardeau, Missouri. Now paper brands were being produced not only at these two new locations but at the older ones in Green Bay and Cheboygan. Later, increased demand required installations at Modesto, California, and Greenville, North Carolina, and purchase of a plant from International Paper Company at Oxnard, California.

"And we were still lagging behind demand," said Vice-President James M. Edwards.

Manufacturing P&G tissues hinged on the availability of a long fiber pulp, much of which came from trees on the eastern slope of the Canadian Rockies. It was this long fiber which contributed the necessary strength without impairing softness and absorbency. Edward Harness was convinced that if the company was to build a sound and enduring paper business it must have control over a major portion of the supply of such wood for its pulp mills.

Howard Morgens fully agreed and pressed this argument with the board of directors. The search for new woodlands was intensified. Forestry experts from the Cellulose and Specialties Division at Memphis, Tennessee, were sent to find the best available timberlands. This time the quest led to vast, untouched tracts around Grande Prairie in Alberta, Canada. Every report marked the region as ideal for Procter & Gamble's needs. But would the Canadian government lease its land to the Cincinnati firm?

Meetings with Canada's national and provincial authorities were long, involved with legalities. Foresters, lawyers, company executives—all participated in negotiations. These were always amicable. And finally the company won the right to lease 7 million acres of Alberta woodlands. There it would build still another plant to process pulp.

"How big is 7 million acres?" said a manager in answer to a reporter's question. "Let me put it this way: try to visualize a highway five miles wide—wide, not long. Then think of that highway running clear across the country from New York to Los Angeles. The land it covers will be just short of 7 million acres."

For the ceremonial opening of the Canadian project Richard Deupree, now in his eighties, flew to Grande Prairie where he made the last official talk he was ever to make. He had prepared notes for the speech; but the ceremonies were held outdoors and a gust of wind blew the notepaper out of his hand, off among the trees. He waved back those who tried to retrieve it. Instead, as all

225

who heard him remember, "He went on talking from the heart. Not about the plant, not about the forest, not about the success of P&G. As always he talked about the company's people. For him, only people, not dollars or size, represented the true wealth of the company."

*   *   *   *   *

P&G and cellulose had come a long way from those days when the cotton linters were an unneeded by-product of crushing cottonseed. By the late '70s the company's paper brands were all among the leaders in their categories—Pampers, Charmin one-ply tissue, White Cloud two-ply tissue, Puffs facial tissue, and Bounty towels.

And cellulose technology was fostering widespread development of other products, too. Among them:

- A new fabric, impregnated with softening agents for use in laundry dryers, resulted in a clothes softening brand.

- The knowledge gained with Pampers led to a second disposable diaper, Luvs. It also helped develop a strikingly beneficial product, Attends, for senior citizens suffering from problems of incontinence.

- As a further outcome of experience with cellulosic fibers, there was a line of surgical drapes and gowns for improved disposable use in hospitals. Under the brand name Boundary, P&G scientists created a three-ply fabric that looked and felt like cloth and provided a barrier against germ migration as well as moisture to prevent infection. To supply hospitals across the U.S., a new plant was built in 1980 at Huntsville, Alabama.

It is easy enough to catalog all these as examples of Procter & Gamble technicians' ceaseless invention and innovation. It is also easy to cite their new and improved products in explanation of the company's growth. But more important in a social sense, as has so often been pointed out, is the fact that one company's activities always compel competitors to devise their own improved products. The ultimate beneficiaries are, of course, consumers.

25
AMERICA'S MOST POPULAR DRINK

"Mrs. Olsen," played by actress Virginia Christine, brought the Folger message to American homes in the 1960s, 70s, and 80s to become one of P&G's most durable brand characters.

According to the U.S. Department of Agriculture, Americans were expending more than $95 billion a year on foodstuffs during the mid-1950s. That meant the average American was annually swallowing $574 worth of victuals, a fantastic sum for the times, probably unique in the world.

So it was not surprising that quite a few P&G executives urged greater attention to this enormous market. Until the 1950s the company had, in a sense, been merely nibbling at the potentialities of edible products. Now it was time for more aggressive action.

Initial steps to establish a strong food business paralleled in many ways the methods which had preceded entry into the paper and cellulose fields. "To get practical experience," W. Rowell Chase said, "we decided to make the kind of acquisitions that facilitate the learning process, then apply P&G improvements as well as marketing and technical skills."

The company had already purchased, in 1955, the small W. T. Young firm in Lexington, Kentucky, which sold Big Top peanut butter. Why buy a manufacturer of peanut butter? Chase explained, "Procter & Gamble had been crushing peanuts for several years as it had been crushing cottonseeds and soybeans. We had been suppliers of stabilizers [which eliminate oil separation] to a number of peanut butter manufacturers. One day one of us—I think it was Morgens—came to a meeting with some new figures on the consumption of peanut butter in American homes. Considering the size of the market, and considering that we were already in the food business with Crisco, didn't it make sense to market our own peanut butter? It would be sold to the same grocery outlets who were buying our other products. In other words, it was a synergistic item in every sense.

"We'd need equipment, of course, and a plant, and we'd have to acquire specialized know-how," Chase went on. "The quickest way to get them was to buy a going business to gain practical experience. Once we had such a subsidiary we could put our research people to work producing an improved peanut butter. We never planned to market a 'me-too' product. Even before we bought Young, the research people had been developing a completely new formulation that was the origin of Jif, the peanut butter we introduced in 1956."

Jif not only drew the attention of consumers, it also drew the attention of the FDA. Howard Morgens, talking to a reporter from

Business Week, described the situation this way: "The Food and Drug Administration wouldn't let us call our product 'peanut butter' because it only had 88% peanuts, not 92%. Then we tried calling it 'peanut spread,' and oh, my God, the grocers would still feature it as peanut butter and call it peanut butter. So the government said we couldn't call it 'peanut spread' either. They wanted us to call it 'imitation peanut butter,' and at that point we gave up and went to 92% peanuts."

The food business was growing in other directions, too. Its experience with shortenings like Crisco and Fluffo had led it to selling bulk products—Primex and Sweetex—to restaurants and bakers. This in turn had inspired interest in cake mixes for home use—an interest which led, in 1956, to the purchase of Duncan Hines cake mixes from the Nebraska Consolidated Mills of Omaha.

"We bought it," Chase went on, "with the feeling that we were expanding into a territory with which we already had considerable familiarity." (In fact, the company's work with edible fats and oils dated back half a century to when Crisco was first sold.)

Then Procter & Gamble had built a strong reputation in the commercial bakery field with its industrial brand Sweetex. Here undeniably was a business the company really understood. Further, it now looked as if convenient cake mixes might widely replace home recipe baking. Given such circumstances, it certainly seemed wise to market prepared household mixes—a field then dominated by two leading flour millers with long experience and well-established brands, General Mills and Pillsbury.

The purchase of the prepared mix business brought control of the brand name made famous by the traveler, Duncan Hines, who had established a reputation as a connoisseur of good food through a widely followed restaurant guidebook. "Recommended by Duncan Hines" had become a highly coveted award by U.S. restaurants.

P&G researchers already had under development a new formula for cake mixes which seemed superior to anything on the market. The experience gained in milling bar soaps with rollers under great pressure was now applied to a patented process for combining dry mix ingredients. The new Duncan Hines Deluxe cake mixes, as they were called, expanded nationally in 1959. Virtually overnight the company had another leading brand.

229

* * * * *

What persuaded Morgens to lead P&G next into the coffee business was an impressive array of facts presented at a 1963 meeting of P&G executives. "The total coffee business in this country, measured in retail dollar sales," Morgens said, "is approximately the same size as the total soap and detergent business." And there were other statistics to whet P&G's interest. The Pan American Coffee Bureau estimated that coffee was the country's largest food import. Over 70% of the U.S. population drank coffee, and an average of three cups were consumed per person per winter day.

So large a market could not be ignored, he maintained, by a company already in the food business. Was coffee a synergistic product for Procter & Gamble? It was indeed. It was a low-price item quickly and steadily consumed. It was distributed by the grocery trade with which the company constantly dealt. P&G researchers had experience with blending flavors. And the buying department was highly proficient in the purchase of a wide range of commodities which, like green coffee, were subject to extreme price fluctuations.

Morgens realized, however, that without solid knowledge about the coffee industry, P&G could not rashly push into competition against such solidly established brands as Maxwell House, Hills Brothers, and many others. What was the quickest way of gaining experience?

The answer came with the news that J. A. Folger & Company, successful veterans in the coffee business, would be amenable to purchase offers.

Folger had a history stretching back almost as far as Procter & Gamble's. It had begun in San Francisco in 1850 during the California Gold Rush. Young Jim Folger had started out to pan for gold but turned instead to supplying coffee to the miners. He built a business that had expanded as far east as Texas and Missouri.

With headquarters in Kansas City and San Francisco, Folger also had plants in Houston and New Orleans. Buying Folger would give Procter & Gamble a rich background of coffee knowledge, a successful regional brand, and the services of experienced management people.

With good will on both sides, negotiations were quickly completed. On November 26, 1963, Procter & Gamble exchanged

1,650,000 shares of its common stock, worth about $130 million at the time, for the Folger assets.

Although Folger's was sold in 52% of the U.S.—most of that west of the Mississippi River—its sales represented only 11% of the total U.S. business. But as Howard Morgens said at the time of purchase, "That is enough to make Folger the second largest coffee business in the United States, and it leaves lots of room for growth."

In the early days progress was slow. There was much to learn. P&G researchers would not revolutionize coffee technology as it had the manufacture of paper and cake mixes.

Flavor being the foundation of any coffee, Folger's was what expert tasters described as "mild, aromatic, with an abundance of high-grown coffee flavor notes." ("High grown" meant the choicest green coffees grown at altitudes over 2,000 feet.) P&G included unusually large portions of high-grown coffees in its Folger's blend. In this way it was able to establish the distinctive difference it sought.

One important learning experience for P&G's people was the exacting care required to blend green coffees so that production resulted in the same flavor each time. As many as fifteen varieties had to be balanced skillfully, and substitutes had to be used when supplies and prices varied. No machines could provide a perfect blend. Only expert tasters could manage that. (Tasters train for years to detect the slightest hints of off flavor. Working like artists, these professionals sip each day's production in a ceremony known as "cupping." They sip, consider, and then pass judgment. Their approval is needed before the coffee is released for shipment.)

As might be expected, P&G also revamped Folger's advertising. It launched a marketing campaign based on a friendly widow with a Swedish accent, Mrs. Olsen, who delivered homely testimonials for Folger's as though she were talking to members of her family. Her commercials continued to concentrate on Folger's superior "mountain grown" flavor. Mrs. Olsen brought a distinctive difference to coffee advertising; she remained a major figure in Folger's marketing plans for many years.

Meanwhile, "freeze-dried instant coffee" was being introduced by a number of P&G's competitors. Although "freeze drying" greatly improved the quality of instant coffee, its high capital investment and operating costs necessitated a premium price.

Aware of this cost factor, Procter & Gamble researchers devised a new technology. It improved the quality of Folger's instant coffee without the expensive freeze drying process. This brought the 1969 introduction of Folger's coffee crystals. The development of High Point decaffeinated coffee soon followed in 1975. Consumer demand for a decaffeinated type at that time accounted for 30% of all coffee sales.

Folger's expansion set off one of the fiercest competitive battles ever experienced in the coffee industry. General Foods in particular, with its leading Maxwell House brand, fought Folger on every front. In the midst of the furious competition a catastrophic frost destroyed almost half of Brazil's coffee trees. Green coffee prices increased by more than 450%. Consumer prices skyrocketed to $4 per pound. People bought less, and P&G felt the sting as did all other marketers.

Despite all setbacks, it continued to push its coffee brands. By 1978 Folger's achieved national distribution with its vacuum as well as instant coffee. An innovative flaked form, designed to squeeze more coffee from a pound, became part of the line—surely a significant addition in an era of high prices. A new decaffeinated brand, High Point Instant, achieved national distribution in 1980, requiring a new plant at Sherman, Texas. Internationally P&G added to its coffee investment by buying an Italian brand from the Società Generale del Caffè in Milan.

*　*　*　*　*

The growing success of Folger's amply demonstrated the value of diversifying efforts within the foods area. Company technology continued to expand. In the gigantic potato chip market, P&G introduced Pringle's potato chips. A unique chip, it was formed from dried potatoes, packed in an airtight can, and shipped through regular dry grocery distribution channels.

Great hopes were held for Pringle's. A giant plant was built for its production at Jackson, Tennessee. But the vagaries of public taste created exasperating problems. By the end of the '70s Pringle's was falling far short of expectations, and P&G's future in such snack foods became cloudy. It was a testimonial to the company's plan for balanced growth that the disappointments in potato chips could be balanced by Folger's becoming the leading U.S. coffee brand.

26

WIN SOME, LOSE SOME

Though P&G ventures into paper products were providing remarkable growth, the soap and detergent business was demonstrating explosive growth of its own. In the mid-'60s a veritable revolution in household cleaning products had literally occurred:

- Liquid detergents largely supplanted granules for washing dishes. Joy and Ivory Liquid from P&G, and Lux Liquid from Lever Bros., were proving how competition could provoke growth of an entirely new category.

- Detergent liquids were developed for other cleaning problems. An entire type—household liquid cleaners—was created, with two P&G brands, Mr. Clean and Top Job, achieving major success. Liquids for heavy laundry jobs also responded to research, but it was years before a truly new satisfactory formula could be invented.

- The laundry process itself was changing. American homemakers were exchanging wringers and old-style washing machines for automatic washers. The clothes line was being replaced with automatic dryers.

- Sophisticated chemists were developing low-suds detergents and new fluorescers (whiteners) and optical brighteners. New technology made possible fabric softeners which took the unpleasant stiffness out of washing in detergents, and they removed the static that caused synthetic fabrics to cling.

For years the nation witnessed races by the competing detergent and chemical companies. How P&G performed in these contests reveals much about the company and its people.

* * * * *

There was a period in which visitors to Procter & Gamble's research laboratories would have been deeply puzzled. They would see discolored old kitchen sinks—heaven knew where they came from—being scrubbed and rubbed by white-coated technicians. Why should grown men and women be scrubbing discarded sinks?

"In those days," a researcher explained, "sinks served also as dishpans. They were made with a glazed, porcelain-like surface. Years of scrubbing with abrasive cleansers left small pits in the surface which were easily stained and hard to clean."

Colgate had been the first to cope with this problem. Its detergent-based Ajax, "the foaming cleanser," captured nearly half the market because of its grease-cutting strength. It was as revolutionary to general cleansers as Tide had been to laundry products. But Ajax relied on the same pumice-like abrasives that other cleansers were using. This was not very effective on difficult food and rust stains.

For some years P&G researchers had been seeking an answer to the problem of removing all kinds of stains—fruit, tea, rust, and so on. They knew that an imitation of Ajax would not be successful.

"In scrubbing away at old sinks with different cleansers," said a technician, "each of us was trying a different combination of ingredients. After hundreds of tests in actual sinks and tubs (and this took years) we finally found a way to create an effective formula containing a chlorine bleach. This was test marketed briefly, but with remarkable success, and then introduced nationally in 1956 under the brand name Comet."

Comet's acceptance was spectacular. No other word could describe its success. It seemed to have magical properties. Television commercials clearly showed its ability to bleach out stains of all types. P&G salesmen were able to demonstrate Comet's amazing effectiveness on the grocers' own sinks. A slight chlorine odor, at first feared as a negative influence, actually helped build (as did a blue-green color) a distinctive impression.

Ajax in its dominant position, having won nearly half the market, was faced with the question of whether to change the formula of its highly successful product to meet Comet's challenge. It elected not to do so, which proved to be a mistake. A technological breakthrough, Comet solved many consumer problems. It quickly became the leading seller across the country and maintained this position through the '70s. (Later Colgate and others did shift to bleach-type products.)

Ivory Babies, from the first in 1887 (inset) to the 1954 model celebrating Ivory Soap's 75th Anniversary, signified Ivory's gentle skin care. As Ivory improved over the years, so did the appearance of the babies.

* * * * *

While Comet was one of those brands which proved dramatically successful from the start, the effort to apply new detergent technology to toilet soaps was, on the other hand, frustrating. As long ago as 1952, P&G researchers had felt they actually had a bar, Zest, which incorporated all the advantages of a detergent. Like Comet, Zest promised to be a sensation at the outset. Its advertising urged, "For the first time in your life feel really clean!"

235

The brand did indeed rise to sales leadership within months. *Consumer Reports*, after making its own tests, wrote: "Zest was the only product that lathered well in hard water; it lathered well even in salt water and left no curd; and it left no bathtub ring."

Despite all such acclaim, something went wrong. Sales began to decline when cold weather arrived. The reason, it was found, was that Zest removed too much of the natural body oils, leaving winter-cold skin itchy and chapped. Evidently the technical problems of putting synthetic detergent properties into a toilet soap were more difficult than anyone had thought. And Procter & Gamble suffered one of its periodic setbacks.

There began a determined effort to find a soap formula which would retain the benefits of detergents. Testing of product after product continued, each with a new feature: A bacteria-fighting ingredient was added to provide a deodorant; the color was changed from white to blue-green. "We tried everything we could think of," said a brand manager. "I used to rub various formulas of Zest into my own arms on the coldest winter days to see the effects. Nothing was altogether satisfactory—at least, not for four long years."

In the meantime, several competitors (notably Lever Bros. with Dove) introduced their own variations of what became known as a "synthetic bar." At P&G, there were temptations to expand Zest whenever some of its tests looked encouraging. But the judgment at executive conferences was that the perfect new Zest formula had not yet been found.

This feeling persisted until tests of new ideas did indeed justify optimism—four years after the first marketing effort. Once launched in 1955 the improved Zest again became successful. It surpassed Camay as a leading soap, second only to the venerable Ivory. (And this confirmed the wisdom of continued testing until a product was deemed decisively "right.")

While Zest was gaining popularity, another soap, marketed by a meat packer, Armour, was achieving its own success. Called Dial, it was advertised as a deodorant soap, promising reduction of odor-causing bacteria because of a new ingredient, hexachlorophene. Dial at first had only Lever's Lifebuoy as competition in the deodorant soap market. It began building sales in that portion of the soap business dominated by complexion bars like Lux and Camay.

Meanwhile consumer interest was stirred by heavy advertising of such toiletry items as underarm deodorants and antiperspirants. Dial was able to capitalize on this trend. "There is no doubt," said one P&G manager, "that we moved too slowly to recognize this widening deodorant market." Once started, however, with Zest and Safeguard (introduced in 1963) P&G was able to establish its own strong position in this segment of the soap field.

(Throughout all these changes Ivory soap continued to maintain its popularity and leadership. Actually, P&G experimented with a detergent bar that had the same ability to float as Ivory, but it failed. Nothing could vie with the original Ivory which, in 1979, celebrated 100 years of success—probably the oldest advertised brand in the world.)

But it was the competition for laundry products that captured the greatest interest. Sales of laundry detergents leaped as American laundering habits changed. Automatic washing machines eliminated the drudgery of an exhausting weekly wash day. Laundering became a simpler household task to be done automatically and frequently.

With the transformation of the nation's laundry habits, detergent manufacturers were in fierce competition to offer consumers a variety of new products. The battle of the low-suds detergents, initiated by All and joined by P&G's Dash, was being waged. And there was more.

The race to produce something new and better also reached into laundry liquids. After Lever Bros. marketed liquid Wisk, liquid detergents became an obvious target for the laboratories of all soap companies. At Procter & Gamble, as elsewhere, a number of formulations were taken to market for testing, yet none did a wholly satisfactory cleaning job. Despite the temptation, the company decided to wait until it had a better product.

Other ideas were explored. One new type of cleaner was introduced by P&G's technicians to be sold in premeasured amounts. This invention was marketed under the brand name Salvo. Salvo was simply a tablet which could be tossed into the water of a washing machine. It was introduced with great éclat in 1960 but never did very well. About the same time, Tide tested small packets of regular Tide which would quickly dissolve in the wash water. These didn't do well either.

237

The problem with all premeasurement was that few washing situations were exactly the same. No predetermined amount of detergent could always be satisfactory. Fabrics were different, wash loads had different amounts of clothes, dirty children's clothes required more cleaning power than light undergarments, soft water required less detergent than hard water, and so on. Consumers had learned to adjust the amount of detergent to their own differing laundry conditions, and so they showed little interest in premeasured portions. In time, Salvo and its competitors disappeared.

Possibly the greatest struggle—one that dominated the detergent field for a decade or more—was the effort to impart maximum "whiteness and brightness" to clothes. This caused a major competitive struggle.

For years women had judged the cleanness of wash by its whiteness. They had developed the practice of boiling clothes, of using bleach, of adding blueing, to give their families whiter wash. Television commercials showed neighboring housewives holding up garments for comparisons of whiteness.

This offered researchers fresh areas to investigate. Fluorescers had of course come into use long ago. Tide's early formulas contained small amounts of brighteners as did its major competitors, Surf, Fab, and so on. Lever Bros. had put a powerful effort behind Rinso, bombarding radio sets with the story of Rinso White. Cheer's addition of blueing represented still another stride in the whiteness race. Oxydol added perborate bleach in tiny colored granules. Even Tide adopted, for several years, a package printed with glowing fluorescent inks to dramatize the brightness idea.

Though most manufacturers simply added greater quantities of brighteners to their existing brands, there were also a number of new products. One of them, from Colgate, made an unusual impact on the entire industry.

At Colgate a new management group decided to use the Ajax name as an overall identifier for numerous other products. It launched this idea with a new detergent and an original, compelling advertising campaign. To emphasize the promise of whiteness, Ajax adopted the symbol of a White Knight, a rider in full knight's regalia mounted on a white horse. It proved to be a brilliant idea. Referred to by advertisers as a mnemonic device, the charging knight was ideally suited to television. He drama-tized Ajax as "stronger than dirt." Its success was immediate. Ajax captured a large part of the detergent market, taking a substantial portion away from P&G brands.

Procter & Gamble had generally resisted launching new products to respond to every competitive effort. But to the White Knight of Ajax the company reacted with speed and strength. Thomas Laco, then brand promotion manager, was given respon-sibility. The result was a new brand, Bold, developed in record time, and entering the market in March, 1965. Bold presented a low-suds formula combined with a high level of fluorescers, a color-safe bleach, and a blueing agent. In short, Bold had every-thing. Nationwide marketing was completed less than a year later. Bold sales increased so rapidly that it rose to replace Cheer as the No. 2 brand behind Tide. When one considers that the entire detergent industry had sought to displace Cheer for over a decade, the quick success of Bold was phenomenal.

These were fast-moving times. Now the textile manufacturers themselves found ways to build fluorescence into their synthetic fabrics. Once this happened, the laundry industry could hardly whiten what was already white. So it now reversed itself and reduced the fluorescers in detergents. Though Bold remained popular, changing conditions did not allow it to maintain its leadership over Cheer.

Nevertheless, the success of Ajax caused some deep soul-search-ing at P&G as Colgate built a whole line of cleaning products under the Ajax name. Not only a detergent, but a liquid cleaner, and then a powdered cleaner rivaling P&G's Spic and Span—all these were introduced by Colgate, as well as a window cleaner and a bleach. All were sold under the Ajax name. All appeared to be growing. *Forbes* magazine questioned P&G's reluctance to follow this pattern of capitalizing on a single name. There were doubts within P&G management as well. Should they follow Colgate's example? It was a question executives debated in long sessions.

True, the Ivory name was used on Ivory Liquid as well as Ivory Snow and Ivory Flakes. The Crisco name has been applied to a new salad oil. But these products were very similar in usage, in formulation, even in odor. Each had been made after considerable research of consumer reactions. No, in this case the extension of a brand name to a different line of products would not be permitted. It strayed too far from the policy, as Howard Morgens had stated, that "Each brand should have its own character—it must stand or fall on its own." He realized that no policy can fit all circumstances. Each case must be examined on its own merits. In this instance, the volume possibilities in each category seemed great enough to support individual brands. The policy would prevail.

27

SETTLED OUT OF COURT

"In the old days," a former sales representative recalled, "there were times when I'd come home at night and drop into a chair, exhausted and frustrated. Our soap and detergent business had spread into so many brands that no one person could handle them all. There were laundry detergents, dishwashing liquids, toilet soaps, liquid cleaners, scouring cleansers, fabric softeners. For each of them, new sizes and new improvements were constantly coming out. You could get dizzy just trying to keep track."

Factories could be built to handle the growing number of products; marketing and research groups could be assigned to separate brands. But when a sales representative walked into a buyer's office, he was expected to sell them all. He simply could not give them adequate attention. Something had to be done. How best to manage the situation?

When foods and toilet goods had been separated from the cleaning products years earlier, the solution had seemed relatively simple. These were completely different categories. But in the case of soap and detergents what was needed was an answer that would provide an immediate solution to this dilemma and also long-term guidance. The problem was threshed around in many management discussions.

Everyone realized that the major trend for the last fifteen years had been toward greater product specialization. Where there had been one or two all-purpose detergents, there were now dozens with high suds, low suds, whiteners, bleaches, and so on. Where there had been a single dry cleaner like Spic and Span, there were many liquids. The same was true in bar soaps. This increase in product specialization was bound to continue. The company's organization had to meet these trends.

Rowell Chase outlined P&G's thinking. "The best thing to do," he reported, "was to separate the soap business by kinds of products so that each division would be expert in its own categories. The split could have been made by cutting the line in half, with each division having half of all categories. The two divisions would compete with each other in every category." While this would have reflected the company's competition-between-brands philosophy, there were problems. "It would have resulted," Chase said, "in each division being a jack-of-all-trades-in-the-cleaning-products business. Instead, the decision was made to allow each division to become a master of its own categories."

These two entities—soap as differentiated from detergents—were established in January, 1966. But it was a year later before the separation of their sales responsibility was completed. "It was not easy," recalled W. W. Abbott who became sales manager of the new Sales Division. "We had to reorganize coverage of the entire U.S. grocery trade. A mammoth recruiting effort for new sales people was mounted. People had to be trained in dozens of new jobs."

Procter & Gamble had discovered long ago that it was one thing to announce such organization changes. It was quite another to obtain support from the people involved.

"In the past, regional sales managers," said one of them, "had clearly understood their responsibilities: to sell; to ship; to employ, train, and motivate a selling force; to extend credit and make collections; to supervise trucking schedules; to arrange for warehousing; to carry out merchandising plans and promotions; to direct clerical help. Always a district sales manager had exercised these responsibilities. But with divisionalization drastic adjustments were made, and some managers viewed the changes as reducing authority for themselves. They disliked it."

They also disliked the idea of having a staff group formed to serve both the new divisions on the corporate level. Yet this was essential. Brad Butler, who supervised the split of the soap and detergent business, explained the value of the move: "As the total load of responsibility of any kind of manager in any kind of business increases, he has no real alternative but to take three steps. First: to establish staff people who can serve as advisers in specialized areas of his responsibility. Second: to formalize policies and procedures which will simplify the decision-making process in many of the routine areas of his operation. Third: to delegate responsibility and decision-making power to subordinates or associates.

"Staff experts," he added, "because of the depth of their specialized knowledge, will prod him [the manager] to do things which he does not quite understand in detail; formalized policies will chafe a bit by reducing his cherished flexibility; and the delegation of decision-making power to other people will appear to dilute his authority." Butler went on to emphasize that the staff experts should be regarded as "liberators of our time and energy, rather than restricters of our prerogatives."

True, with any organization, large or small, business or government, these problems exist. Perhaps more than most, P&G has diligently explored the relationships between division and corporate responsibilities. There seems little question that the close interplay of these two functions explains much of the company's success.

The specialization within each operating division certainly permits greater knowledge of that area of the business. As an illustration of how this interplay could work, Butler cited the case of Pampers.

"Several years ago," he said, "it became apparent that Pampers had to provide adhesive tapes on diapers instead of pins. Now there's nothing unusual about producing products with an adhesive tape attached. There were suppliers available who could easily provide the equipment. But once these applicators were installed, we discovered that our machines simply could not be operated at their accustomed speed. The entire line had to be slowed down to match the speed of the tape applicator.

"This was the kind of problem that could not be solved solely by our diaper people. They had to bring together experts from throughout the company and combine their individual talents. Innovative members from engineering, product development, manufacturing, technical buying services, and purchasing were brought in. Competitive activity was lending real time urgency to the effort. Finally the decision was reached that modification of the existing system wouldn't do. An entirely new system had to be invented.

"Again people of line and staff tackled the problem together. Within three months a totally new, far faster, more reliable device was ready for installation on the Pampers line. In short, in well under a year Procter & Gamble experts, working together, invented and brought to completion a new machine, a new system, for which no need had heretofore existed."

*   *   *   *   *

In the clamorous, extremely dramatic days leading into the 1970s it was astonishing that any company could do "business as usual." Distractions were endless. The war in Vietnam sapped the strength of American youth by sucking 543,400 young men into its vortex. In the Sea of Japan trouble loomed when the North Koreans seized the U.S.S. *Pueblo* with its eighty-three man crew. Meanwhile, in the United States, opposition to the Far East conflict became ever more pronounced. One day 250,000 shouting, fist-waving demonstrators marched in Washington in protest against the war. Even the incredible exploit of Neil Armstrong, the first human being to walk on the moon, could not draw attention away from domestic disturbances. One might have thought this was one of the worst periods in the annals of America.

Yet these were some of the company's most prolific years. Increased sales generated a continuous need for new detergent plants: at Augusta, Georgia (1963), Lima, Ohio (1968), and Alexandria, Louisiana (1969). The laboratory technicians conceived one new product after another. A fabric softener, Downy, was followed by another softener, Bounce. Bounce offers an intriguing example of how the company's growing cellulosic technology could be applied elsewhere. P&G researchers had discovered how to impregnate softening ingredients into a nonwoven sheet made from cellulose. Inserted into a clothes dryer, the sheet released its ingredients, softening the clothes as they dried. Bounce quickly became the second largest-selling fabric softener after Downy.

Other products followed in an endless display of laboratory creativity: Era, in the heavy-duty laundry field; the dishwashing liquid, Dawn, which soon rivaled P&G's older Joy and Ivory Liquid. In soaps there was the outstanding success of the highly perfumed deodorant bar, Coast.

Approaching the '80s Procter & Gamble's future seemed bright in spite of all the country's troubles—except for abrupt blows that came from the United States government. Not that government challenges were anything new. The company had been forced to deal with several adverse decisions by the Federal Trade Commission. One resulted from its acquisition of the Clorox Chemical Company far back in 1957.

Just a week after Howard Morgens had become president, the Federal Trade Commission charged that the purchase of Clorox was in violation of Section 7 of the Clayton Act in that it "might tend to create a monopoly in the household bleach industry." Morgens and Deupree were shocked. They saw dangerous implications for all business in the FTC contention. With considerable indignation, Deupree described the situation at a dinner commemorating the fiftieth anniversary of the Staten Island plant. Facing some 250 civic leaders, he gave them a detailed account of what was happening, and his voice shook with anger.

"Last spring," he said, "Procter & Gamble was offered the opportunity to buy a going company, one whose product seemed to fit very well into our organization and our marketing structure. It was Clorox Chemical Company, headquartered in California . . . We studied the proposed purchase at considerable length. Near the middle of May—and bear that date in mind," Deupree urged, "we told the staff of the Federal Trade Commission in Washington about our plans. A great deal of information was given to them both by us and by the Clorox Company. On October 7, the FTC staff filed a complaint. The complaint doesn't accuse either P&G or Clorox of monopoly or restriction of competition. It admits that the two companies weren't competitors, that the bleach was a new addition to P&G's product line. The real basis of the complaint was this: 'Procter & Gamble is a successful company. It advertises widely. It makes products which are broadly accepted by housewives and other consumers. In other words, Procter & Gamble has been a successful competitor in its business fields and, as a result, has grown and prospered.'

"But, and here's the key," Deupree said, shaking a finger for emphasis, "the complaint charges that this very success, this kind of business competence by Procter & Gamble, makes it illegal for us to acquire the Clorox firm because P&G's competence, to quote the press release written by the FTC staff, 'may substantially lessen competition or tend to create a monopoly.' They claim this may, I repeat *may* happen some time in the future."

There followed a legal contest that continued for years at considerable expense to all involved. Decisions were rendered favorable first to the FTC, then, on appeal, to Procter & Gamble. The issue was re-argued and the FTC ordered divestiture. Finally the case went to the United States Supreme Court, and the high court ruled against the company. Procter & Gamble had no choice but to divest itself of Clorox.

The acquisition of Folger's coffee was under similar FTC pressure. The company had acquired Folger in 1963 but it wasn't until 1966 that problems arose. On June 22, 1966, the FTC served formal notice on P&G: It intended to seek the company's divestiture of Folger!

Cincinnati executives were stunned. Some expressed outrage. They called in lawyers, and for months there were hearings and conferences with government representatives. In the end, in an effort to avoid lengthy litigation similar to that in the Clorox case, P&G and the FTC reached a consent decree. On February 9, 1967, Morgens announced to employees and the press:

1. The company has agreed that, during the next seven years, it will not acquire—without prior consent of the Federal Trade Commission—any business in the United States concerned with household consumer products which are generally sold through the grocery store.

2. We have agreed that, within the next five years, we will sell our present Folger coffee plant in Houston, Texas, to a purchaser approved by the Federal Trade Commission. This means that we will move promptly to replace our Houston capacity and to find a purchaser for our Houston plant.

3. We also have agreed that for the next five years we will not do two things which we have not done in the past. Specifically, we have agreed not to engage in price discrimination on Folger, and we have agreed not to promote Folger coffee jointly with other Procter & Gamble products.

"We continue to believe," Morgens said, "that Procter & Gamble's acquisition of the Folger business was completely lawful. Our settlement with the Federal Trade Commission specifically states that there is no admission on our part that we have violated the law in any way . . . Procter & Gamble is in the coffee business to stay and to grow. This settlement with the Federal Trade Commission does not mean any slackening in our efforts to move ahead in this highly competitive field."

There was another field, too, that demanded development.

* * * * *

For a long time it was a curious anomaly at Procter & Gamble that few of its officers discussed the company's industrial and institutional sales. These were still regarded as by-products. But in 1975, when total P&G revenues reached $6 billion, a reporter questioned a P&G executive about this bulk business.

"It must be big," the interviewer said. "I see cakes of P&G soap in every hotel room. And I was told you sell products of all kinds in bulk to restaurants, bakeries, hospitals, hotels, schools, military installations, car-wash places, and heaven knows what else. How big is the business?"

The executive waved the question aside with a casual, "Oh, it's only 15% of our volume. We don't talk much about that."

"*Only* 15 percent?" The reporter was incredulous. "Fifteen percent of $6 billion is $900 million a year! Your industrial business alone would rank among the biggest firms in the country!" (Indeed, five years later, in 1980, the industrial business of P&G, viewed separately, could at the time be placed near the midpoint ranking of the *Fortune 500* companies.)

In describing Procter & Gamble's industrial and institutional business to security analysts, Ed Harness once said, "The company is in only two kinds of business—consumer products mainly related to cleanliness and diet, and industrial products that tend to be closely related to our consumer products. There is a common tie of technology that binds them all together. Additionally, there is a fundamental set of management concepts that pertains to both our consumer business and our industrial operations."

The industrial sector had been operated primarily to maximize profit opportunities emerging from consumer products. The soap and detergent business created the knowledge leading into the industrial chemicals field. Industrial cleaners and soaps for hotels grew directly from consumer products. Industrial foods were based on knowledge of edible fats and oils, which resulted in products for restaurants and bakeries.

One exception was the cellulose business. Though it began as an offshoot of the crushing of cottonseeds, the pulp mill at Foley had propelled the cellulose business into widespread opportunities of its own.

Still, by and large, the industrial business had relied on opportunistic product growth as contrasted with careful market studies.

247

This might have been adequate while the company was concentrating on establishing its domestic and international consumer business. But by 1970 it was clear that more would be required for industrial expansion.

The first step was to separate industrial products from the consumer divisions. They were grouped together under a newly formed Industrial Products Management Committee headed by Group Vice-President Bill Snow. Management attention to industrials was intensified. R&D effort was increased. Added funds were allocated for plant and manufacturing facilities. The company was clearly making its first real effort to seek greater growth in the industrial field. By the mid-'70s new opportunities became surprising realities.

Cellulose pulp not only supplied part of the company's own paper needs but also chemical ingredients for detergents such as carboxy methyl cellulose. At the same time it fulfilled growing demands from textile, cellophane, and photographic film manufacturers.

Industrial foods were also finding a special market because of the nation's changing eating habits. More and more meals were being eaten away from home. With some 90 million people holding jobs, many of their lunches had to be taken at or near their places of employment. In the evenings, millions of working women were too weary to cook. So P&G bulk products for restaurants found a ready reception, especially in chains like Burger King, Wendy's, Marriott, and Sheraton. The fast-food chains were selling, in 375,000 outlets nationwide, over $40 billion worth of meals. Procter & Gamble became one of their steady suppliers.

In all, the Industrial and Institutional Divisions were soon marketing some 200 products. If the public seldom heard of them, it was because they were never advertised in consumer media. Their specialized customers could be reached only through trade publications. Nevertheless the first decade of intensified attention to the industrial business confirmed that opportunities were waiting to be developed, and P&G plunged into the task.

28

THE POLLUTION PANIC

There came a time, however, that truly tried men's souls. "We were being accused," a P&G officer recalled, "of being among those who were despoiling the country because of our use of chemicals in detergents."

Synthetic detergents did indeed necessitate increased use of chemicals in cleaning products: Surfactants, builders, tri-polyphosphates, optical brighteners, tarnish inhibitors, suds depressors—all grew out of chemical technology. (Simultaneously, chemicals became major factors in agriculture as well, with the increased use of herbicides, insecticides, and fertilizers.)

It was true that some of these chemicals did not fully "degrade" or decompose as they flowed away through sewage systems to be washed into streams and lakes. Traces were detected in drinking water and wells. Some of these substances, ingested by fish, birds, and animal life, were found to have reached toxic levels. And minute amounts of some substances were discovered in the general food supply for humans.

A landmark book published in 1962—*Silent Spring* by Rachael Carson—helped spur a nationwide protest movement which affected P&G and many other major companies.

Procter & Gamble could not escape harsh attacks. The company had pioneered in the use of a cleaning agent called alkyl benzene sulfonate (ABS). Because of its effectiveness and lower cost, it was used by other manufacturers, too. But ABS had one serious drawback: Residues of the compound, not completely breaking down during sewage treatment, occasionally left white foam along the banks of some rivers and streams. That visibility served to intensify public outcries.

Congressional committees held hearings at which company scientists testified that there was no health hazard in the

249

detergent residues. What problems existed were entirely aesthetic. Much of the industry was already committed to an alternative surfactant called linear alkyl sulfate (LAS). These firms argued that the best way to accomplish change was voluntarily, not to wait for government edict—and they were changing.

Still, sudsing along waterways persisted, and whenever such foaming was viewed in streams, detergents were blamed. The detergent manufacturers never made much effort to correct this impression even when they changed their formulas.

*　*　*　*　*

Other ecological forces were also at work. The analytical tools used by scientists were being refined. Studies, while often preliminary, raised questions which were reported by the media. They created widespread public fear and demands for government controls.

As cries for action grew louder, small public interest groups became adept at using new scientific data to increase public concern through the impact of TV. Commentators put extreme pressure on government at all levels—local, state, federal—seeking to force quick solutions to complex problems. The mood of the times was that technology was out of control. Therefore, anything that controlled technology was regarded as beneficial.

Throughout this time P&G and the entire detergent industry were exploring product improvements with new applications of chemical technology. Inevitably they found themselves everywhere on a collision course with environmental fears.

And suddenly a new discovery appeared overseas. Thomas Bower, supervising P&G operations in Europe, found a laundry soaking product that used enzymes to remove stains. According to reports, these enzymes (organic derivatives which originated in living cells) could break down a remarkable range of substances that left stains in fabrics. Bower investigated. Bringing back samples, he asked P&G's research center in Brussels to study them with regard to their possible use in detergents.

Researchers found that enzymes did indeed help to eradicate some of the most stubborn laundry stains. They were particularly effective on organic materials such as blood, grass, tea, and coffee. Bower at once forwarded this information to Cincinnati, together with samples for further study. Before long, on orders from headquarters, he journeyed to Copenhagen to persuade a Danish pharmaceutical company to sharply increase production of enzymes to fill P&G's needs.

Soon, all major European manufacturers rushed to incorporate enzymes in their products as European consumers came to recognize their benefits. The U.S. followed, first with presoak products, then by incorporating enzymes directly into detergent formulas. The presoaks required the added step of soaking clothes before laundering in the machine. P&G's presoak product was Biz, which had only modest success. But by the late '60s most U.S. manufacturers were including enzymes in their detergents. Their advertising chanted claims of stain removal never before possible. Some portrayed the enzymes in TV commercials as tiny organisms (which they were not); but the graphic depiction of mysterious "things" eating at stains helped build apprehension more than sales—just when warnings from another source arose.

There were reports that a few workers in European as well as U.S. plants were developing allergic symptoms when exposed to enzyme dust during the manufacturing process. The problems proved correctable and no lasting harm resulted. Clearly a householder, pouring a spoonful of granules into a washing machine, was hardly in the same situation as a worker involved day in and day out with enzymes. Nevertheless public alarm swelled to such proportions that the Federal Trade Commission issued a press release in 1969 announcing a "non-public investigation."

John Smale, who was then vice-president for detergent products at P&G, recounted that the "non-public investigation quickly became very public, indeed." Newspapers across the United States carried headlines warning that enzymes were unsafe.

The industry did everything it could to reassure homemakers. A yearlong study by the National Academy of Sciences, the nation's leading scientific group, showed that "enzyme detergents are not hazardous when used in the home, are entirely safe for the environment, and that enzyme detergents remove many protein-based stains, and soil in general, better than those without enzymes."

It didn't help. Consumers' fears continued. Trying to correct their misunderstandings proved futile. By 1971, P&G concluded—as did many of its competitors—that enzymes should be removed from its detergents in the U.S. Ironically, the uproar did not reach Europe, where enzymes remained in wide use with no evidence of consumer hazard.

251

The company's decision to drop enzymes, even though proven safe, marked a recognition that when a product was caught in controversy it could be wiser to eliminate the material causing the argument rather than attempt to carry on the fight in public. P&G had learned long ago it could not be successful selling products people did not want, whatever their reasons.

This policy was put to the test in the controversy that arose in the late 1960s over the use of phosphate builders in detergents. Public concern centered mainly in Canada and the states of the Great Lakes basin, though it eventually spread across the U.S. There was little question that the quality of Great Lakes water was deteriorating as the discharge of improperly treated sewage increased. Runoff agricultural wastes and fertilizers also added to the problem.

An international commission made up of representatives of Canada and the U.S. was appointed to study the situation. One of their early conclusions was that lake quality was dangerously declining as a result of "accelerated eutrophication." (This is caused by over-fertilizing of algae. Its decay consumes the oxygen in the water that normally sustains fish and other marine life.) Eutrophication, a natural process, had of course gone on always, but the report said the heavy influx of fertilizers, especially phosphorus, was now speeding up the process and threatening important water sources. Worse, the report identified detergent phosphates as a major source of the trouble. The idea quickly grew that one essential step toward improved water quality would be to require the detergent manufacturers to eliminate phosphates from their formulas.

Howard Morgens described the widespread fear as "a case history of how confusion and misunderstanding can sweep across the country." Some companies tried to escape losses by quickly producing nonphosphate detergents. True, their cleaning qualities were diminished. Yet advertised as safe, they quickly won a considerable share of the market.

Procter & Gamble refused to join the stampede. Its reasons were clear. Company scientists insisted that phosphate was not a pollutant; it was a safe ingredient commonly found in food. The primary source of water pollution, they maintained, was improperly treated city sewage. Also pouring impurities of all kinds into lakes and streams were hundreds of waterfront factories.

252

Such arguments had little effect. Householders were more familiar with their laundry products than with the emissions of distant factories. Besides, while they could not control what industrial plants were doing, they could curtail their own contributions to pollution. Individuals cut back their usage and pressed their village and city councils to ban all detergents containing phosphates. To do so became almost a patriotic rite. And Procter & Gamble, refusing to change formulas in which it had faith, experienced a sharp drop in sales.

This was a time when P&G was faced with one environmental setback after another. First had been the public outcry against enzymes; now phosphates were being attacked, as was a promising new phosphate substitute, NTA. NTA (sodium nitrilotriacetate) had been developed some years earlier as an additive bringing potential improvement to detergent performance. P&G had been gaining regional experience with NTA even before the phosphate uproar began. Now as the threats to phosphates grew ever more serious, NTA seemed to offer the ideal safe avenue for reducing phosphate content without loss in cleaning performance. P&G ordered large quantities of NTA. Suppliers began a sizable expansion of factories to produce it.

But government scientists claimed they detected a possible health hazard in NTA, too. This raised new questions, not about NTA itself, but about its possible interaction with other materials in lakes and streams. Such doubts were taken to the U.S. Surgeon General who reviewed the data, then called in the three major detergent manufacturers. He had no legal jurisdiction in the matter, he said, but nevertheless he asked, in December, 1970, that the three major manufacturers "voluntarily" cease using NTA.

They had no choice. The publicity that had been stirred up effectively ruled out NTA's public acceptance. Next day, Howard Morgens personally approved the public statement outlining the company's position. It pungently expressed his feelings as well as those of the P&G research staff:

"The Surgeon General's statement does not claim any lack of safety for NTA itself," he wrote. The release went on:

> It does claim that when NTA is combined with mercury pollution or cadmium pollution already in the water it might lead to a third substance that would be harmful. It bases this claim on a study involving an extremely high concentration

253

of these metals and NTA—a concentration that does not exist in nature and that has no relevance in our opinion to what could happen in the natural environment.

As for the quantities of NTA in certain of our products, we are absolutely confident of their safety. Our research on NTA started in 1961. We believe there has been more research supporting the safety of NTA than there has been supporting the safety of most, if not all, of the materials going into the nation's food products.

The Surgeon General does not suggest there is cause for concern about the limited quantities of NTA now in use. However, once the Surgeon General has made the statement he has, public confidence in products containing NTA is bound to be adversely affected. Regardless of the facts, the future usefulness of this material has been largely destroyed. Therefore, we have already moved to phase out the use of NTA as rapidly as possible.

This is too bad. NTA offered us and the world our best hope for a no-phosphate detergent. At no time did this entail anything approaching a complete substitution of NTA for phosphates. However, NTA was one of the building blocks for an effective phosphate-free product that was both safe for humans and the environment. We must now start all over again in our research efforts to develop phosphate-free detergents.

It was a bitter setback. Though NTA was permitted for use in Canada with never any evidence of a human health problem, it continued to be questioned throughout the United States. P&G then launched a massive search for other replacements for phosphates, a search that for several years diverted R&D energy from other developmental work. (In 1980 the U.S. Environmental Protection Agency finally concluded, a full ten years later, that NTA should not be prohibited from use as a detergent builder. But there were still those who raised questions clouding the future for this new material.)

At the height of the phosphate controversy, worried P&G stockholders asked questions. What was wrong with the company? Why was it not emulating other firms by producing its own nonphosphate products? Why was it sacrificing markets and money, allowing others to lure away former P&G customers?

Howard J. Morgens

In the face of such pressures, Procter & Gamble had to reply with a restatement of two pertinent facts: First, nonphosphate detergents did not clean as efficiently as products like Tide. Test after test confirmed this. Second, nonphosphate detergents, at that time relying on highly alkaline and corrosive ingredients, could be hazardous. A number of physicians had reported their harmful effects on children who had somehow had their eyes and mouths exposed to the cleansers.

Nevertheless there were P&G shareholders who still could not understand why the company stubbornly pursued a course that led to a loss of sales. There were so many questions that Procter & Gamble's annual report for 1971 published an explanation by Howard Morgens.

"The introduction of many nonphosphate detergents," he acknowledged, "clearly took some of the business that might otherwise have been ours. Because of this, Procter & Gamble found itself in a most unusual position. We know how to make nonphosphate detergents. We could have introduced one or more at any time. Why, then, didn't we follow this policy?

"It was certainly not because we are indifferent to ecological matters. Both as a company and as individual citizens we yield to no one in our concern for the environment." [He could have

255

reminded stockholders that P&G was spending millions a year seeking ways to prevent its own plants from discharging pollutants.]

"We did not introduce nonphosphate detergents because we felt strongly that it would be irresponsible for us to do so. The present nonphosphate detergents, as we view them, fall into two general classes. There are those that just won't get dirty clothes clean, and we feel housewives will quickly recognize their ineffectiveness. Then there are those that are dangerous to use in the home."

For a company that had never deliberately tried to market a poor product in almost a hundred and forty years, its present attitude was understandable. P&G had no intention of undermining its principles by selling what the founders would indignantly have called "shoddy goods."

While the furor over phosphates continued, company scientists went on experimenting with any number of possible substitutes. They spent over $130 million on the quest. Yet fear about phosphates continued to grow, often approaching panic. The Federal Trade Commission threatened to require that detergents be labeled as pollutants. It conducted extensive, highly-publicized hearings in Washington at which Howard Morgens personally testified to the safety of phosphates and the lack of suitable alternatives.

It did little good. Several cities passed laws banning detergents with phosphates. These included Chicago, even though its sewage flowed not to Lake Michigan, but to the Mississippi River. Others like Miami and Buffalo followed, and then the state of Indiana. The company hadn't yet found satisfactory substitute formulas. Morgens reluctantly concluded they should withdraw their detergents from sale in these areas until they developed efficient alternatives.

Five other states and local governments soon joined the move to prohibit phosphates in detergents. By then P&G researchers had indeed found alternatives. While none proved to be fully effective, they were as safe for home use as phosphates themselves, and they cleaned as well or better than competitive products. P&G reluctantly began using these formulas in areas where phosphates had been banned. The company was frank about the inferior quality of the substitutes; and made repeated efforts to get states to rescind their bans.

In areas which had banned phosphates, other data showed that consumers were using more cleaning aids at added costs to compensate for the decreased performance of the nonphosphate detergents. And mineral deposits, once effectively controlled, were building up on the insides of washing machines and in the fibers of clothing. One manufacturer reported a 15% jump in repair calls in nonphosphate areas. As one state considered banning phosphate detergents, it was estimated that the cost of removing detergent phosphorus at the sewage plant level would be no more than $2.50 per year per household—far less than the estimated costs of a detergent phosphate ban ($60), clothes wearing out, and increased washing machine repairs, which would not deal with the full problem.

Eventually, however, as proper sewage treatment was expanded over the years, the quality of Great Lakes water began to improve. Fears about phosphates began to subside, though many states retained their prohibitions.

Finally, in 1979, the joint Canada-U.S. commission published the results of years of analytical work. These contradicted many of its earlier conclusions. The gist of the report was that 53% of all phosphorus entering the Great Lakes came from groundwater runoff. Sewage accounted for 24% and was labeled "a major contributor of the pollution now affecting the Great Lakes." Airborne dust brought 19%. There were other minor sources, but detergents accounted for no more than 2% of the phosphates in the lakes.

* * * * *

Throughout this time laundry habits continued to change. Energy shortages resulted in cooler water for washing laundry. New textiles required special care. Product improvements continued: Bold-3, with a built-in fabric softener; Cheer, with a wrinkle-relaxing ingredient; Downy fabric softener, with a longer lasting fresh scent.

Commenting on the way P&G had clung to its principles during the phosphate crisis, Ed Harness said: "Hardly a day passes when each of us doesn't have the occasion to make a decision, large or small, involving a choice between the expedient and the principled. Making the hard decision, the decision based on principle, usually seems to involve a short-term sacrifice on the part of the company. Our history clearly demonstrates that we've gotten where we are through a consistency in making our

257

decisions on a matter of principle. In difficult times the company must continue operating on the principle of what it believes is right rather than what will make everyone happy next week." The bitter and costly phosphate experience has been called a test of company character. For many it was more than that. It was a revelation of company character.

29

MATTERS OF PRINCIPLE

In reviewing the phosphate matter some years later, Howard Morgens was asked how he and his associates were able to reach a conclusion on the right posture for P&G to take.

"It wasn't that complicated," he said, "once we had isolated the principles involved. There were really only two in this case. The first is that Procter & Gamble obeys the law. The second is that we sell products that are safe for use under normal usage conditions." Following these principles left P&G no choice during those crucial months but to comply with the law and withdraw its products from sale until they were recognized as safe.

But was it really so simple for a company to permit principles to guide its operations through all kinds of situations? If principles shape the character of a company, how do they develop?

The matter of "character" for Procter & Gamble was, fortunately, not something that had to be construed hastily to fit the situation of the moment. The principles by which Procter & Gamble operated had been of major importance since the beginning of the Procter and Gamble partnership in 1837. Matters of ethics and attitudes toward employees, toward suppliers, and toward customers had in truth been of concern to the company's leaders for generations. Scarcely a year had passed when character was not the subject of a major talk by William Cooper Procter. Deupree, McElroy, and Morgens had followed the same ritual.

Many attempts had been made through the years to define P&G's character. All recognized that it was difficult for those who were currently part of the organization to appraise it objectively. However, unless they defined their goal, they knew it would be that much more difficult to reach it.

259

At a time of momentous change, there came an opportunity for P&G executives to reflect on the nature of their company. Howard Morgens began preparing for his eventual retirement and for the orderly transfer of authority to his successor Edward Harness. The process would take several years, in itself indicative of P&G's practice of planning for the long-term.

The elections of 1971 gave Neil McElroy the titular position of chairman of the executive committee, while Howard Morgens became chairman of the board. Morgens remained in charge as chief executive officer, while Ed Harness became president with responsibility for all U.S. operations.

In his first address as president to P&G's assembled management organization, Harness spoke emphatically of P&G's character. "We are built," he said, "on sound principles and practices and are not dominated by a group of individuals." Recalling a theme laid down by his predecessors, he said, "Though our greatest asset is our people, it is the consistency of principle and policy which gives us direction."

As Harness reviewed this subject he too recognized it was an impossiblity to define the P&G character completely. Many in the past had included such descriptions as "responsible," "aggressive," "noncompromising," "dedicated to constant improvements," "creative." Others had emphasized the company's dedication to long-term growth.

"Thoroughness," too, was often repeated, and now it was something Harness chose to stress. "Many outsiders say thoroughness and self-discipline are our most distinguishing features," he said. "Sophisticated competition for millions of buying decisions makes vital finding of the little extra to amplify the small difference and the avoidance of small mistakes."

"The art of finding the principle" was another quality he mentioned. "Making the hard decision, consistent with principle, usually involves two things—hard thinking by a disciplined mind and short-term sacrifice on the part of the company."

Harness also emphasized management by penetration as another important P&G trait. "At every level we expect our managers to penetrate the operations of those reporting to them. One way we can give young people a sense of responsibility so early is for their managers at all times to be knowledgeable of our principles and to stress them for the young people reporting to them."

* * * * *

Reliance on age-old ethical tenets was important indeed whenever P&G had to cope with social pressures. These pressures reflected changes in the country's own attitude toward its traditional ways and institutions. As examples:

- The civil rights movement, after violent urban riots in the '60s, brought new attitudes and laws regarding the hiring of racial minorities.

- The women's movement intensified demands for equal treatment of women in hiring and promotion.

- The Vietnam War and later the Watergate scandal generated suspicions of government itself, with questions rising about the undue influence of large U.S. corporations.

- Environmental concerns constantly assumed new urgency affecting every P&G plant's relation to its community.

- Rising consumer aggressiveness was directed at the quality and safety of products.

Procter & Gamble weathered these challenges as well or better than most major corporations. For years the company had prided itself on being able to cope with changes. It had proven, during the detergent revolution for example, that it could improve its competitive position even in times of stress. These factors and more confronted Harness when he became head of the company.

He also faced this challenge: During Morgens' administration of seventeen years, P&G had experienced greater growth than it had known in any previous period of its history. Business analysts regarded it as phenomenal—especially since *Fortune* magazine consistently ranked P&G among the twenty-five leading American industrial corporations.

In those seventeen Morgens years the company's total sales had increased from $1.1 billion to $4.9 billion, almost five times what it had been in 1957. Net earnings of common stock went from 86¢ to $3.85. (Twice, in 1961 and 1970, there were two-for-one stock splits.) Net assets of the company more than quadrupled from $462 million to almost $2 billion.

Yet during these seventeen years there had been vast capital expenditures for new plants, products, and research and development facilities in the United States and overseas. Nevertheless, throughout these years of high expenditures net earnings as a

261

percentage of sales had never varied by more than 1%, the average being 6.8%.

Such a record explains the statement Harness made at the time he assumed the duties of chairman and chief executive officer in 1974. "The period of Howard Morgens' stewardship," he said, "is best characterized as the era in which Procter & Gamble became, in truth, a world corporation rather than a U.S. corporation, and a diversified corporation rather than a soap company with some adjuncts."

It was the year 1974 in which John Smale became P&G president; Brad Butler, vice-chairman; and William Gurganus, president of P&G International. The new top management team found itself in the midst of the most severe U.S. recession since World War II. James W. Nethercott, senior financial vice-president, underscored the problems at that time of inflation, price controls, energy crisis, and high interest rates. "Nineteen-seventy-four was a year," he said, "that tested business organizations everywhere, including ours."

Nevertheless, management reported capital expenditures of $246 million, the highest to that point in company history. Obviously, growth for the future remained its paramount concern.

Unquestionably, as P&G executives pointed out to inquiring reporters, this spectacular record resulted from the efforts of company-trained people. It was the best possible refutation of those who criticized P&G's policy of making promotions from the ranks of its own personnel, of heavy reliance on its own people.

Brad Butler, vice-chairman of the board, recalled his first company meeting at which Richard Deupree spoke. "If you leave us our money," Deupree had said, "our buildings, and our brands, but take away our people, the company will fail. But if you take away our money, our buildings, and our brands, but leave us all our people, we can rebuild the whole thing in a decade."

With this thought in mind, Butler leaned back from his desk and described a special characteristic of P&G that had been nourished for 140 years. That was, he said, "the sense of pride and proprietorship in the company that is shared by the tens of thousands of people who develop, and produce, and sell, and ship our products, and who handle the countless administrative details that keep this business running.

(Above) P&G managers confer on ways of promoting better relationships among employees of diverse backgrounds. Edward G. Harness (left) stepped down as Chief Executive Officer in 1981 to become Chairman of the Executive Committee of the Board of Directors. He was succeeded as CEO by John G. Smale. Owen B. Butler became Chairman of the Board.

"We talk proudly," he continued, "about our executives spending their entire business lives with the company, but in many of our nonmanagement families the relationship with the company also goes on from generation to generation. It is those people and the quality of their relationship with the company which is perhaps our greatest single asset."

The formula for developing and nurturing such an asset was expressed in the company's 1976 annual report:

- Find and hire good people—men and women of high character.
- Treat each employee as an individual who has individual talents and life goals.

263

- Provide for each employee a working environment which encourages, recognizes, and rewards individual achievement.

It was in essence a distillation of what P&G had been practicing from the time William Cooper Procter convinced the founding families that the interests of the company and the interests of its employees are inseparable.

* * * * *

One of the many new demands being made on corporations was to exhibit a greater sense of social responsibility. Corporate leaders were being asked to help solve many of society's ills, including the creation of more jobs, hiring and promoting more members of minorities and women, giving more money to charities, solving housing problems and school problems. All these and more were being presented to business for solution. Was society asking too much of industry? Facing some two hundred of his associates, P&G's chairman assessed the situation.

"In this decade of the '70s," Harness said, "both in the United States and abroad, the role of the public corporation has been so discussed, debated, and belabored that it isn't easy for anyone, including people like ourselves who manage businesses, to keep his mind focused on the jobs which our shareholders are paying us to do."

After reviewing the historical basis for the laws that make a corporation possible, Harness said, "The state provides a corporation with the opportunity to earn a profit if it meets society's needs. However, in recent times critics of our business structure seem to be losing sight of the primary purposes of the corporation. Some even want to blame the corporation for all of society's ills."

Calling the role of corporations "one of the most phenomenal success stories in the evolution of the free world," he conceded that it was the duty of corporations to "raise the expectations of mankind in general and of government, educators, and thought-leaders in particular. This is understandable," he said, "considering some of the roles that corporations have come to fill in the non-communist world. For example, corporations in the United States pay nearly 40% of all the taxes collected at the federal, state, and local levels. Corporations in this country furnish over half of all the jobs, generate about two-thirds of the gross national product, and a similar share of the payroll dollars. In the last sixty

264

years, corporations of the Western democracies have built the hardware to win two world wars and to put men on the moon."

And what of those critics who argued that corporations should put citizenship responsibilities ahead of their profit-making responsibilities? "I am not aware," Harness replied, "of any bankrupt corporations which are making important social contributions.

"Procter & Gamble has succeeded throughout the 140 years since its founding for many reasons. Key among these is the fact that company management has consistently kept profit and growth objectives as first priorities while recognizing that enlightened self-interest requires the company to fill any reasonable expectations placed upon it.

"Somehow we have managed to keep our priorities straight and yet have the sense of civic responsibility to achieve many important secondary objectives. Somehow our predecessors were wise enough to know that profitability and growth go hand in hand with fair treatment of employees, of customers, of consumers, and of the communities in which we operate." He was in a sense describing the corporate conscience of America.

* * * * *

One of these efforts of P&G to serve community and society in general is the Procter & Gamble Fund. Established in 1952, the fund has been distributing well over $5 million annually in the U.S., primarily to higher education and to health, welfare, and cultural agencies.

In the field of higher education, the company was a business pioneer. Its program started as scholarship aid for outstanding students at private universities and colleges. Later it was altered to give direct grants to some seventy private institutions of learning, generally to those providing the largest number of graduates to P&G. Though the number of graduates from nonprivate schools also became sizable, the fund continued to focus most of its attention on helping preserve private education. It relied on company taxes to aid tax-supported universities.

A separate grant program, one of the few in the U.S., was developed for the leading women's colleges. Special awards were also made to the many state associations formed to help private universities. And the company became a major supporter of the United Negro College Fund, with several senior executives taking an active part in annual fund raising efforts. The shortage of

John G. Smale   Owen B. Butler

minority and women engineers—a universal phenome-
non—resulted in another program, one which offered scholar-
ships to these groups to attend engineering colleges.

Apart from such educational grants, by the late 1970s over 40%
of fund gifts were going to community activities in cities where
the company had large numbers of employees. A notable example was a gift to the city of Cincinnati in bicentennial 1976 for the
planting and perpetual maintenance of Yeatman's Cove Park on
the city's riverfront. Though P&G's financial contributions to
Cincinnati social institutions, hospitals, and so on had been highly generous for decades, it had seldom sought publicity for these
efforts. But the 200th anniversary of the country clearly was
something special, justifying an unusual step. John Smale had
championed this project and Harness and others gladly offered
support.

The $1 million gift was announced by Smale in a televised
news conference. "When Procter & Gamble was founded in
Cincinnati back in 1837," Smale said, "the riverfront played a key
role in the development of the city and of our company. The
beautification of this area will preserve the riverfront's historic
importance to the community and serve Greater Cincinnati's
long-term interests by strengthening the downtown area."

Harness later described the company's rationale for the gift this way: "The future earnings of this company rest first and foremost on our ability to attract to Cincinnati bright, capable, dedicated, and concerned people as our employees. If nearly one-quarter of those people are expected to spend their careers in Cincinnati, then it serves the interests of the stockholders for us to support soundly-conceived efforts to maintain and enhance this community as a good place to live and raise families."

*   *   *   *   *

"Affirmative action" was of course a phrase born to accentuate the need of racial minorities for expanded opportunities for employment and advancement. It was eventually established as an American principle by the President's Executive Order of 1965.

As with most companies, Procter & Gamble had long sought to recruit the most capable people available. Racial unrest, beginning in the early '60s, fixed the nation's attention not only on discrimination in voting, seating in public places, education, and housing, but on bias in job opportunities as well.

P&G managers recognized a need for change and progress. They set out to bring a larger number of racial minorities into the company. As part of a national voluntary effort called Plans for Progress, P&G took steps to enlist minority employees in production, in sales, in a wide variety of jobs.

It was not easy. There was a cynical lack of belief in the black community that jobs were indeed available, a view influenced by the fact that no members of minorities had previously held the jobs in question. One senior P&G sales executive told of extensive recruiting efforts with the Urban League and other agencies. The credibility problem business had among blacks created difficulties in finding recruits. College education was a requirement for many jobs, and at that time minorities enrolled in colleges generally had greater interest in nonbusiness careers in education or government.

Then in 1968, American companies with the cooperation of the U.S. Labor Department organized the National Alliance for Business, an outgrowth of Plans for Progress. It established specific job goals. It set out with heavy publicity and the cooperation of many social agencies to fill jobs in private industry. Howard Morgens accepted the NAB chairmanship for the Metro-Cincinnati area. He committed Procter & Gamble's top management to this effort

267

and provided personal leadership to the Cincinnati business community. Though the initial efforts of the NAB resulted in meeting its national goals (Morgens exceeded by nearly three times the jobs goal for Cincinnati), all concerned learned that the problems involved would require years to solve.

As minority communities came to realize that added education could result in better job opportunities, college enrollment of minorities increased. So did enrollment in high schools and vocational schools. The 1965 executive order required that hiring goals be established for minorities at least proportional to their availability for the work force. Later, similar requirements were applied to women. By the late '70s P&G made major strides in the employment of minorities. Each year reports on hiring and advancement were published and made available to employees.

In 1971 Harness reiterated his feelings on this matter: "I have no idea what the federal government is going to do over the next few years toward improving the role of minorities in America, but I am perfectly clear on what the company is going to do.

"It will remain the policy of Procter & Gamble to seek out and employ members of racial or ethnic minorities. We will educate our incumbent managers on the aims and the proper execution of this program. We will maintain working conditions where minority employees will find peace, dignity, challenge, and equal opportunity for advancement. We will advance, on a merit basis, members of minority groups. Black will work for white and white will work for black.

"Without getting into any questions of ideology, there is a simply overpowering reason for our course of action. The brains and the hands of minority groups in America are a vital national resource, a vital raw material. We cannot and will not attempt to move ahead in American business without utilizing this valuable asset.

"Be assured that we expect in the years ahead, in all U.S. departments of the company, to have effective implementation of this program to the point where it will no longer be a subject worthy of anyone's concern."

* * * * *

There was another problem. Among the most shattering revelations growing out of the Watergate incident were reports of large contributions to the presidential campaign of 1972, some made illegally with corporate funds. The news was shocking. The media had a field day. Further investigations led to payoffs made by U.S. firms to foreign governments or agents in an effort to get contracts abroad. Some U.S. businessmen were indicted, a few convicted. Others were forced to resign as top officials in their companies. How did P&G fare with its far-flung foreign operations?

Harness felt it important to tell a meeting of company managers: "There is no question that some corporations have been guilty of such practices, and I make no excuse for them. I suspect that the corporations involved are a relatively small minority of U.S. companies.

"Regardless of what I suspect about others, ladies and gentlemen, I want to report to you on the one company about which I have full knowledge, and that is our company. I want to assure you simply and flatly that this company has made no illegal political contributions to anyone in this or any other country, that this company makes no unethical political contributions anywhere in the world, that this company pays no bribes to anyone anywhere in the world, and that this company does not deal under the table with customers or suppliers here or abroad. That is the way this company has operated; that is the way we will continue operating."

What more needed to be said? Managers realized that new employees required forceful reminders of how they were expected to conduct themselves within P&G policies and principles. For this purpose, practices which had existed for many years were digested into brief statements in a booklet which was required company reading. A letter from Harness accompanied the booklet. It said in part, "The principal foundation on which Procter & Gamble has been built is the character of the people in the organization. From its people, the company itself has developed a strong tradition of character. Honesty, integrity, fairness, and a respect and concern for others have been characteristics of P&G people and company activities ever since our founding in 1837. While Procter & Gamble is oriented to progress and growth, it is vital that employees understand that the company is concerned not only with results but with how results are obtained. We do care. And we will never tolerate efforts or activities to achieve results through illegal or unfair dealings anywhere in the world."

*   *   *   *   *

269

It was from this sense of social responsibility that P&G management developed a conviction that its business activities were the primary contribution it could make to society.

It was true that a major portion of capital expenditures was intended to expand production capacity. How else could the constant flow of new products be insured? But it was also true that great store was placed on the importance of cost reductions. In a time when the United States was showing a slowdown in productivity, what could be more vital than reducing costs?

As many managers saw it, steps to improve productivity were the highest form of "corporate responsibility." The "superior total value" the company sought for consumers was not only superior quality and innovation for its products but lowest possible costs as well. One without the other clearly was not satisfactory.

Certainly employees gained a great deal from this constant emphasis on a lean operation. Cost reductions largely through capital investment, permitted maintenance of good working conditions, better benefits and retirements, and highly competitive wage rates. In its training programs the company had worked closely with employees for years on adopting changes to fit the needs created by new equipment and machinery.

It was, in fact, the close cooperation between management and employees that explains operations today throughout P&G.

James M. Ewell had spoken of this years earlier, emphasizing "the need to initiate changes before being forced into change." Ewell, who headed staff manufacturing and employee relations, recognized that "one of the major qualities men and women want in their jobs is to know their ideas are welcomed." Possibly this explains the great attention given to training and education that P&G provides for its employees. Countless special seminars and classes are conducted each year on company time. In addition, over 700 young men and women each year work on their own time toward advanced college credits with P&G paying the tuition.

Thus efforts to reduce costs and improve efficiencies are constantly attacked. Dating back to the depression days of the 1930s, these efforts provide savings ranging from several hundred dollars to many millions. In nearly every case the key question is: Will an added investment pay for itself, or "pay out" in a reasonable length of time? As many as 400 projects can be underway at any given time throughout the company.

"One of the best examples of how all this works," it was pointed out, "can be seen in our ten-story high detergent towers, where wet detergent paste is spray dried into granules. The first P&G tower was built in 1946, and by the late '70s thirteen towers were in operation in the U.S. Without the engineering improvements over the thirty years, a total of 108 towers would be needed to do the job of the thirteen we actually have."

There are countless other examples. Paper machines are running at incredible speeds; Cascade production was increased 60% by P&G design development; millions are being saved in plant construction throughout the world by the use of detailed models to replace blueprints. Moreover P&G's rapid strides in turning out its products more efficiently were taken while achieving impressive increases in employee safety. There was personal commitment throughout the company which verged on a crusade for safety.

True, P&G's record had once been dismal. In 1930 the company's injury frequency rate was 36.25 per million man-hours, compared to an all-industry average of 18.47. That same year, the company appointed the first of its plant safety engineers, and the program began to instill safety awareness in all employees. By 1952, the Chicago plant became the first in P&G to hold a world safety record in the soap and glycerin industry. By 1955, P&G's rate hit an all-time low of 1.01. Other plants followed with world safety records in their respective industries: Buckeye Cellulose, Long Beach, Ivorydale, Kansas City, Sacramento, Mehoopany, and Jackson. Internationally, the Philippines manufacturing plant became a shining example. By 1971, when the Occupational Safety and Health Act (OSHA) was passed, the national all-industry frequency rate stood at 8.47 per million man-hours worked. P&G's rate was 1.4.

There were also areas where P&G achieved impressive results in increased productivity. As energy costs rose in the 1970s, the company investment in energy savings began to pay. Waste products from coffee processing provided fuel savings of $200,000 yearly; wood chips at Foley achieved dramatic savings as well. By 1980 Procter & Gamble's U.S. energy usage per unit produced had declined 28%, well above the 1980 goal of 16% set by the Department of Energy for the ten highest energy-consuming industries in the country. The example was often cited that if comparable energy reductions were made throughout society, significant reductions in imported oil could be achieved. Creative use of capital was proving to be as innovative in evergy saving as in product development and marketing.

*   *   *   *   *

When Ed Harness had outlined his thinking on P&G's character, he had chosen to highlight one point as the "art of finding the principle." Perhaps that was what he had in mind in 1977 when he rose to review the company's response to social demands of the past ten years.

One of the main roles assigned to manufacturers, he said, is the creation of jobs. Any contributions to society that a business can make first require earning a profit, and that usually generates jobs.

What was the impact of a single new product in creating jobs? The figures were hard to project, but a financial analyst at P&G agreed to try. He based his estimate on one of P&G's most successful brands, Pampers.

"At the volume Pampers are doing, I estimate perhaps 2,400 jobs are required to manufacture Pampers," he said. "To that we must add the R&D people involved in maintaining quality and in making further improvements; the engineers who design and improve equipment; sales representatives, advertising, purchasing, traffic, and financial people. It looks to me like between 2,850 and 2,900 P&G employees directly owe their jobs to Pampers. And that ignores sales in foreign countries. Outside P&G, I estimate an added 31,000 jobs are needed by various suppliers, equipment manufacturers, truckers, and retail outlets to support Pampers. That is a total of 34,000 jobs on Pampers alone."

This amazing figure, he reported, did not include all the other disposable diapers being sold, largely the result of the market Pampers helped to create.

30

P&G'S
PARTNER, THE CONSUMER

"In looking over the long list of people who have made Procter & Gamble what it is today," a retired vice-president was asked, "whom would you pick as the most influential?" The answer came without hesitation: "The consumer."

Obviously it was not the expected reply. Neither was it flippant or evasive; without favorable consumer response in the form of purchases any company must collapse. In the case of Procter & Gamble, practically every product it has marketed has been founded on what the company defines as consumerism: a response, after comprehensive market research, to what consumers need and want.

There were many people, however, who had a different concept of consumerism. To them it meant government regulation of what was offered to the consumer. Naturally, companies like P&G objected to constraints. Procter & Gamble's executives recognized an increasing conflict between "government regulation on the one hand and freedom of initiative on the other." Proposals for a new federal consumer protection agency represented the very antithesis of freedom of initiative. Yet such proposals were being made.

One of those who felt most strongly about all this was Vice-Chairman Brad Butler. At a national meeting of women's clubs he emphasized the fact that many nations operate from the premise that there is an elite class who should make decisions for others. "In the American democratic system," he said, "the very concept of an agency for consumer advocacy is wrong because it is based on a philosophy that there is one national consumer interest. In fact, there are countless consumer interests based on each of our personal needs and wants."

273

As a matter of record, there were thirty-nine agencies and 400 bureaus running hundreds of consumer-oriented programs in the United States, many with overlapping jurisdictions. Arguments against a new government bureau rose from countless sources. A determined effort, extending over several years, finally led in 1977 to a decisive vote in the House of Representatives. It turned back the idea of a new consumer agency. For the time being at least, the rejection seemed to mark an end to such reforms. Government had by no means stopped growing, but a sense of balance seemed to be emerging.

As Butler put it: "Consumerism is an integral and fundamental characteristic of our company. In seeking to learn what consumers want, and what quality or products they are entitled to receive, I believe we have become the world's first and leading consumer advocate. That's our stock in trade. It is only by becoming a consumer advocate that we have come to be what we are now."

To underscore this point, company people in market research often cite their own extensive studies—over 1.5 million interviews annually by phone and mail. "P&G alone," one executive said, "doing less than 1% of the disposable consumer goods business in the U.S., did the equivalent of nearly 1,000 Gallup polls in a single year."

Harness summed it up in a different way. "The job of homemaker must be one of the most challenging and most creative to be found anywhere. The homemaker is a business manager, an efficiency expert, a budget control specialist, a child psychologist, a human relations expert, a buyer, a cook, and on and on. These consumers are continually testing our products against their own standards and their own needs, and are continually looking for something better. At relatively low cost they can sample other products to see whether they perform better. In this way our products are subjected to continuous tests week in and week out in that toughest of all testing laboratories, the American home."

One example of Procter & Gamble's sensitivity to consumer views has been the handling of communications. Some letters brought complaints from which the company gained insights for improvements; a larger number were requests for information about a product or how to use it. Routine questions about cake baking, removing stains from dresses, giving home permanents, or the proper brewing of coffee were quickly answered. For this the telephone was used more and more. By the late '70s P&G had become one of the first companies to include a toll-free telephone number on its packages. Consumers could simply pick up their telephone and ask their questions directly of a member of the company's consumer services group. (By the early '80s every P&G package listed a toll-free number, and a large staff of men and women were giving prompt responses to calls. Others were answering thousands of letters every month.)

Another consumer innovation occurred when several states passed laws requiring consumer education in their schools. The company realized that many students as well as their teachers were not aware of the positive steps taken by P&G and other companies to meet consumer needs.

Why shouldn't there be a better channel of information to the schools? After extensive consultation with educators in many states, the company's educational services group—as part of its consumerism program—offered teaching aids free to teachers. Soon some 50,000 educators were using P&G teaching guides and P&G films. One reason for the broad acceptance of the program was its noncommercial, objective tone. Emphasis lay on how new products are tested, on the importance of consumer reaction, and on the role of advertising behind a brand.

Despite all efforts on the part of American industry to foster public understanding, demands for more stringent government controls stubbornly continued. Products previously thought to be safe came into question as new analytical equipment revealed fresh data. P&G deodorants, for example, became embroiled in an argument about one of their active ingredients, zirconium. This had safely been used for years. Now it was being attacked because of theoretical long-term health effects. As had happened with enzymes, such warnings received wide publicity. The company was forced to stop using zirconium in its aerosol sprays even though no solid evidence of a hazard existed.

All aerosol sprays were soon subjected to challenges. Studies suggested a possible effect on the ozone layer by chlorofluoro-carbon propellants high in the atmosphere. Because of this the entire industry was forced to switch to an alternate propellant.

Harry Tecklenburg, director of the company's R&D efforts, described the impact of the increase of regulations on the company's overall research effort. "Including both direct and indirect costs," he said, "at least 25% of our R&D expenditures are now involved with satisfying one type or another of government regulation." He added that one in every eight members of the R&D staff was involved in dealing with regulatory agencies. "What this really has forced us to do," he said, "is to put much greater emphasis on seeking breakthrough projects rather than the surer but less dramatic improvements of older products."

* * * * *

Like Neil McElroy before them, Howard Morgens and Ed Harness were staunch defenders of widespread advertising. In the late '70s the media were reporting that Procter & Gamble was spending millions annually on advertising—almost three-quarters of the entire sum going to television. The *New York Times* reported that: "The truly enormous extent to which Procter & Gamble is committed to television is underlined by the fact that it leads all U.S. companies in television expenditures." The *Times* listed such large advertisers as General Foods, General Motors, Bristol-Myers, Ford Motor Company, Philip Morris, General Mills, and Johnson & Johnson all well below P&G. The *Times* continued:

> *A keystone of the P&G television effort has been its company-produced soap operas—"Search For Tomorrow," "Guiding Light," "As The World Turns," on CBS; "Another World" on NBC; and "Edge of Night" on ABC.*

> *The key to P&G sponsorship is upbeat, whether it is the froth of the Miss Universe contest or the People's Choice Awards, or more serious dramatic efforts like Katharine Hepburn's "The Corn is Green," or "Wilma," the inspiring story of Olympic gold medal winner Wilma Rudolph's triumph over crippling childhood illness.*

> *In regular [evening] entertainment P&G sponsors shows such as NBC's "Little House on the Prairie" and CBS's "The Waltons."*

> *"We look for quality, family-oriented programs with broad appeal," a P&G spokesman said. "We have guidelines that our people and our advertising agencies use. We look for programs in good taste that will appeal to the people who buy and use our products—which is just about everybody. We avoid anything with gratuitous violence, sex, or profanity."*

276

Officers of Procter & Gamble are sometimes challenged to explain why the company spends such large sums on advertising. The answers reveal one of the least understood of P&G operations.

"Since we run our business by brand," executives say, "we make advertising appropriations by brand, not by division and not for the company in total. The overall corporate figure is largely meaningless to those who operate the business. It is simply the total for our individual brands. On most of our brands we estimate competitors' spending with great care, with the objective of spending less per unit than the closest competitor."

There were other pragmatic answers as well to questions about advertising expenditures. One is that there is nothing profligate about television advertising which reaches individual consumers by the tens of millions every day, each contact costing a fraction of one cent. Any appraisal of the company's history shows that as advertising budgets have been increased, sales and earnings have risen. That has been true ever since Harley Procter launched his first major advertising campaign with $11,000. And if television has become the principal recipient of the company's advertising expenditures, it is because television, according to all surveys, has yielded the highest results in sales.

One thing young P&G brand managers learn early in their careers is that it is seldom the amount spent to advertise a brand that spells success. If it were that simple, P&G or one of its competitors could simply increase advertising expenditures and be assured of an immediate upswing in sales. It is the idea and the product quality behind the advertising that make the difference.

As television grew, all advertisers learned what they had previously learned from radio and magazines: Great ingenuity is required to find the exact messages which will convince a skeptical consumer to try and then continue to use a product. P&G's brand people rely heavily on their advertising agencies for the creativity needed to achieve this. The close relationship between the company and its agencies, often enduring decade after decade, has become legendary in a business where agencies and clients separate all too frequently. One agency executive put it this way: "It's a full partnership. Once they give us a brand, they expect us to know and care as much about it as they do. And then they damn well make sure we do."

277

It works. Compton Advertising has been associated with P&G since 1922; Dancer Fitzgerald Sample since 1933; Benton & Bowles since 1941; Young & Rubicam since 1949; and Leo Burnett Company since 1951. These set the records for longevity. But others would follow: Grey; Tatham-Laird & Kudner; Cunningham & Walsh; Doyle Dane Bernbach; and Wells, Rich, Greene.

One agency veteran who had served on a number of P&G brands over the years was asked, "What would you say distinguishes P&G from other advertisers?"

"There are several things, but I'll list three," he said. "First, they never forget the consumer is making the buying decision; they are fanatics on this and they'll research consumers' reactions on virtually anything. Second, they know the importance of a consistent brand personality. They'll stay with the same advertising strategy for years and rarely allow themselves to be distracted. And third, they insist that the product be the star of the advertising."

He cited the long-term dedication of Ivory to "mildness," of Tide to "superior cleaning," of Crisco to "more digestible food." And he recounted the years Mr. Whipple had squeezed Charmin toilet tissue to dramatize its superior softness.

"Some people think P&G buys its way into the market with big ad and promotion budgets or has some other secret for success," said Leonard S. Matthews, president of the American Association of Advertising Agencies and himself a former executive on P&G advertising accounts. "I don't think there's any secret to it. The company simply is tuned in to what consumers want and it does a good job of making products that satisfy those wants."

Harness once gave his views on this to a group of analysts: "Outside observers of our business frequently conclude that the success of a product like Pampers, for instance, is the result of a high level of consumer demand which we have somehow pumped up through large-scale advertising and promotion campaigns." The truth, he said, is: "While advertising and selling are terribly important, we have never been able to build a successful brand through these skills alone . . . If people do not perceive any real performance benefits in a product, no amount of ingenious advertising and selling can save it."

* * * * *

In the days when Procter & Gamble produced and controlled its own evening TV programs (as it still did in the '70s with its

278

daytime TV serials), the company could sponsor shows produced by its own staff and its agencies. But today the networks control evening programming. They choose programs which companies sponsor unilaterally or in cooperation with other firms. For P&G this has created problems.

It had always tried to make its position clear through an editorial policy first developed to guide radio programming, then expanded to meet the more complex problems of TV. In sum it says: "While it is not Procter & Gamble's desire to control the kind of programs or program content broadcast by the stations or the networks, support through our sponsorship of programs imposes a right and an obligation to choose, to the best of our ability, that programming with which we want to be associated commercially. We try to apply the same standards to these network-produced shows as we do to our own daytime shows."

In line with this commitment, the company has long demanded the right to preview shows on which its commercials might appear. If its representatives found any segment of a performance objectionable, the commercial or sponsorship was withdrawn.

"Is this censorship? Not at all," said a member of the television staff. "We can't rule a program off the air and we don't try. We simply withdraw our association with it. It's not only a matter of good taste, it's a matter of practical common sense. We direct our messages to the American household. We believe most American homes prefer wholesome programs to those which glorify eroticism or viciousness. We want to be welcomed, not switched off."

As the world's inflationary forces continued their pressure, advertising expenditures were often attacked by those who charged they were inefficient and raised product costs. One response from Howard Morgens seemed to silence most of these charges. "Advertising used properly lowers costs to the consumer," he said. "This is a point that never seems to be understood adequately. By producing a large volume of sales for standardized items, advertising makes the mass production of such items possible. And mass production brings about savings in manufacturing costs; the high volume it creates also lowers distribution costs per unit."

For the retailer, "advertising spurs a more rapid turnover of goods. This makes lower retail profit margins possible, thereby reducing prices for the consumer." In addition, he pointed out, it

279

tends to create a more stable volume of sales week in and week out, and such stability also improves efficiency and economy.

The *Wall Street Journal*, reflecting that the 143-year-old company has, on average, doubled its earnings every decade, quoted a top company officer: "There's no doubt in my mind that we wouldn't be the company we are if we didn't have our close contact with consumers through advertising and market research. We've never added it up, but I'm sure the feedback we get from consumers brings suggestions that save us many millions a year."

31

BEYOND THE SEAS

Business commentators have often expressed amazement over Procter & Gamble's international growth. Their reaction is understandable. From 1955 to 1979 the company's foreign sales multiplied from $238 million to over $1.3 billion. Its earnings increased eightfold, while its overseas assets quadrupled from $81 million to $320 million.

It was indeed a remarkable feat. In effect, in twenty-five years the company had created an organization which promised soon to rival in size a domestic P&G it had taken 140 years to build. How had it been achieved?

In the mid-'50s the Procter & Gamble company outside the United States was in relative infancy. Earnings were derived mainly from mature businesses in the United Kingdom, Canada, and the Philippines, all of which were entered well before World War II. In Latin America, Mexico, and then Venezuela, P&G operations were just getting started, and a small foothold had been established with factory acquisitions in southern France and Belgium.

By 1960, the company in the U.S. had expanded into paper, toilet goods, coffee, edible fats, and cake mixes. Outside the U.S., the concept was to build first, as Jake Lingle had outlined in 1955, "an exact replica" of the U.S. soap and detergent business in each country to be entered. The same policies which had led to success in the U.S. were adopted to build the international business. The initial target was the newly formed European Common Market (1957) which was rapidly recovering from the ravages of war.

The first Procter & Gamble subsidiary formed in Europe after World War II was Switzerland's Procter & Gamble A.G. Many countries would be opened by this "export division," headquartered in Geneva. The Swiss group would manage sales in

lands too small to justify the establishment of full-scale subsidiary operations. For example, Camay manufactured in England would be sold in the Middle East, and Philippine Camay would be shipped to Hong Kong or Singapore. Some of these export businesses, like Venezuela or Peru, would thrive and blossom to a size at which a local organization would later be established. On the Continent, the Geneva office had developed a small Belgian business which had led to the purchase of a plant in Malines, Belgium, to serve the Benelux countries.

Two events several years later proved decisive in accelerating P&G's entry into Europe. The first was the establishment of the European Technical Center in Brussels in 1963 to serve Common Market subsidiaries in product research, process development, purchasing, engineering, and manufacturing. The other was the successful entry into the German market. Initial German experi-

The international flavor of P&G products as they appeared in Lebanon during the mid-1950s (opposite page), and in Germany (this page) in the 1960s and 70s.

ence was obtained through a work agreement with Rei-Werke, A.G. It served as P&G's sales agent in Germany beginning in 1961 and operated a detergent plant of its own in Koblenz. Rei-Werke was subsequently purchased in 1965.

P&G had learned time and again that it was rarely possible to formulate a single detergent to match all laundry conditions. This was a major reason for the number of different brands offered for home laundry use even in the U.S.—Tide, Cheer, Oxydol, Bold, and so on. Company researchers knew what U.S. homemakers knew—all laundry conditions are not the same. The hardness of water varied widely depending on area, well water, and soil formations; laundering habits varied as did the size of families; there were wide ranges of synthetic fabrics which required specific treatments. Despite criticisms from those who said "all cleaning products are the same," scientists and homemakers knew differently. As one foreign manager reported, "We now have eighteen major detergent and edible fat formulations in the United States. The international divisions have fifty-five, and they require engineering and design of countless variations in equipment, buildings, and detergent towers."

William R. Gurganus, president of P&G International, summarized the first years in Europe as the "story of suds levels." Gurganus had begun his P&G career in brand management and had been closely identified with the success of Cheer in the U.S. To Lingle and Howard Morgens he seemed an ideal choice to lead the establishment of the German business. He was named its general manager in 1963. Gurganus quickly discovered that direct transfer of U.S. detergent technology would not be enough for success in Germany. For the manufacturers of German washing machines were not emulating those in the United States. Their machines could not work efficiently with the high suds levels of Tide and other American detergents. For them a new detergent formula had to be devised, one producing less suds.

The research scientists in Brussels had to work fast, for two formidable competitors, Unilever and Henkel, were rushing to develop detergents of their own for German machines.

Procter & Gamble's technicians achieved the goal first, developing a completely new low-suds formula with the brand name Dash. (German Dash was unlike any other P&G detergent, even its American namesake.) And Dash proved to be superior to anything then on the European market. But it involved a high-priced risk.

Normal procedure would have demanded thorough test marketing before making a major financial commitment. Yet here was an opportunity to leap ahead of all competitors. The risk of failure was undeniably great. But so was the risk involved in waiting until others caught up with (or surpassed) P&G's efforts. And so even before Dash was thoroughly tested, major appropriations were approved in Cincinnati, and the construction of a new plant at Worms was begun.

In a new country not yet recovered from a disastrous war, this was indeed a "bold decision" of the type Morgens had outlined several years earlier. Variations of its low-suds formula thereafter provided a base for the company's European business in Italy, France, and elsewhere on the Continent.

* * * * *

By 1968, Thomas C. Bower, who had played a major role in developing the European business and was then manager of the Common Market Division, was able to summarize the nature of things in Europe: "We now have plants in four nations of the Common Market," he told P&G managers. "These are located in Marseilles and Amiens in France; in Malines, Belgium; in Pomezio and Bariano, Italy; and in Worms and Koblentz, West Germany. All do a considerable amount of intercompany business. To avoid duplication of effort, they make certain products for each other. For example, France supplies perfumes for the other Procter & Gamble companies as well as the all-important base mix of ingredients for detergents now being made in Italy."

The ability of the different P&G subsidiaries in each country to complement each other led to increased efficiencies and reduced costs everywhere. It also led to an ability to extend success in one country quickly to others. Dash was one example. Another was the spread of the company's first enzyme detergent. All these demonstrated the wisdom of establishing a technical center in Europe.

The safety questions that had caused so many problems with enzyme detergents in the U.S. were in sharp contrast to the public acceptance in Europe. P&G's European managers had brought enzymes to the attention of the U.S. company in the first place, and it was in Europe that enzymes were to become most successful.

285

The benefit of enzymes offered particular advantages in certain laundry situations, and so it was decided that Germany would be the initial market for a new formula containing enzymes, Ariel. It proved an instant success, and Ariel was soon expanded throughout the Continent, then to Britain, and beyond. It was enthusiastically received in Latin America and the Middle East, and by the late '70s it had become so popular worldwide that it had surpassed U.S. Tide as the company's largest single detergent brand. It was ironic that public fears in the U.S. about enzymes would still prevent acceptance of enzyme detergents by U.S. consumers.

In addition to Germany, France, and the Benelux countries, P&G's European expansion soon extended into Italy, Austria, Spain, and Scandinavia. Tom Bower liked to dramatize the close relationships among the European companies with a story of how they had worked together to respond to a major strike in France in the late '60s.

"Our international operations were suddenly threatened," he said, "when wildcat strikes began to spread industrial paralysis across France." Bower realized that if the French plants were closed by a general strike they would be unable to supply Ariel ingredients to the P&G factories in the other Common Market nations. All P&G installations in the Common Market would come to a standstill.

"With the only long-distance telephone line still open to us," Bower said, "we called the other plants and arranged for united action. We hired every truck that was available. We loaded them with the reserves of perfumes and detergent mixes we had on hand in France, as well as with thousands of cartons for Ariel. We sent them all speeding across the borders to Belgium and Germany. From there they could be reshipped to Italy where we had a detergent tower." By the time the French strike paralyzed all activity, the other P&G plants had been supplied and continued to operate.

Bower realized that the end of the long French strike would bring a wild demand throughout France for all the household products that had disappeared from grocery shelves. It would take French plants weeks to replenish the supply.

Foreseeing this, the combined resources of the P&G factories in Italy, Belgium, and Germany were mobilized to deposit huge supplies of soaps and detergents in warehouses close to the

French border. Trucks were hired and kept on stand-by. The day the strike ended and the borders were opened the loaded trucks rushed into service.

"We flooded the starving retail trade with a high volume of deliveries and created a wonderful opportunity for a wide consumer retrial of Ariel. We avoided a sizable local loss by intercountry cooperation," he concluded triumphantly.

* * * * *

Although Procter & Gamble's international growth took the company to many countries during the 1960s, there was one major foreign market it had not attempted to penetrate. That was Japan. One reason was that Japanese customs and traditions differed so completely from those of America. How would an alien company like P&G fare in so unfamiliar an atmosphere? Would it be welcomed or barred by the government? Despite such doubts and many others, there were executives in Cincinnati who argued, "Here is a vigorous, prospering country of 100 million people, the third-largest detergent market in the world, next to the U.S. and Europe. We ought at least to try to build a business in Japan." As a result the company sent an exploratory mission to Tokyo. Its purpose was to learn if there would be an appropriate Japanese partner for a joint venture, a joint venture being the only way approved by the Japanese government for an outside company to launch an operation in Japan.

They did not have an easy time. The country's two largest soap and detergent manufacturers, Kao Sekken and Lion Yushi, were polite but disinterested. They were doing well enough without affiliating with an American firm. On the other hand, after these disappointments the visitors found the smaller Sunhome company of Osaka quite amenable to the idea of a joint venture. It would certainly strengthen Sunhome's competitive position with fresh capital and products.

Any discussion of a joint enterprise, however, had first to win government approval. Getting that approval was neither quick nor easy. For months P&G emissaries found themselves involved in long talks with one ministry after another. The Japanese officials were polite, stiff-bowing, attentive. They could not be hurried. But eventually they granted official sanction to the deal. In 1972 the firm of Procter & Gamble Sunhome Company, Ltd. began its Japanese operations, with P&G owning 50% of its stock.

Trouble developed immediately. The two leading Japanese companies increased their advertising to meet P&G competition. Almost concurrently the 1973 Arab oil embargo struck Japan a severe blow. Japan was completely dependent on imported oil, and this action caused energy prices to rise to levels which made the manufacture of detergents costlier than had ever been anticipated. Neither Kao nor Lion raised its prices to meet these added costs, one way of challenging Procter & Gamble's stamina in their country. On top of that, Japanese housewives began hoarding detergent in anticipation of shortages. Obtaining trial of new products in such circumstances was a great marketing challenge. There followed several years of difficult competition with losses mounting. Were the tough Japanese manufacturers once again to succeed in staying the entry of foreign competitors, as they had beaten back earlier efforts of Colgate and Unilever? The answer was no; P&G had come to stay. Eventually it was to have the leading detergent in Japan, All-Temperature Cheer.

For companies doing business in foreign countries, the Watergate scandal in the early '70s had unexpected repercussions. As the investigations of improprieties in political contributions grew, alarming evidence emerged that a few major U.S. companies had illegally contributed to U.S. political campaigns. These led to revelations of corporate contributions and kickbacks in numerous foreign countries as well. These events received extensive publicity, and new regulations by the Securities and Exchange Commission were laid down putting tight restrictions on future contributions. Fortunately, P&G emerged from this period with its reputation unblemished.

That was no accident. As the company expanded its operations—from new plants in the U.S. to acquisitions and to plants in foreign countries—senior managers were made aware of the ethical heritage of the company and of the vital importance of assuring that this heritage was not obscured as new employees were added. Historic ethics and integrity must not be lost as the company grew around the world.

P&G executives discussed this regularly. Bill Gurganus outlined what he termed "good corporate citizenship" abroad and emphasized some principles which had guided foreign expansion from its beginning.

"In a foreign country, never forget we are a guest," Gurganus told his listeners, "we are bound by its laws." But he also emphasized the need to follow P&G policies as well, which called for fair treatment of employees, of the trade, of customers, and of suppliers, as well as the ultimate consumer. He likened the supplying of quality consumer products to that of fulfilling a social responsibility. "However," he said, "providing consumers with superior products, fairly priced, is far more than a social responsibility; it is essential to our success."

It is fundamental policy at P&G that line managers have the final responsibility for seeing that their business is operating within P&G policies. But policy guidance is one of the roles of a strong staff. Senior managers quickly learned that close involvement of corporate staff groups would assure that U.S. policies were woven into operations abroad.

There were other benefits of staff participation in foreign operations. One such example was the success of U.S. engineers in reducing the construction costs of new plants. Working closely with their local counterparts, the U.S. engineers insisted on using advanced construction techniques which had been developed elsewhere. Though these techniques often conflicted with practices favored by local contractors, patient insistence achieved sizable cost and time savings.

The role played by the U.S. purchasing department offers another example: When the company entered Japan it found that competitive bidding by suppliers, a normal practice in the U.S., was far from common. In fact it was actively resisted. Seemingly, many suppliers consulted with one another prior to bidding, removing much of the competitive incentive. The company worked to introduce new procedures and patiently won point by point. A leading American investment firm marveled that "P&G Sunhome has significantly improved profits via two steps in the purchasing area." The report stated, "Contrary to general practice, P&G has succeeded in implementing competitive bidding. And second, an exhaustive analysis, supplier by supplier, revealed they too were benefiting from favorable exchange rates in the costs of their imported materials. When faced with this fact presented by P&G, meaningful price reductions followed."

Such steps to control costs, the report concluded, helped P&G to build a stronger Japanese operation in its detergent business. In turn, it discouraged the major Japanese detergent manufacturers in their efforts to prevent P&G entry.

*   *   *   *   *

289

In the late '70s company managers were able to say rather proudly that within the entire area where P&G had established local operations it had become the leading manufacturer of laundry detergents. Quite an achievement in just two decades.

This sharp international growth stemmed almost completely from the successful application of American detergent technology and marketing skills to local conditions.

And the Geneva-based export business continued to thrive. It moved into northern Africa, the Middle East, and much of Latin America. By 1979 these operations had spread to more than 100 markets. They included supervision of seven smaller plants where P&G had licensing agreements.

Of course, products other than detergents were introduced: dentifrice and shampoo into Britain, Venezuela, and parts of the Middle East; Crest into Mexico; in Italy there was the purchase of a small instant coffee brand, Splendid. Closer to home, Canada, with living standards similar to the U.S. and within range of U.S. television broadcasting, soon was selling most of the P&G products sold in the U.S., including shortenings, cake mixes, and toiletries.

But as the '50s and '60s were the decades of detergents for the international business, the '70s were dominated by Pampers.

*   *   *   *   *

Lacking their own disposable diapers, world markets seemed ready. But as far as Cincinnati was concerned, how could the people be found and trained to research the disposable diaper markets throughout the world then oversee manufacturing and sales?

In headquarters conferences several conclusions were reached. One was that throughout the world, "a baby is a baby." With few exceptions the same product could be sold everywhere. The laborious market-by-market evaluation necessary for cleaning products would not be needed for diapers. Another conclusion was that international expansion need not wait for plants to be built abroad. Pampers would be supplied, at least initially, from U.S. installations operating seven days a week. New plants abroad could follow as the business was being built.

Preparations began for production in Germany. Senior Vice-President David Swanson reported: "A number of bilingual German recruits and a few experienced managers from the

German company were brought to America. A training school was set up for them at the Cape Girardeau Pampers plant in Missouri. Twenty of the Germans and their families were moved to this location. The blitz course was a complete success. Within twelve months every German manager was trained to operating competence. The result was that eventual production at the German Pampers plant grew 40% faster than at a comparable plant in the U.S."

Though Procter & Gamble established Pampers sales in seventy-five countries by 1979, the first such steps occurred in Canada and Puerto Rico. Puerto Rican acceptance was especially gratifying. Many families lived without ready access to washing machines. Washing diapers and drying them on a clothesline was an onerous chore in a land of high humidity. Puerto Rico became one of the most successful Pampers markets.

Although "a baby is a baby," diapering methods did vary somewhat from one country to another. Disposable diapers had been widely used in Germany, but with an unsatisfactory absorbent pad inserted in plastic pants. Swedish mothers disliked pins anywhere near a baby and kept the diaper in place with a plastic sheet called a *snib* tied around the diaper. Japanese mothers used a thin cloth, not very absorbent, which resulted in Japanese babies being changed nearly twice as often as babies in other countries. But, with these exceptions, U.S. Pampers—in five sizes—satisfied needs everywhere.

As international sales increased, a Pampers plant was built in Canada, two in Germany, and another was scheduled for Japan. A company publication concluded: "Whether they live in a bustling city in Japan, a desert village in Saudi Arabia, or a mountain chalet in Switzerland, millions of babies around the world are staying drier because of Pampers."

* * * * *

One of the major problems faced by Lingle and Gurganus was staffing the rapidly growing international subsidiaries. In the early years, managers were shuffled from country to country. Initially, the United States and British companies supplied most of these people. Neil McElroy had started this pattern back in 1930 when he was sent to handle the business at Newcastle upon Tyne, and the pattern continued.

Now, as each subsidiary became established, it began recruiting from its own country, offering opportunity within that country as

291

well as worldwide. Soon virtually every international company could find its nationals serving in other countries. At one time in Japan the management team was made up not only of U.S. people, but natives of the Philippines, United Kingdom, Canada, Switzerland, and Belgium. "If the pattern holds," said one senior executive, "it will not be long before Japanese are not only filling many spots in the Japanese company but supplying management talent to other countries as well."

With deep satisfaction, Gurganus was eventually able to note that six of the company's top officers had begun their careers in the international business.

* * * * *

By 1979 the company had full-fledged operations, including manufacturing plants, in twenty-two countries, and its products were being exported to more than 100 other nations.

Studying these figures as he sat in the garden of his suburban Cincinnati home, retired Walter Lingle—who launched international expansion—might well have murmured, "Not bad, not bad."

Not that this was the culmination of a triumphant achievement. No ultimate goal had been reached. No effort was being relaxed. The beginning of the year 1980, if it marked anything at all, was merely another point in the long history of the company. It reaffirmed a constant determination to grow, to enter new fields of interest, to make the most of the opportunities offered by the American system of free enterprise.

As one veteran employee of Procter & Gamble expressed it, "In this company no year ever brings the end of anything. Every year is simply a new beginning." And so the last words in this history should not be the conventional "The End" but rather "The Beginning" for a company forever fixing its eyes on tomorrow.

EPILOGUE

The eleventh floor of the Cincinnati headquarters, the executive floor, has an atmosphere unlike that of any other part of Procter & Gamble. As hushed as a cathedral, its wide, green-carpeted corridor leads past the offices of the corporation's top executives, past beautifully appointed conference rooms, past the life-size portraits of former presidents and chairmen. One is tempted to walk on tiptoe. In the first of many visits to that floor I felt it would be sacrilege even to clear my throat.

For weeks I had secret doubts about some of the things I heard said there. One officer after another discussed the "thoroughness" of every P&G undertaking, the high ethical standards the company observed. That made me wonder. Being thorough was understandable. But in a pragmatic age of fierce industrial competition, when leading businessmen were often pictured as tough and ruthless, could these quiet men really be so devoted to unimpeachable standards of corporate conduct?

Yet as I delved into the archives I realized that beyond the words were many corroborative actions. I recalled Procter & Gamble had once deliberately sacrificed millions upon millions of dollars when it withdrew its best-selling Tide detergent from many states rather than reduce it to an inferior product. Month after month while I studied the record, it became clear that what might sound like pious words truly reflected the unchanging character of Procter & Gamble.

There were, too, some thoughts I had about political attitudes. I had heard from outside sources that the company was "a hidebound, conservative, unbending Republican organization" which linked its success to Republican policies. Surely there was nothing reprehensible in this. But was it true?

The answer came in a revealing statement from Chairman Edward Harness. "Starting at the end of World War II," he said,

293

"we had about seven years of a Democratic president in the White House, eight years of a Republican in the White House, eight more years of Democrats, and then eight more years of Republicans. If you look at each of those two-term stretches as potential business cycles and attempt to match those cycles with P&G's progress, you will find no meaningful correlation. The volume growth of the company's U.S. business seems to have been essentially unaffected by the presence of one party or the other in the White House."

He might have applied the same observation to the thirty administrations which had preceded these since 1837. Procter & Gamble's growth had never been dependent on or interrupted by political victories. Individuals within the company had supported candidates of various parties as was their right and obligation as citizens, but such political activity had no connection whatever with the business of Procter & Gamble.

And then there was the astonishing, almost unbelievable optimism of every company executive, especially as it pertained to future growth. "There are always new and synergistic fields to enter," they said. Was this too optimistic? Yet even as they spoke Procter & Gamble went into the soft drink business. It acquired the U.S. and international business of the Canadian-based Orange Crush Co. with its venerable Hires root beer and Orange Crush brands.

Remembering the vigor with which the company progressed from soaps and detergents to foods, to toilet goods, to paper products, one can hardly doubt that its new soft drink division will soon add its own impressive share to annual sales which, in 1980, exceeded $10 billion with earnings over $600 million.

A most significant indicator of optimism was the increase in capital spending. In 1980 this amounted to three-fourths of a billion dollars, a sum far greater than any ever reached before— and surely an impressive testimony to confidence in the future.

After one spends a number of months with P&G's people, one comes to understand their enthusiasm and their confidence. These are ingrained in the company's character. It will not change as long as Procter & Gamble's eyes are fixed on the opportunities of the years ahead.

True, as an observer and chronicler I did my utmost to maintain a detached perspective. I even questioned the age-old policy of making all promotions from within the company's ranks—until I realized that this very policy accounted for much of Procter & Gamble's success. Even as this history was being completed the reins of leadership were being passed from Chairman Edward Harness to a new group, all of whom had spent essentially their entire careers with Procter & Gamble. John G. Smale, president since 1974, was elected chief executive officer. Owen B. Butler was elected chairman of the board. In addition Edwin L. Artzt and Thomas Laco had recently been elected executive vice presidents. How could any outsider be more familiar with or more devoted to the aims, the character, and the spirit of the company? How could any outsider be expected to understand and perpetuate the heritage with which these men had lived for decades?

For me, the Procter & Gamble story has been a revelation. To recount it has been an extraordinary privilege. I cannot bring this task to a close without expressing my profound gratitude for the opportunity that was afforded me.

O. S.

Appendix A

These brief biographical notations include the executive responsibilities of the persons listed as well as the years in which they served in their highest, or most recent corporate capacities.

William A. Procter (president, 1890-1906)

James N. Gamble (vice-president, 1890-1932)

Harley T. Procter (vice-president, 1890-1895)

David B. Gamble (treasurer, 1890; secretary, 1895-1905)

William Cooper Procter (general manager, 1890; president, 1907; chairman of the board, 1930-1934)

J. H. French (treasurer, 1895-1903)

Herbert Greer French (treasurer, 1904; vice-president, 1919-1942)

Hastings L. French (secretary, 1906-1914)

John J. Burchenal (vice-president, 1911-1925)

Clarence H. Gamble (secretary, 1915-1917)

Ralph F. Rogan (secretary, 1918; vice-president, 1940-1954)

A. Edward Anderson (vice-president, 1919-1921)

Wallace E. McCaw (vice-president, 1919-1924)

George S. Woodward (treasurer, 1919-1939)

Richard R. Deupree (general manager, 1927; vice-president, 1928; president, 1930; chairman of the board, 1948; honorary chairman of the board, 1959-1974)

Stockton Buzby (vice-president, 1931-1933)

Floyd M. Barnes (vice-president, 1931-1954)

Renton K. Brodie (vice-president, 1931; administrative vice-president, 1954-1955)

Clarence J. Huff (vice-president, 1938-1943)

Walter H. Tuttle (treasurer, 1939-1950)

William R. Huber (comptroller, 1939-1942)

H. Truxtun Emerson (secretary, 1940-1950)

Kelly Y. Siddall (comptroller, 1942; vice-president, 1954; administrative vice-president, 1955-1961)

Harvey C. Knowles (vice-president, 1942-1961)

Neil H. McElroy (vice-president, 1943; vice-president and general manager, 1946; president, 1948; chairman of the board, 1959; chairman of the Executive Committee, 1971-1972)

Thomas J. Wood (vice-president, 1943-1961)

Walter L. Lingle, Jr. (vice-president, 1948; executive vice-president, 1954-1962 and 1964-1969)

Howard J. Morgens (vice-president, 1948; executive vice-president, 1954; president, 1957; chairman of the board, 1971; chairman of the Executive Committee, 1974; chairman emeritus, 1977-   )

J. Gibson Pleasants (vice-president, 1948-1969)

Samuel Benedict (secretary, 1950-1962)

George S. Woodward, Jr. (treasurer, 1950-1964)

C. Kenneth McCracken (comptroller, 1955; vice-president, 1957-1968)

W. Rowell Chase (vice-president, 1955; executive vice-president, 1960-1970)

James M. Ewell (vice-president, 1955; vice-president, group executive, 1973; senior vice-president, 1976-1979)

H. Schuyler Cole (vice-president, 1956-1963)

Mark Upson (vice-president, 1956-1963)

Donald H. Robinson (vice-president, 1956; vice-president, group executive, 1962-1967)

Dean P. Fite (comptroller, 1958; vice-president, 1961; vice-president, group executive, 1972-1975)

Edwin A. Snow (vice-president, 1959; vice-president, group executive, 1962-1972)

Richard S. Runnels (comptroller, 1961; vice-president, 1967-1973)

Edward W. Merkel (secretary, 1962-1967)

J. Spencer Janney (vice-president, 1962-1968)

Albert N. Halverstadt (vice-president, 1962-1969)

John W. Hanley (vice-president, 1963; vice-president, group executive, 1967; executive vice-president, 1970-1972)

Edward G. Harness (vice-president, 1963; vice-president, group executive, 1966; executive vice-president, 1970; president, 1971; chairman of the board, 1974-)

Alan C. Fite (treasurer, 1964-1978)

Milton P. Link, Jr. (vice-president, 1966-1968)

Eugene W. Gilson (vice-president, 1966-1969)

William M. Ittmann (vice-president, 1966-1970)

Thomas C. Bower (vice-president, 1966; vice-president, group executive, 1973-1975)

Charles M. Fullgraf (vice-president, 1966; vice-president, group executive, 1973; group vice-president, 1976-)

James W. Nethercott (comptroller, 1967; vice-president, 1969; senior vice-president, 1976-)

John G. Smale (vice-president, 1967; vice-president, group executive, 1970; executive vice-president, 1973; president, 1974-1981; chief executive officer, 1981-)

Richard W. Barrett (secretary, 1968; vice-president, 1971-1975)

William R. Gurganus (vice-president, 1968; vice-president, group executive, 1969; executive vice-president, 1972; president, P&G International, 1974-1980)

Owen B. Butler (vice-president, 1968; vice-president, group executive, 1970; executive vice-president, 1973; vice-chairman of the board, 1974-1981; chairman of the board, 1981-)

Edwin L. Artzt (vice-president, 1969; vice-president, group executive, 1970; group vice-president, 1976; executive vice-president, 1980-)

George H. Perbix (vice-president, 1969-)

Edgar H. Lotspeich (vice-president, 1970-1976)

Harry Tecklenburg (vice-president, 1970; senior vice-president, 1976-)

W. Wallace Abbott (vice-president, 1970; senior vice-president, 1976-)

Bryce N. Harlow (vice-president, 1971-1977)

Thomas Laco (vice-president, 1971; vice-president, group executive, 1973; group vice-president, 1976; executive vice-president, 1980-)

Donald I. Lowry (vice-president, 1972; group vice-president, 1976; senior vice-president, 1980-)

Kingston Fletcher (vice-president, 1972; group vice-president, 1980-)

Morgan V. Hunter (vice-president, 1973-1975)

John W. Collins (vice-president, 1973-1975)

Edwin H. Shutt, Jr. (vice-president, 1973-1976)

William O. Coleman (vice-president, 1973-)

George M. Gibson (comptroller, 1973; vice-president, 1978-)

William E. Forbis (vice-president, 1973-)

James M. Edwards (vice-president, 1974-)

Anthony D. Garrett (vice-president, 1975-)

Albert E. Harris (vice-president, 1975; group vice-president, 1980-)

Samih A. Sherif (vice-president, 1975-)

Robert E. Cannon (vice-president, 1975-   )
Powell McHenry (vice-president and general counsel, 1976-   )
Charles L. Jarvie (vice-president, 1976-1979)
David S. Swanson (vice-president, 1976; senior vice-president, 1979-   )
Fred M. Wells (vice-president, 1977-   )
Geoffrey Place (vice-president, 1977-   )
Charles A. Ferguson (vice-president, 1977; group vice-president, 1980-   )
Gerald V. Dirvin (vice-president, 1977; group vice-president, 1980-   )
Edwin H. Eaton, Jr. (treasurer, 1978-   )
Charles C. Carroll (vice-president, 1978-   )
John E. Pepper, Jr. (vice-president, 1978; group vice-president, 1980-   )
Wahib N. Zaki (vice-president, 1979-   )
R. Marvin Womack (vice-president, 1979-   )
Robert V. Goldstein (vice-president, 1979-   )
Charles E. Eberle (vice-president, 1979-   )
Ashley L. Ford (secretary, 1980-   )
Sanford G. Weiner (vice-president, 1980-   )

Appendix B
Plant Locations in U.S. Cities

(The kinds of products manufactured in these cities are indicated by this code: L = laundry & cleaning products; P = personal care products; F = food products; O = other, including pulp, chemicals, and animal feed ingredients. Subsidiary names are included next to the cities in which they operate. Year of start-up or acquisition is in parentheses.)

Albany, Georgia—P (1972)

Alexandria, Louisiana—L (1969)

Augusta, Georgia—L (1963)

Baltimore, Maryland—L,P,O (1930)

Cape Girardeau, Missouri—P (1969)

Cheboygan, Michigan—P (1957)

Chicago, Illinois—L,P,F,O (1930)

Cincinnati, Ohio, and vicinity:

    Ivorydale—L,P,F,O (1886)

    St. Bernard—L (1928)

    Cincinnati Toilet Goods—P (1947)

Dallas, Texas—L,P,F,O (1921)

Evanston, Illinois (Crush International [U.S.A.], Inc.)—F (1980)

Foley, Florida (Buckeye Cellulose Corporation)—O (1954)

Fort Worth, Texas (Traders Oil Mill Company)—F,O (1942)

Green Bay, Wisconsin (1957):

    East River—P

    Fox River—P

Greenville, North Carolina—P (1975)

Huntsville, Alabama (Buckeye Cellulose Corporation)—O (1980)

Iowa City, Iowa—P (1956)

Jackson, Tennessee—F (1971)

Kansas City, Kansas—L,P,O (1904)

Kansas City, Missouri (Folger Coffee Company)—F (1963)

Levelland, Texas (Buckeye Oilseed Products Company)—F,O (1979)

Lexington, Kentucky—F (1955)
Lima, Ohio—L (1968)
Long Beach, California—L,P,F,O (1931)
Macon, Georgia—F (1909)
Mehoopany, Pennsylvania—P (1966)
Memphis, Tennessee (Buckeye Cellulose Corporation)—O (1921)
Modesto, California—P (1971)
New Orleans, Louisiana (Folger Coffee Company)—F (1963)
Omaha, Nebraska (D.H. Food Company)—F (1956)
Oxnard, California—P (1973)
Portsmouth, Virginia—F (1931)
Quincy, Massachusetts—L,P,O (1940)
Sacramento, California—L,F,O (1953)
St. Louis, Missouri—L,O (1927)
Sherman, Texas (Folger Coffee Company)—F (1979)
South San Francisco, California (Folger Coffee Company)—F (1963)
Staten Island, New York—L,P,F,O (1907)

Appendix C
International Operating Companies

Austria:	Procter & Gamble Vertriebsgesellschaft m.b.H.
Belgium:	Procter & Gamble Benelux
Brazil:	Inter-American Orange Crush Company
Canada:	Procter & Gamble, Inc.
	Procter & Gamble Cellulose, Ltd.
	Procter & Gamble Specialties, Ltd.
	Victory Soya Mills Ltd.
Federal Republic of Germany:	Procter & Gamble GmbH
Finland:	Procter & Gamble OY
France:	Procter & Gamble France
Greece:	Procter & Gamble Hellas A.E.
Great Britain:	Procter & Gamble, Ltd.
Ireland:	Crush International (U.S.A.), Inc.
Italy:	Procter & Gamble Italia, S.p.A.
Japan:	Procter & Gamble Sunhome Company, Ltd.
	Procter & Gamble Japan K.K.
Lebanon:	Procter & Gamble Manufacturing Company of Lebanon, S.A.L.
Mexico:	Procter & Gamble de Mexico, S.A. de C.V.
Morocco:	Moroccan Modern Industries
The Netherlands:	Procter & Gamble Benelux
Peru:	Deterperu, S.A.
Philippines:	Procter & Gamble Philippine Manufacturing Corporation
Puerto Rico:	The Procter & Gamble Commercial Company
Saudi Arabia:	Modern Industries Company
Spain:	Procter & Gamble España, S.A.
	Crush International (U.S.A.), Inc.
Sweden:	Procter & Gamble Aktiebolag
Switzerland:	Procter & Gamble A.G.
Venezuela:	Procter & Gamble de Venezuela, S.A.

INDEX

*Page numbers in italics
indicate an illustration.*